MUSTERED!

Foot Soldiers of the 12th

J P FAHEY

This Book is a Limited Edition.

It is One of Fifteen Hundred

First Edition Books of the First Printing of

MUSTERED! FOOT SOLDIERS OF THE 12TH

J P Fahey #1229

Hampshire House

P.O. Box 1573, Port Richey, FL 34673-1573

Hardcover edition published in 2001 by Hampshire House.

MUSTERED! Copyright © 2001 by J P Fahey. All rights reserved. Printed in the United States of America. No part of this book may be used or reproduced in any manner whatsoever without written permission from the publisher. For information and permission address requests to Hampshire House, P.O. Box 1573, Port Richey, FL 34673-1573

Battle site maps from THE CIVIL WAR BATTLEFIELD GUIDE, edited by Frances Kennedy. Copyright © 1990 by The Conservation Fund. Reprinted by permission of Houghton Mifflin Company. All rights reserved.

COVER: MICHAEL MOORE, DESIGN GRAPHICS ADVERTISING ASSOCIATES, PORT RICHEY, FLORIDA

Publisher's Cataloging-in-Publication of this hardcover edition for standard library cataloging is as follows: (*Provided by Quality Books, Inc.*)

Fahey, J.P.
  Mustered! : foot soldiers of the 12th / J.P. Fahey.
  -- 1st ed.
  p. cm.
  Includes bibliographical references.
  ISBN 0-9713313-5-9

  1. United States. Army. New Hampshire Infantry Regiment, 12th (1862-1865) 2. New Hampshire--History--Civil War, 1861-1865--Regimental histories. 3. United States--History--Civil War, 1861-1865—Regimental histories. I. Title.

E520.5 12th. F34 2001   973.7'442
                            QB101-701079

DEDICATION

*To the memory of
foot soldiers of the 12th New Hampshire
and all foot soldiers North and South
who fought each other
for their country*

ACKNOWLEDGMENTS

To Ruth Herron, artist and writer, who inspired me to write this book by sending articles and news clippings; and who, in her eightieth year, became my editor and confidante;

To Linda Gray, my lifelong friend, who walked and talked with me, empathized and sympathized with me, and even listened while I read to her.

To Ruth Lamos Crouse, a family friend for over fifty years, who encouraged me to write during my darkest hours and who always believed in me;

To Michael Bradshaw, who has guided me through time and distance;

To the memory of my mother, Louise Musgrove Pickering, who cherished her heritage and passed it on to my sisters and me.

Contents

Foreword

CHAPTER I	**Preparing for War**	1
	Formation of the 12th Regiment	5
	Mustered In	10
	Farewell New Hampshire	13
	Off To War	15
CHAPTER II	**Tenting on the Old Camp Ground**	18
	Foraging Expeditions	24
	Near Fredericksburg	33
CHAPTER III	**Defeat at Fredericksburg**	41
	First Scenes of War	47
	Near the Front	50
	An Eerie Evening	53
	Left Behind	54
	Someone Had Blundered	56
CHAPTER IV	**Camp and Hospital**	60
	Mud March	64
	Fighting Joe Hooker	67
	Lincoln Reviews the Army	70
CHAPTER V	**Chancellorsville**	73
	May 2, 1863	83
	Left Behind Again	85
	Jackson's Advance	86

	May 3, 1863	87
	Until the Last Man Falls	90
	Hospital and Wounded	113
CHAPTER VI	**After the Battle**	111
	Battle Reflections	111
	Battlefield Humor	114
	Knee Deep in Mud	117
CHAPTER VII	**Marching North**	125
CHAPTER VIII	**Gettysburg**	138
	Saving the Colors	151
	Pickett's Charge	161
	The Wounded	162
	After the Battle	167
	South Again	170
	Wapping Heights	175
CHAPTER IX	**Point Lookout**	181
	Religious Rebels	186
	Treatment of Prisoners	193
	Arrival of the Subs	200
	A Deserter's Confession	209
	A Trip to Washington	211
	Furloughs for Home	216
	Election Day	219
CHAPTER X	**Bermuda Hundred & Swift Creek**	223
	Battle of Swift Creek	233
	Brotherly Love	240
CHAPTER XI	**Drury's Bluff**	242
CHAPTER XII	**Cold Harbor**	256
	A Comrade's Cry	256
	Visions and Presentiments	260

	Slaughter at Cold Harbor	265
	June 3, 1864	265
	Battle Observations	268
	Rescuing the Dead and Wounded	276
	Capt. Nathanial Shackford	282
	William Welch	282
CHAPTER XIII	**Siege of Petersburg**	285
	Cemetery Hill (Battle of the Mine)	291
CHAPTER XIV	**The Bermuda Front**	299
	Battle of Fort Harrison	303
	Election of 1864	309
	Capture of the 12th Regiment	310
	Escape from Libby Prison	314
CHAPTER XV	**Chapin's Farm: Last Winter in Dixie**	336
CHAPTER XVI	**Richmond**	347
	A Blazing Celebration	350
	A Starving City	353
	Unwelcome Captors	354
	Welcome Heroes	355
	Libby Prison	356
	President Lincoln Arrives	357
	General Lee Returns Home	359
CHAPTER XVII	**Manchester and Danville**	361
	Assassination of Lincoln	361
	Captain Bedee's Lament	364
	Testimonial to the 12th Regiment	370
CHAPTER XVIII	**Concord—Home!**	372
	Handing Over the Colors	377
	Independence Day Farewell	380

List of Illustrations

Commissioned officers of the 12th Regiment	*8*
Howard Taylor: "The Little Corporal"	*14*
MAP: Fredericksburg, December 11-13, 1862	*42-43*
MAP: Chancellorsville, May 1-3, 1863	*72*
Lieut. Rev. John Durgin: "The Fighting Parson"	*84*
Sergt. McDuffe, Sergt. Tasker, Lieut. Bedee	*93*
Maj. Savage, Capt. Savage, Lieut. Cram	*94*
Capt. Keyes	*94*
Lieut. French	*99*
Surgeon Flower, Capt. Fowler, George Fowler	*103*
Albert Nelson, Dan Nelson, Major Nelson	*112*
Chaplain Thomas Ambrose	*113*
Sergt. John Piper	*116*
Alonzo (Lon) Jewett	*119*
Warren Tucker	*129*
Charles Smith	*123*
Orrin Colby and James Marshall	*131*
MAP: Gettysburg, July 1, 1863	*137*
MAP: Gettysburg, July 2, 1863	*141*
Lieut. French, Sergt. Howe	*152*
Sergt. Parker, Corporal Brown	*152*
Lieut. Fernal	*154*
MAP: Gettysburg, July 3, 1863	*156*
Lieut. Asa Bartlett	*159*
Charles Drake	*163*
Albert Jones, Sergt. Lawler, Christopher Joy	*183*

Woodbury Sanborn	*173*
"Irish Ed Ryan"	*187*
Sergt. Osgood	*189*
Howard Taylor	*200*
Louis Rowe and George Currier	*232*
Sergt. Osgood	*241*
DIAGRAM: Drury's Bluff	*243*
Lieut. Dunn	*260*
David Sanborn	*262*
MAP: Cold Harbor, June 3, 1864	*264*
Sergt. Clarke's Positional Diagram of Cold Harbor	*267*
George Place	*272*
John Emerson	*273*
Capt. Shackford	*282*
William Welch	*283*
Almon Farrar and William Gray	*304*
Albert Bacheler and Benjamin Thompson	*334*
Edmund Tebbetts ("Old Teb")	*337*
Capt. Bohonon	*345*
Newell Davidson	*350*

3 Major Contributors to *Mustered!*

Asa Bartlett, *Historian of the 12th Regiment Association and author of the History of the 12th*

T. E. Barker, *Commander of the 12th, gave his war documents, letters and accounts to Bartlett.*

R.W. Musgrove, *author of the Autobiography of R.W. Musgrove, at the time of his enlistment*

R.W. Musgrove *at the time of writing his autobiography & History of Bristol, in 1904.*

Foreword

When I was a teenager, my mother showed me a hand-bound manuscript entitled *Autobiography of Richard W. Musgrove*, but it was of little interest to me at the time. Nearly four decades later, in the summer of 1999, my cousin Ruth sent word that the State of New Hampshire was dedicating a bridge to Captain Musgrove in my home town. Information on him was being requested, and I knew that my mother had saved the manuscript along with a lot of other "stuff".

In an old trunk in the attic, I found a box full of diaries, letters, accounts, and anecdotes written by Musgrove and his comrades in the 12th New Hampshire. They were covered in dark blue paper to preserve them from fading. Underneath were two manuscripts containing sketches, portraits, and accounts of events, marches and battles. One was the autobiography, the other a huge book of nearly a thousand pages, published in 1897, entitled *History of the Twelfth Regiment, War of the Rebellion* by Capt. Asa Bartlett, another foot soldier in the 12th.

The regimental history contained many of the accounts, sketches, anecdotes, and diary recordings I had found in the trunk. And it contained something else—portraits of the foot soldiers of the 12th along with an old lithograph of their battle-scarred flags.

I hauled everything down from the attic, locked the doors, unplugged the phone and hunkered down to read, beginning with the autobiography—written nearly one hundred years ago by my great grandfather, Capt. Richard Watson Musgrove.

It was a meticulous account of a regiment of foot soldiers who fought in the Virginia campaign. The regimental history contained a collection of accounts written by officers and soldiers of the Twelfth, and thus held a broader regimental perspective, particularly on events which occurred after Musgrove left the regiment in May of 1863 to lead a brigade of "Galvanized Yankees" into the western frontier.

These are the sources I have used in writing this book. All of *MUSTERED!* came from that trunk.

My objective was to present an accurate, personal, unembellished chronicle of the regiment as experienced and recorded by its own members. I have edited sparingly, using the style, form and parlance of the original writers wherever possible. (Clarity and readability were the only criteria for exceptions.) Where context was lacking, I have provided information from the regimental history and placed it in italics.

Although *MUSTERED!* chronicles the life and time of only one regiment of foot soldiers, it is every foot soldier's story. For behind the battles commanded—and blunders ordered—by generals at headquarters or on horseback, stood a brotherhood of foot soldiers, North and South, carrying knapsacks, muskets and the weight of war on their shoulders.

It is my hope that your journey with the boys of the 12th will bring new insight; that along the way you will find yourself living vicariously with them, sharing their history, their humor, their hardship and their heart; and that you will keenly see and long remember two enemy soldiers lying side-by-side, one wiping the sweat and blood from the face of the other whispering, *"We are not enemies now, we are brothers, each fighting a cause the other believes in."*

J P Fahey

*Map showing the Seat of War
from Harper's Ferry to Suffolk, Virginia*

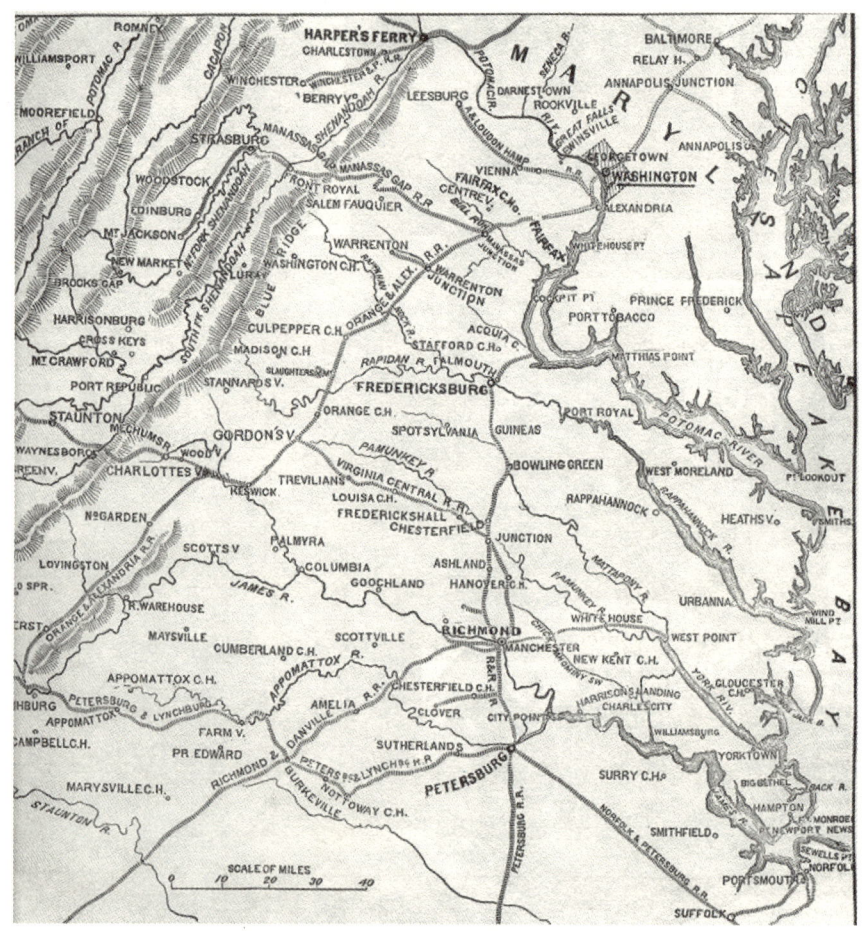

Taken From *Campfire and Battlefield: An Illustrated History of the Civil War*
By Rossiter Johnson, 1894, p. 141

CHAPTER I

Preparing for War

December 1860. *Following the political campaign of 1860, northern towns were bustling with excitement and apprehension. Nestled in the valley of the White Mountains of New Hampshire is the town of Bristol (population 1,124, in 1860). The townsfolk are a hardy people, independent yet united in pride of character, community and country. One of these is Richard Watson Musgrove, an eighteen-year-old mill worker and seminary student.*

It is at this time and place that our chronicle begins, narrated by Captain Richard Watson Musgrove, fifty years later.

In 1860 the American people were being prepared for the great national struggle that was looming in awful proportions from the south; yet I little realized then the humble part my comrades and I were to play.

The months following the election of Abraham Lincoln brought only gloom and apprehension, as preparations for the great war ahead went on. Discussion of the great crime of slavery entered into every phase of society life and application to study under such circumstances was well nigh impossible. The debates in

Congress, platform, pulpit and the press of the day kept the public conscience at fever heat. In our society meetings at the seminary some phase of national affairs was each week discussed, and extracts from the orations of the great masters were no longer used for declamations, but extracts from Wendell Phillips, William Lloyd Garrison, and Charles Sumner predominated discussions.

One by one the southern states passed ordinances of secession. The 1st of February 1861, the papers announced the withdrawal of Texas from the Union, when a young man by the name of Middleton, who was a student from that state, announced that he was then a resident of a foreign nation. This called forth indignant retorts that were not complimentary to him or his state, whereupon he attempted to draw a revolver. This action caused such a demonstration among the boys present that he was soon convinced that the wisest course for him was to keep his revolver in his pocket.

When on the 12th day of April 1861, the fact that Sumter had been fired upon was flashed over the wires, the North rose as one man. The people gave themselves over to demonstrations of patriotism. Mass meetings were held, martial music was heard in every town, and recruiting for the army went on faster than the volunteers could be organized. At Tilton School a mass meeting was held; the band furnished music, and many patriotic addresses were made. With few exceptions the people were a unit in favor of forcibly preventing any state from withdrawing from the Union; and yet underneath all the excitement and enthusiasm deep gloom rested on the people as they saw preparations for war going on. Yet few caught more than a glimpse of the immensity of the struggle ahead.

MUSTERED!

One public man, thought to be more extravagant than any other, was quoted as saying that the Union was worth the expenditure of fifty thousand lives. The sentiment was quoted by the daily press in display type to show how the judgment of a great man could be warped in times of great excitement, in others to show the value of the Union. Yet more than ten times fifty thousand men would be sacrificed to prevent the disintegration of the nation. Little did the vision of even the most far-seeing grasp the immensity of the sacrifice required.

The summer of 1861 found me again at work in the paper mill. As the Fourth of July approached, some of the boys suggested the hanging of Jeff Davis in effigy on the Fourth as a diversion. Accordingly, an image was made and duly hung on the flag staff in Central Square on the evening of July 3d. The image was clothed, including boots, with clothes left by workmen at the paper mill. At three o'clock the next morning commenced the greatest conflagration in the town's history and the hand engine of the fire department was used for the first time. The entire west side of Central Square was swept away. As the fire lit up the square, there hung the effigy of Jeff Davis; and the clothes and boots he wore, all covered with lime, plainly disclosed where this man had been put together.

This fact under ordinary circumstances would not have occasioned any regrets; but now the authors did not enjoy their identity being known because the fire had not half finished its work ere the boys were accused of being the cause of it all, and Jeff Davis told who some of the boys were. Gossip was wild for a few days and there was talk of a town meeting to see what could be done with the boys. It was charged in the leading state paper published in

Concord that the fire was caused by a fireball being thrown by a boy through a window. There was no truth in this account, but of course the story told by the boys was not, for a long time, believed.

I was one of the boys interested and was on the street that night and knew that no glass was broken, unless it was the glass of the winebibbers in the basement where the fire originated. There was some good reason to believe that dissipation by men in the basement named was the cause of the conflagration, but this was never known.

On the 2d day of July 1862, President Lincoln issued a call for 300,000 men. The news reached the people of Bristol through the daily press at five o'clock in the afternoon on the third. I remember the impression it produced: People were beginning to realize that all the resources of the government would be needed to crush the rebellion and were preparing to nerve themselves for the sacrifice.

I worked at the paper mill from twelve o'clock midnight to twelve o'clock noon and recall that the first man I met on my way to the mill after supper that night was Captain Daniel Mason. His salutation was "Well, Richard, what would you give if you were out of it?" My reply was, "I would not give anything." There was a common patriotic feeling that animated all, or nearly all, the young men at that time. Those who sought to evade the responsibilities of the hour by going to Canada were few indeed compared with the many who were ready to respond to the call of the government when duty seemed to demand it.

During the third week of July, my brother, Abbott, who was at work in a hosiery mill at Cohoes, New York, enlisted in Company H, 115th Regiment, New York Volunteers, and came home to spend a few days on a furlough. These were the last days he spent at home. It was well that the curtain concealing the future was not lifted, or else more than a shadow would have rested on the family circle

On the 4th of August, Bristol held a special town meeting and voted to pay all who should enlist on the quota of the town before the twentieth of that month, the sum of $200. There were a few in town who were bitterly opposed to the war. Among these, one of the most rabid was Abbott Lovejoy, who was one of the few Democrats in town opposed to coercing the South. When Judge Fowler moved that the sum of $100 be paid to each man who should volunteer on the quota of Bristol, Mr. Lovejoy promptly moved to amend by making the amount $200. He sought to prevent any action by presenting an expensive bone of contention. He took his hat and started for home with the remark, "There now, fight over it." But he misjudged the spirit of the meeting, and before he reached the street, the amendment was adopted; and so Bristol paid $200 to its volunteers under the call of the President.

Formation of the 12th Regiment

At that time two local men from Laconia, Colonel George Stevens and Colonel Thomas Whipple, were agitating for the raising of a regiment. A meeting in the interest of the movement was held at Laconia on July 25th and excitement ran high. The advantages of belonging to a regiment, the companies of which would be composed of men from adjoining neighborhoods, appealed strongly to the people of this section and large numbers signified their intentions of enlisting. Arrangements were made with the state authorities to allow the men to select their own officers.

Under this arrangement, enlistment papers were sent out from the statehouse on Tuesday, August 12th, and on Saturday, August 16th, Governor Berry was notified by Colonel Stevens that a full regiment had been enlisted. This fact gave rise to the claim that the 12th Regiment, New Hampshire's largest, was raised in three days. It cannot be denied, however, that nearly all of these men had, during the ten days previous, signed a paper agreeing to enlist as soon as the opportunity presented, and so affixed their names to enlistment papers as soon as they arrived. Thus, within this small sparsely populated territory, enough men enlisted within three days to fill the ranks of the regiment, one thousand strong—a record claimed at the time to be without a parallel in the entire country.

Within the three days named, Blake Fowler enlisted seventy-one men, who became a part of Company C, 12th Regiment, of which company Mr. Fowler was chosen captain. David Everett enlisted forty-three men, who became a part of Company D, and he was made first-lieutenant of that company.

I remember the circumstances of deciding to join my fortunes with the many others from Bristol who were proposing to enlist. In Central Square one day, I met Alonzo Jewett. We sat down on the grass outside the fence in front of the residence of Hon. Samuel K. Mason, and for half an hour discussed the subject in all its bearings. Our decision was to enlist. We shook hands and parted, and August 12th, within an hour after the enlistment papers reached Bristol, we affixed our names and became recruits for the United States army.

MUSTERED!

I cast my lot with the recruits of David Everett. These were merged with others enlisted by Bradbury Morrill, and a larger number enlisted by J. Ware Butterfield, a young lawyer at Sanbornton Bridge. A meeting for the election of officers of Company D was held in the old chapel at Piper's mill in Sanbornton a few days after our enlistment, but there is no fact or record that enables me to give the exact date. At this meeting Mr. Butterfield was elected captain; Mr. Everett, first-lieutenant; Mr. Morrill, second-lieutenant; Alonzo Jewett, first-sergeant, and I was chosen third-corporal.

On the 20th of August a meeting was held at Laconia by the line officers of the regiment for the election of field officers. Colonel Thomas. J. Whipple was elected colonel; George W. Stevens, lieutenant-colonel; and Dr. George Montgomery, assistant surgeon. None of these men were commissioned for the places to which they were elected. Colonel Whipple was a brilliant lawyer and a capable, fearless soldier. He had served in the Mexican war as lieutenant-colonel of the 1st Regiment, New Hampshire Volunteers, but his personal habits had resulted in his retirement from the service in March previous, and therefore Governor Berry declined to commission him. This gave great offense to a majority of the men of the regiment and resulted in a bitter controversy that came near making serious trouble in the regiment. This was stayed only through the advice of cool heads, including Colonel Whipple himself. Day and night the cry of Whipple! Whipple! rang from all parts of the encampment, but beyond the protest, Captain John Potter of the Regular army was commissioned as colonel, and the men were not reconciled to his appointment to command them till after the battle of Fredericksburg. John Marsh was commissioned as lieutenant-colonel, and Reverend Thomas L. Ambrose was elected chaplain. The others elected at this meeting and commissioned were Dr. Hadley Fowler, as surgeon, and Dr. John Sanborn, as assistant surgeon.

B. B. L. 5-9.
GEN. JOSEPH H. POTTER.

B. B. L. 5-10.
BVT. COL. JOHN F. MARSH.

B. LB. L. 5-8.
CHAPLAIN THOMAS L. AMBROSE.

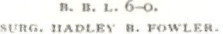

B. B. L. 6-0.
SURG. HADLEY B. FOWLER.

DB. B. L. 6-0.
ASST. SURG. CHARLES W. HUNT.

During August, after our enlistment, there was little to do, and the time was passed visiting friends, making preparations for our trip south, and in occasional meetings at Sanbornton Bridge and elsewhere of those who composed Company D.

About the first of September, we rendezvoused at Sanbornton Bridge for drill, and on the fourth of that month took the train to Concord. From the station, we marched to the old fairground, where each man was furnished with a blanket; then each company was assigned one of the barracks erected for our reception. Each of these barracks provided fifty bunks, giving accommodations for two men each, two bunks to a section, one above another. Louis Rowe and I shared one bunk. The cooking was done over an open fire a little way off, and there was a small cookhouse where the food was protected from the weather.

That first night in camp was a memorable one. Leaving the environments of home had a sobering effect on all and that there were many sad hearts cannot be denied. Many spent the evening around the campfire singing and in other ways trying to keep up their spirits, and as the hours passed, this was changed to a prayer meeting led by Reverend Asa Witham, a Free Baptist local preacher of Company D. Some, true to other instincts, sought relief in strong drink. Adversity and a hard experience drive some men to seek relief in strong drink, while it makes others more religious. So in the army, men who never drank before became intemperate, while others became men of prayer.

Many in the company were greatly annoyed by the actions of some when under the influence of liquor. The one giving the greatest offense was in Company D. He had seen active service and showed such proficiency in drill and in the manual of arms that he had been elected sergeant. For a sergeant to act thus was considered by many as particularly scandalous, and a self-constituted committee was organized that waited on the company officers and asked that he be dismissed from the company. We were told that he was too good a soldier to be thrown overboard, but if he continued to offend after being mustered or reaching the seat of war, he would be disciplined. This reasoning satisfied the committee of enlisted men, but the interview had hardly terminated when an officer arrived in camp who arrested him as a deserter from the navy and we saw no more of the drunken sergeant.

Mustered In

Dr. Hadley B. Fowler, surgeon of the regiment, was the first to receive his sealed parchment of authority and acted as examining surgeon, passing or rejecting each and every man who presented himself as a volunteer for the 12th Regiment. In the regimental history Captain Asa Bartlett, an enlistee at the time, describes the mustering procedure:

The examination, as it should be, was careful and thorough . . . After running in single, "undress" file safely through the gauntlet of Surgeon Fowler's eyes and hands, each supposed himself all right for the muster-roll, but the final test was yet to come . . . C.aptain Charles Holmes, U.S.A., was mustering officer . . . and he required each man to walk along in front of him while his sharp eyes watched every motion and scrutinized every feature, judging the fitness of the man for the business required of him quite as much from his motive as his physical power. He would commence on the right of the company, and when it was seen that he began to challenge and throw out some of the men

MUSTERED!

before he had got to the center, it made some of the smaller ones think that their chances were few and fast growing less; and when their turn would come to step out and march up the company front, each one did so, expecting, surely, his fate was sealed. But Captain Holmes was not so green as his subjects and knew from experience that it was in the left wings of the companies that the toughest and most lasting material of every regiment is found.

H. B. F. 5-4.
SERGT. HOWARD TAYLOR.

Fifteen-year-old Howard Taylor, having boldly written his name on the enlisting paper and taken the oath of allegiance, found he could rely on Doctor Fowler, not only for safe passport under his hand but for aid and assistance in running safely past the final inspection of the mustering officer. To do this successfully a pair of shoes was made for him, big enough to admit of extra inner soles an inch or more in thickness, which with height of heels and thickness of taps outside to correspond was sufficient to stilt him up three inches beyond his natural perpendicular. Thus toed and heeled, with pant legs long enough to cover, he walked resolutely up to the company front from his place on the extreme left, faced and saluted like a West Point cadet and passed unchallenged into the service of his country.

On Friday, September 5th, after our arrival in Concord, Company D marched to the city and in the statehouse yard was mustered into the service of the United States. It was an impressively solemn occasion. The company stood in the north side of the yard facing south and with uplifted hands swore to defend the flag of the Union and to obey all lawful orders of our superior officers. Every man seemed to realize the full import of that oath. They thought also that they had some conception of the work before them, but, alas, they had not.

This ceremony over, we were informed we could have a furlough and go to our homes and remain there till Monday. This offer all accepted with pleasure. On Wednesday following, we drew our uniforms and a few days later, our arms. Another furlough of two days was granted the next Saturday and, indeed, it was very easy to obtain a leave of absence during the first three weeks in camp. Then as the day of our departure from the State drew near, the grip of military discipline was tightened.

On the 11th, I went to Franklin from camp with Captain Butterfield, Lieutenant Everett, Alonzo Jewett and was initiated into the mysteries of Free Masonry. This work was done by the officers of Meridian Lodge at a special meeting that day and on the afternoon of the following day. As may be supposed, no time was spent in lectures or in examination of the candidates as to their proficiency as they progressed.

Life in camp at Concord was filled with squad, company and battalion drills, dress parades, guard mountings and various other duties, all intended to prepare the men for active service. On the 23d of September the routine of camp duties was varied by the arrival of a large delegation of the friends of Companies D and C from Bristol and neighboring communities. A sword was presented to Doctor Fowler and another to Lieutenant David Everett, while a suit of clothes was given Captain Blake Fowler.

On the 24th came friends from Sanbornton, who presented tokens of regard to the officers and men from that section of the State. On this occasion a dinner was served by the visitors and speeches made. One man said that all the offices of the towns and state would be at the disposal of those who returned from the war. His remarks were somewhat prophetic, for he himself got left soon after the war when running for an office against a veteran.

Farewell New Hampshire

On Thursday, September 25, an order was issued stating that the regiment would start for the seat of war Saturday morning, September 27, at seven o'clock.

Then came preparations for the march. No more furloughs were to be issued and few passes from camp, but the number of visitors increased rapidly. The camp was crowded with those interested in the welfare of loved ones in the regiment. There was little sleep for any one the last night in camp. Some spent the time in noisy demonstrations, some spent hours in writing good-bye letters to friends, and all devoted much time to packing their knapsacks to the utmost capacity. The art of getting along with little had not then been learned. As it was, much had to be left behind and this furnished food for bonfires kept burning all through the night.

The last evening, Louis Rowe and I went to the city and called on friends and bore back to camp from them a good stock of edibles for our coming trip. These friends were strangers who had invited us to their homes that evening. They took our names that they might keep track of us at the front. At the depot on our departure, I was presented with a box by Miss Hobbs, a teacher at the seminary at Sanbornton Bridge, and Miss Lucy A. Way, a niece of Bishop Baker and a recent graduate there. On opening the box on the train it was found to contain among other things, fruit, a looking-glass and comb and two letters. The comb was carried in my pocket all through the war and for thirty-five years after the war and then was given a place among other war relics in my cabinet. The letters contained words of cheer and appreciation; and in my journal of that day I find recorded these words, "How it does lighten the burdens of life to know we have friends who appreciate our motives and sympathize with us."

The march to the depot that Saturday morning was the first in heavy marching order. With gun and accoutrements, knapsack, haversack and canteen, each man carried about sixty pounds and from that time, the work of lightening the load commenced and was continued till many disposed of the knapsack entirely and carried the blanket in a roll over the shoulder.

> *Though the morning pack is easy and light,*
> *Woe, woe to the back before it comes night;*
> *For the soft and the light, ere the long day has sped,*
> *Will grow hard as a rock, and as heavy as lead.*
>
> **History of the 12th Regiment**

A thousand men in ranks make a great showing; and the 12th Regiment, marching by platoons, extended almost from the Concord covered bridge to the railroad station. Thousands of people lined the sidewalks, cheered and waved handkerchiefs and flags as we marched along. At the station there were many sad scenes of parting between the soldiers and wives, sisters, aged parents, and other friends.

Off To War

With a train of twenty passenger cars, the regiment moved from Concord for the South. Its passage was a continuous ovation. All along the route crowds had gathered to see us pass and saluted us with cheers and the waving of flags and handkerchiefs. At Worcester, the regiment left the train and marched to the park, where long tables were loaded with a substantial meal, of which we partook with great enjoyment. Norwich, Connecticut was reached at dusk, where the regiment embarked on the steamer *City of New York* and arrived at Jersey City at two o'clock Sunday morning. Here my brothers, John and William, met me for a long, last visit, as the train that was to bear us south was not ready till 9:00 a.m.

We arrived at Philadelphia at three o'clock Sunday afternoon, where we disembarked to march from one depot to another. We marched to Coopers Volunteers Refreshment Saloon. Here were conveniences for all to have a generous wash and then take seats at tables loaded with the best of the markets, including luscious peaches and pears from the orchards of that section. The hour was near the closing of the afternoon services, and all the churches emptied their congregations en masse to greet the soldiers from New Hampshire. The hearty meal and the royal greetings extended by the people brightened the faces and lightened the hearts of all the boys; and, for me, has afforded a bright theme for thought in all the years that have since come and gone.

The latter part of the afternoon the train pulled out of Philadelphia, and at three-thirty the next morning we were in Baltimore. While waiting here, a few miles outside of Baltimore, another train passed from which salutes were fired at our train. As a result of the firing, Darius Robinson of Company I, who was standing in the door of one of the cars, fell dead. A lieutenant, Henry Ashbey, of the 84th New York Volunteers was arrested on arrival at the Relay House, but he proved his innocence by the fact that the fatal bullet would not fit his revolver. The guilty party escaped arrest and whether the shot was actually fired by a Rebel sympathizer or as a salute was never known.

All day Monday we waited in Baltimore for a train to take us to Washington. There was little evidence of disloyalty to be seen here because the city was completely under military control, but one private of the regular army moved among the boys and expressed his opinion in most emphatic and bitter words that the government was seeking to liberate the slaves by the war.

The ride from Baltimore to Washington during Monday night was one of the first memorable events in the history of the regiment. The entire regiment, officers and men, were loaded into freight cars. The night was warm and the men not located near the doors soon began to pant for breath. "There is plenty of air outside, let's get some," said one; and the butts of muskets began to play. The same impulse moved the men in every car to action at the same time, and all along the train the bombardment continued, and pieces of the boarding on the sides of the cars were constantly flying into space until ventilation was ample. The regiment left its mark on that train; and if it was ever afterward used for the transportation of troops, it was in better condition for that purpose than when the Twelfth took possession of it.

The boys looked forward to their arrival in Washington with interest, expecting something of the same reception accorded them in Philadelphia, but they were sorely disappointed. No words of greeting or demonstration of gladness were accorded the regiment and this had a depressing effect on us all. Washington was as cold as Baltimore, and what added to the disappointment was the fact that the regiment was marched to the Soldiers' Rest (or Soldiers' Retreat) for breakfast where the place was found to be deserted.

Then came the march of seven miles across Long Bridge to Arlington Heights. The fierce rays of the Virginia sun in late September beat without pity upon men unaccustomed to marching and struggling along under a heavy load. The march, though short compared with many taken later, was one of the hardest for us as raw recruits. Arriving at our destination, the regiment went into camp.

CHAPTER II

Tenting On The Old Camp Ground

October 1862. *The encampment on Arlington Heights, called "Camp Chase" after one of New Hampshire's most honored sons, was pleasantly located on General Lee's estate overlooking Georgetown and Washington. The second day, after pitching tents, the men received their first lesson in changing base by moving their camp a short distance across the road. On October 6th, by virtue of a special order from General Wright, another change of base was made. The regiment moved about three miles to near Fort Corcoran (later called Fort Meigs) where it joined General Whipple's division of the Third Army Corps as an independent command.*

On Tuesday, October 7, we moved camp close to Fort Corcoran on Arlington Heights, but further up the river. Here we had an opportunity to bathe in the Potomac.

On the following Thursday, we marched to Washington, about eight miles, and exchanged our old arms for new Springfield muskets, carrying a large ball and three buckshot. Our route was over Long Bridge to the city and back through Georgetown.

Letters about this time informed me that the 115th Regiment, New York Volunteers, in which was my brother Abbott, was at Harpers Ferry at the time of its surrender by General Miles and that they were paroled and were then in Chicago.

Little time was given in camp for reflection. There was something to do nearly every hour in the day from reveille at 5:00 a.m. to taps at 9:30 p.m. There was breakfast call at 6:00 a.m.; call for policing the grounds and sick call at 6:45; squad drill 7:00 to 8:00; guard mount at 8:00; company or battalion drill 9:00 to 11:00 a.m.; dinner call, inspection of quarters, regimental drills in the afternoon; dress parade, supper calls; and schools for officers in the evening. In the evenings there were usually some religious services or social meetings in the open air. On Sunday morning there was always inspection and usually a sermon by the chaplain.

A number of amusing incidents happened here involving the training of the raw recruits. The following, recorded in the regimental history, is an example:

He proved to be a good and trusty soldier of Company G, but as yet he was a mere tyro in the military camp. When seeing Colonel Potter about to cross his beat one day at Arlington Heights, he cried: "Halt! halt! halt! You can't pass here without saying 'Concord.' This took the army discipline all out of the colonel, and it was some time before he could command his own countenance sufficiently to inform the guard that he was put there to *receive* and not *give* the countersign.

It was here that the men found rare sport in trying to break in a lot of mules that were as green in knowing what to do as their instructors were in knowing how to teach them. Walter Libby, one of the drummer boys, who was heedless and always ready to make sport for the boys, thought he would show a specimen of his horsemanship. So, mounting a spirited animal without saddle or bridle, he gave a Comanche yell which so frightened the mule that Walt soon found himself riding at break-neck speed up the length of the parade ground and heading directly for a wide, deep ditch that had just been dug out for a hospital reservoir. The officers and boys, whose laughing shouts helped to scare the mule, now stood in fearful silence expecting to see both beast and boy go headlong into the open reservoir. But with one tremendous bound, the noble mule landed himself and rider safely on the other side to the glad cheers of all. The remarkable part of this incident is that one of the men afterward measured the ditch and swore that it was seventeen feet wide.

One evening soon after our arrival in Virginia, the Masons of the regiment went outside the camp lines and spent an hour under the blue arch of Heaven in consultation as to the best methods to assist each other in time of trouble. I was one of the party, and I found later that the members of the fraternity were of great assistance to each other in many ways. The leader of this party was Rev. Captain John Durgin. A few months later, when left for dead on the battlefield at Chancellorsville, he gave the Mason sign of distress, and his life was saved by brother Masons of the Confederate army. Because of the assistance of his enemy brother, he recovered and lived many years.

MUSTERED!

About this time, one of my company was outside the regimental lines practicing with his gun, as he claimed, when one of his fingers was blown off by a premature discharge of his gun. There was a difference of opinion as to whether or not this was really an accident, but the man secured his discharge thereby a few weeks later.

On the 10th came orders to pack up and be ready to march at a moment's notice. The notice to move did not come, and we remained in camp that night. That was fortunate, for during the night we had our first experience with a Virginia rain storm. The rain fell in torrents and those who did not have proper ditches around their tents suffered consequence. The rain continued during the next day. We remained in camp waiting for orders to move and continued to wait for a week.

In camp here we had A-tents. I had four tent mates Louis Rowe and the three Nelson brothers, Major, Dan and Albert. These men were farmers, handy with the ax, and they laid a floor in our tent. This was made of round wood cut in the woods near by and split, the flat half being at the top. Though rough, this floor was a great improvement over the bare earth.

We now had shelter tents issued to us. These consisted of pieces of cotton cloth about five feet square, each piece being provided with buttons and button holes. Each man had one. Two pieces buttoned together formed the two sides of a roof and sheltered two men; a third piece closed one end and a fourth the other end, and so sheltered four men. In stormy weather, four to a tent was a common arrangement, though four had to lie snug together to have the cloth cover all. The addition of two other pieces doubled the length of the tent but only added two more to its occupants. In this way the tent could be extended any length desired, but as all the occupants had to crawl in from one end or the other, tent companies of more than six were unusual.

On October 16 we heard the first shot fired in actual warfare. Some rebel cavalry made a reconnaissance near our lines and were shelled when they hastily departed without returning the fire.

At three o'clock on the morning of October 17, the long expected reveille sounded and the order to march was again issued, and this time the line of march was taken for Washington where we arrived at seven o'clock in the morning. Previous to our departure it had rained enough to make the roads muddy—and the mud of Virginia is something fearful. In traveling, one sinks to the bottom of the mud and it is only with great difficulty that the foot is removed for a forward step, and then large masses adhere to the feet making traveling extremely difficult and tiresome.

About noon, the regiment boarded a train of freight cars at Washington, and we were soon in motion. We passed through Beltsville and White Oak Bottom to Annapolis Junction, where we took the rails of the Baltimore and Ohio Railroad, and proceeded west to Knoxville, Maryland. This crooked road and its deep cuts through ledges and the high hills that towered above the track were the marvel of all. I lay down on the bottom of the freight car and with my knapsack for a pillow got some much needed sleep. Knoxville was reached soon after midnight. Here the regiment finished the night in bivouac, its first experience in sleeping on the ground without shelter.

Knoxville was a station on the B&O railroad about three miles from Harpers Ferry. It had a few dwellings and a church on the hillside under which was a schoolroom. No services were held in the church the Sunday morning we were there, but every seat in the schoolroom and many in the church were occupied by the boys writing letters home. Later in the day one fellow, who had rolled off the top of a freight car the night before while asleep and was supposed to have been killed, came into camp growling because he had been left to walk so many miles.

During the day many amused themselves trying to pitch their shelter tents on poles cut near by, but towards night the order to fall in was given; so tents already pitched were struck and the line of march taken up, and we moved some three miles to the east side of South mountain near Petersville. From this mountain was named the recent battle in which the Union forces were victorious. There we remained till the evening of October 24.

On the 23d, Lieutenant E. T. Case, Abram Brown, and A. E. Huntoon, all of the 9th Regiment., visited me. They were fellow students at Sanbornton Bridge, and we all were expecting to graduate there in June 1863. This was the understanding when we last separated, but instead we met in Virginia—all in the army.

Here we learned of the death of William. P. Harlow of Bristol. He was taken from our camp on Arlington Heights to the hospital at Washington, sick with brain fever and died the night after his arrival. His was the first death in Company C.

At ten o'clock, on the morning of October 24, we marched to Berlin, Maryland five miles, arriving about midnight, where we bivouacked till morning. The night was cold and the men suffered much. Just before starting on this march a member of Company I died, and his remains were hastily buried in a shallow grave by the roadside wrapped in his blanket. This seemed shocking to our sensibilities, but it was only another lesson in the hardening process that was going on. But for these preparatory scenes, the hard work ahead of us could not have been performed.

On the 27th of October we crossed the Potomac on a pontoon bridge and were again on the sacred soil of Virginia. During our march of three miles the rain fell copiously and the tramp of the army soon churned the soil into deep mud, and we welcomed an order to go into camp, though on the steep hillside. We were encamped near the bridge, evidently as guard, and here we remained till the army passed. We left behind at Berlin my close friend, Sergeant Alonzo Jewett, who was sick. He received a furlough home and did not rejoin us for some months.

Foraging Expeditions

Now we were in Hillsboro county, Virginia, (now Loudon county) at a place the men nicknamed "Starvation Hollow". Here we remained for four days without rations.

Local farmers were Confederate sympathizers who claimed to be "good Union men" and it took but few denials from these farmers to make "smart thieves out of poor beggars"; soon the fields and the orchards were found to be much more liberal than their owners.

The plantation houses, widely separated, showed marks of prosperity; the blight of an army had not till now fallen on this section. Since leaving Concord not a pound of fresh meat had been issued to the 12th Regiment, and some whose consciences troubled them at the thought of foraging used this fact to justify the act. Others had no qualms of conscience to silence and so all, as far as practicable, went in for some of the delicacies the section afforded, despite the fact that stringent orders had been issued from army headquarters against foraging, and that those caught in the act were threatened with hard work on fortifications then being constructed.

A hive of honey was brought to our camp one night; and turkeys that unwisely defied the soldier with a gobble, did so no more, sweet potatoes started from the ground wherever found, and sheep and cattle came to an untimely end.

A prank was played by Company D men on the men of Company C one night. A squad from Company C had captured a fat steer and were busily dressing it when they were discovered by Louis Rowe, the Nelson brothers and myself and others from Company D, also in quest of fresh meat. Hastily taking in the situation, we went back to camp, got our muskets, and returned. By this time the work of dressing the steer by Company C was nearly completed. Looking up, those at work saw in the starlight a party of armed men descending upon them whom they doubted not were the patrols scouring the country for just such offenders as they were, and they instantly sought safety in flight, leaving every pound of meat behind. This meat Company D bore triumphantly into camp, and in the morning generously presented a portion to our friends in Company C who had dressed the creature.

That there was cause for nervousness when on such expeditions may be seen from the fact that a dozen of the 12th Regiment in one squad were arrested one day by the provost guard at the insistence of a cantankerous sheep farmer and taken to division headquarters. This arrest did not please Lieutenant Colonel Marsh, and he mounted his horse at once, took a detail of twenty men and started out to see what he could do at foraging. Soon after, finding a flock of sheep, he commanded his men to fire but the only effect the firing had was to put the sheep to flight. Fortunately they took refuge in a corner of the field where the men, after laying down their arms, surrounded them and captured a dozen which they bore to camp.

There is a sequel to The Sheep Story: A day or two after the old Virginia farmer had hunted in vain for his lost sheep that he was sure had been gobbled up by the Twelfth boys, one of them (the boys, not the sheep) by the name of Ben Thompson, gathered up the sheep pelts (that he knew better where to find than the farmer did), carried them over to the farmer's house and tried to sell them to him, offering to take Confederate money for them at the low price of one hundred dollars per pelt. This was about an equal thing in surface measure, said Ben to the farmer, but the bare skins were worth much more than the paper, for by an equal exchange of square inches, the latter would be getting the wool, which was more than half grown, for nothing. But the dividing line between *meum et tuum* often takes a devious and tortuous course in times of war, and Ben's bargain was busted.

Another incident occurred here which will be told in anecdotal form, as recorded by the comrade concerned, and often repeated:

A LIVE WATERMELON

It was just about dark enough to see but not be seen and the melon patch was but a few rods in front of our line, as carefully located by one of the Company F boys before night. So he quickly but noiselessly creeps over the breastwork and crawling along on all fours, soon finds himself among the vines where he squints and feels for the luscious fruit; but finding only some small green specimens left, he ventures a little farther out; still finding none worthy of capture. Not wishing to return to be laughed at for so much danger and pains with nothing to show for it all, he concludes, after holding a council of war with himself, that he will reinforce with new courage, crawl beyond the middle line and prove:

> *That he, alone, is sure of luck*
> *Who shows himself most full of pluck.*

Scarcely has he commenced to put this resolution into motion when, as if already proving the truth of the couplet, he espies dimly through the darkness, but a few feet ahead of him, a large melon. But now he halts, stretches and flattens like a toad, for he thinks he hears the click of a gun lock. In breathless silence he lies and listens and gazes into the darkness. He hears nothing now but the beating of his own heart and sees nothing but a dark spot on the ground which he now fully believes must be nothing more or less than a big watermelon. What else can it be? No longer willing to borrow fears of his imagination, he draws himself up into creeping posture again and commences to advance; when all at once out of a vedette hole (that our young hero had mistaken for the big melon) springs a full grown and well armed Johnny reb exclaiming: "Now I've got ye, yer damn Yank," as he thought he had, and was intending, doubtless, to take him prisoner. But the game was too quick for him and he only had the satisfaction of sending a bullet after the retreating form of the melon hunter who, having thus opened the ball of a regular fusillade for some distance up and down the lines, contented himself to remain quiet behind the works the rest of the night, for if his pluck did not get him the melon, it was certainly his good luck that the melon did not get him.

At this time the army was moving south and the long expected advance on Richmond had once more commenced. Here we saw General McClellan and General Burnside as they passed us riding to the front. This was the first time we had seen our commander-in-chief or Burnside, and so all hats came off and all joined in a hearty hurrah to which the generals replied by uncovering, a formality not repeated at subsequent meetings. That very day orders were issued at Washington for the removal of McClellan and the promotion of General Burnside to be commander of the Army of the Potomac.

After two or three days in camp on the south bank of the Potomac, while the army was passing, the regiment fell in the rear of the army and moved two miles to Lovettsville and the following day ten miles to Hillsboro, which place we reached Thursday, October 31. There we remained till Sunday when the march south was resumed. During the following week we marched about fifty miles. Each day firing was heard a few miles south of us, a constant reminder of the work we had in hand. Our march took us by easy stages to Snicker's Gap, thence to Orleans.

Many nights on this trip our regiment was on picket. This service brought extra duty but with it additional opportunity, for the picket line was remote from the main line of travel and here the country had been foraged less. Among the luxuries of the picket line was a fricasseed chicken, when I officiated as cook. These were palmy days for the forager.

Waterloo was a village of a dozen negro huts or shanties and the remains of a woolen mill—about the only one seen by us south of the Potomac. Here we remained four days.

Since leaving Arlington Heights, no mail had been received by the regiment from New Hampshire and the boys were becoming impatient for news from home. Captain Butterfield had a brother-in-law for clerk by the name of George Pecker, and someone conceived the idea of sending him to New Hampshire for news. The idea was quickly acted on. Each man of Company D contributed sixty-two cents, and he promptly started to bear tidings of the boys to their friends and bring tidings from them to us. He made the trip, delivered his mail, talked with our friends in their homes and answered many anxious questions that could not be answered by mail, and returned. The trip was well worth what it cost, for the next day after he left the accumulated mail of four weeks was received and all came in for a share. This mail brought the intelligence that Comrade Robert Easter, who was sent to Washington sick when we left Arlington Heights, had died of typhoid fever there.

It was at this time that Sergeant Osgood received the following verse written by Miss E.N. Ladd entitled "Ode to the 12th New Hampshire Mountaineers":

> *Go then brave soldier, go fight for the right,*
> *And drive Secession far out of thy sight;*
> *And when thou returnest, then shalt thou see,*
> *That fighting for country is honor to thee.*

Her verse so inspired us that we committed it to memory and took the title "12th New Hampshire Mountaineers" as our own.

Sunday, November 16, we marched ten miles to Warrenton. On arriving in camp, the sick were removed from the ambulances and placed in a large tent erected for their reception. Here several died within a few hours of their arrival. Among the number was Edward Pratt of Company C. It had been intended to send him and others to some hospital to the rear from our last camp, but for some reason this was not done and the sick were loaded into ambulances and brought along. Comrade Pratt was suffering from a high fever, and the ride to Warrenton was more than he could endure. He walked from the ambulance to the hospital tent and soon after breathed his last. I was with him when he died.

Had these men been afforded the comforts of home their lives might have been spared. But this was impossible. Riding in ambulances over rough roads or over the fields afforded hardly a moment of quiet or rest, and the roadside must occasionally be visited, efforts which required strength far beyond what the sick men had. No wonder many often succumbed as soon as they found themselves no longer obliged to nerve themselves to meet the necessities of the hour.

We were informed that the remains of those dying here were to be sent north, but after we had started on the march the next morning, I learned that all had been buried. Obtaining permission, Louis Rowe and I returned to the scene of our encampment and marked Pratt's grave by nailing to a nearby tree a piece of a hardtack box on which we wrote his name, company, regiment, and also his residence—all we could do for our deceased comrade. His remains were later removed to his native town of Hebron.

MUSTERED!

When the regiment left Waterloo, there were more sick men than could be carried in the ambulances; some were allowed to ride on the baggage wagons, while others had to walk. Among the latter was Harlan Paige who was sick with jaundice and unable to keep up. W.H. Sleeper was detailed to help him along. The following account of their adventure was recorded by Paige:

We only made about two miles the first day. . . . The next morning, we saw just across the road five Rebel cavalrymen who at the same time saw us; but just then a squad of our own cavalry came dashing up the road A brisk skirmish ensued during which we made off as fast as we could. . . . The next morning we were met by Captain Fowler who was going back to bury Edward Pratt who had died of disease the day before. We called his attention to the danger of so doing, telling him he would surely be captured. He could not believe that Rebel soldiers were so closely following until he found himself a prisoner in their hands.

Each day the rear guard of our army was skirmishing with the enemy; and several times we were passed by our cavalry who told us we should surely be picked up by the rebel cavalry...for we would now be left between the two lines. After passing Catlett's Station . . . Stewart's cavalry was all around us . . . In just one week we arrived at Bull Run where we found our forces guarding the bridge, and learned that seventy-two of our men had come in before them, but all as paroled prisoners. I was now nearly well but Sleeper was sick and was admitted to Baptist Church Hospital where he died in a few weeks . . . the saddest of all was that he who had so faithfully nursed and watched over me when sick should so soon sicken and die himself.

Warrenton was the first town of considerable size within the enemy's line that we had visited and the secession spirit was very manifest. In the town few people were seen, and the heavy wooden shutters with which most of the houses were provided were tightly drawn and the doors locked.

Just outside the town, near where we encamped the night of our arrival, was a plantation house. As we passed it the next morning, the owner was walking the front porch in dressing gown and slippers with marks of scorn and contempt on every line of his features as he saw his fences down, his fields and even his front lawn deeply cut up with the wheels of the artillery and baggage trains.

We now experienced a succession of rainy days. The roads and fields over which we marched were badly cut up, the supply trains were a long distance in the rear and the army was decidedly short of rations. The wet earth was soft but unhealthy for beds and various expedients were necessary to keep our bodies from the wet ground. At one place poles and bushes were cut, and at another two immense stacks of straw and one of hay disappeared as if by magic.

On the 19th of November, while on the march near Hartwood, our regiment was for the first time drawn up in line of battle to repel an expected attack; but no attack came, and after being under arms for a couple of hours, we resumed our march.

This little incident brought out the real stuff of which some of the men were composed. Most were ready to commence the real work of service as became men, while some trembled with fear. Especially noticeable among the latter was one of the officers whose blanched face indicated that he was hardly a man to lead a charge.

Near Fredericksburg

Sunday evening, November 23, 1862, we reached a point about four miles east of Falmouth, which lies on the north bank of the Rappahannock, opposite Fredericksburg. We were near the railroad that runs from Falmouth to Aquia Creek where, as events proved, we were to remain for the winter.

For some days previous to reaching Falmouth, the army was extremely short of rations, causing much suffering. This was occasioned by the bad condition of the roads in our rear, or to the change of base of supplies from our rear to Aquia Creek, or both combined. Many a man made a day's march on a single hardtack. Individual foraging was out of the question in so large an army constantly on the move, but the commissary department gathered in for the use of the army what the country afforded, which was but little compared with the demand. One evening I and several of my tent's crew, by tramping two or three miles to where cattle had been slaughtered, secured the head of a steer just butchered. We took turns on duty that night, keeping it boiling, and when morning came were surprised and rejoiced at the large amount of meat that we secured from the bones.

The next morning I started out with plenty of rations for the day. A few hours later while resting by the roadside, I noticed one of my comrades, Hiram Philbrick, looking exceedingly haggard and said to him, "What is the matter, Hiram? Are you sick?" "No, but I have not had a mouthful to eat since yesterday morning," he replied. My haversack was instantly opened and the poor fellow given a meal, which lasted in memory a long time, for as we have met at reunions and at other times in later years, he has never failed to allude to the food furnished him that day.

Another incident showing human nature in the army might be mentioned. While on the march, all luxuries secured by foraging were shared with the officers. On arriving at Falmouth I was suffering slightly from jaundice and longed for something to eat besides my daily rations. I could think of nothing at the commissary, where supplies were sold the officers, that would fit my case better than dried apple; so I applied to an officer, to whose mess I had contributed, to give me an order for the same, offering to pay for it, of course. He replied he would be glad to give orders, but he was afraid if he did, he would not be able to get supplies for his own mess as he needed.

We passed some days near Falmouth in the open, south of the railroad, but soon moved to the north side of the track into a growth of pine where the trees on the average were about a foot in diameter. As showing the rapid growth of the pine in Virginia, it may be stated the rows were plainly visible where corn had grown when this land was cultivated.

The trees were rapidly felled for firewood and for building winter quarters. Before many weeks had passed, every tree had fallen and then the stumps and finally the roots gave way to the soldiers' axes for fuel.

Quite comfortable quarters were here erected by the men. The company streets (about forty feet wide) were laid out parallel with each other, and the tents were on both sides of the street facing inward. These tents were about eight feet long by six wide. Walls about three feet high were built of logs and on these were pitched the shelter tents. Four men to a tent furnished four pieces of shelter tent cloth which, buttoned together, made the roof.

The ends above the logs were closed with a rubber blanket, pieces of hardtack boxes, or by other devices. On one side or end was a fireplace, the chimney built of wood and daubed with clay to prevent its being destroyed by fire. Two bunks in one end, one above the other, occupied about one-half the space, leaving the other half for a living room. New Hampshire boys were skillful in the use of the ax and took great pride in their work. Our quarters were among the best in the army.

In a letter to his wife, Corporal Clarke of Company G described his new quarters:

> We laid it out seven feet square and built it up three feet from the ground with pine sticks or small logs, and in one end – the front, next to the street – we built a fireplace, projecting out the size of it in true southern style and opening into our room, which is a kitchen, dining, sitting and bed room, parlor, chamber, cellar and attic all in one. The fireplace is about three feet wide and two and a half feet high in front and then commences the chimney, tapering in as it goes up four or five feet about the ridge-pole and is topped out with a barrel. The chimney takes up about half the front end, and the other half is left open for a door. After logging up three feet high all round, except the doorway, we put on the ridge-pole and cover with our shelter tents for a roof. Next we take the clay mud, of which there is no stint here, and chink up the crevices in the log walls and plaster up our chimney. Our three rubber blankets answer well for the two gable ends and a door, and our house is completed. Our bedstead is a rack of limber poles covered with cedar boughs for a feather bed, and our woolen blankets and overcoats answer for sheets and coverlids. We sleep feet to the fire.

General Whipple stopped and looked us over, as he was riding past the other day and suggested to Colonel Potter that others take pattern by us . . . I am writing this by the light of our fireplace.

Soon after arriving at Falmouth, we learned that Captain J. Ware Butterfield, Captain Blake Fowler, Dr. Fowler and his son, George had been captured at Warrenton. They had remained there after the army left on account of sickness and were all promptly captured by the enemy. Captain Fowler, Dr. Fowler, and his son rejoined the regiment some months later and with them came Sergeant Jewett, who was left behind at Berlin. Captain Butterfield was a very capable officer, but he never rejoined his company, and this act of his occasioned some bitterness towards him

Thursday, November 26, was Thanksgiving in New Hampshire. We in the army had plenty of hardtack and beans to sustain the inner man, but the thoughts of all were turned to home. At the time of the usual afternoon drill, Lieutenant Colonel Marsh marched the regiment to the drill ground as usual, but instead of a regimental drill he formed the men en masse and addressed them, and then called for three cheers for home. These were given with a will, and the regiment was marched back to the encampment where three cheers were given for Colonel Marsh.

Later in the day the remains of Benjamin Weeks of Company D were buried. He had died the night before; his was the first death in camp of a member of my company. His death made quite an impression on the men. According to military usage, when a private is buried, the order of march is first the privates, then corporals, sergeants, and, last, the commissioned officers of the company, the whole under the command of a corporal. As corporal, I officiated on this occasion. In the absence of a coffin, Weeks' body was placed to rest on a bed of evergreen; and evergreen was his covering before the cold earth filled the grave.

One of my duties as corporal was to take turns with the other corporals and sergeants in drawing rations. It was not long before the boys discovered that they fared better when I drew the rations. An explanation was found in the fact that each day when my turn came, I took the morning report giving the number of men present and figured from that just what rations we were entitled to, and I insisted on having this from the commissary sergeant. On one occasion the commissary sergeant gave me less quantity of sugar than I claimed and refused to make good the shortage. Taking along one man of my detail as a witness, I carried the sugar to the division commissary, had it weighed and got a certificate of the amount. With this, I appeared at the colonel's quarters and stated my case, with the result that the commissary sergeant was reprimanded and made good the shortage. This led to my being detailed to attend to the drawing of all rations for the company.

Daily life often brought encounters with southerners whose culture was foreign to the New Hampshirites' rank and file. The following anecdote from the regimental history illustrates:

> One day while Colonel Potter was standing outside his tent, he noticed a queer looking specimen dressed in a semi-military costume sauntering across the parade

ground in that lazy careless gait that bespeaks anything but the trained soldier. Having several times before noticed the same fellow hanging around the camp, the Colonel determined to interview him:

"Who are you, sir, and to what company do you belong?"

"W-a-l-l, Colonel, to answer yer last question fust, so I sha'n't forgit and git mixed up, I don't exactly belong to any company jest neow, but kinder go it alone, yer see? Though before this ere pesky war split us, we used to hang out as Ben Thompson & Co."

"I perceive, sir, you are more rogue than fool, and–"

"Thank yer, Colonel, for the compliment, but–"

"But *what*, sir? I want to know what you are hanging 'round in this way for."

"W-a-l-l, yer know, Colonel, a good coconut will chitter when yer shake it, but yer can't git the milk nor meat out til yer crack the shell."

"What do you mean, sir, by such silly subterfuge? Do you want me to order you under arrest as an idle camp follower and suspicious character?"

"Oh, no, Colonel, I don't want any orders to 'rest anybody, though I jest guess yer right about these 'ere idle camp fellers acting mighty 'spicious. And that's the reason, yer see, Colonel, that I can't train in theya company, for there's nothin' 'spicious or speckled 'bout me, but I'm jest as full of fun as two kittens and a fiddle."

"Will you answer my questions, or will you not, sir? I give you one more chance to explain yourself and your business here."

"W-a-l-l th-a-r, Colonel, since yer so mighty pertikeler to git a wee sip of the coconut milk, I'll jest tell yer, that if this 'ere regiment should happen to git turned wrong side out before it gits through, and go back to New Hampshee *tail end tu*, I should then be Colonel instead of you."

One day while picketing on the banks of the Rappahannock, J.B. Leighton of Company G was hailed by a Rebel picket across the river and asked if he had any coffee.

"Plenty of it," responded Leighton, "come over and get some."

"Wish I could," replied Johnny, "but I tell you what I will do, Yank. I'll exchange a cargo of the weed for one of the berry."

"All right, rig up your transport, Johnny, and send her along."

In a few minutes a little dug-out with rudder set to hold it against the current and laden with a twenty-ounce plug of tobacco, is pushed out into the stream and slowly makes its way toward the opposite shore . . . and the witty reb again shouts to Leighton:

"Oh! Yank, did you know we'uns have got a new general?" .

"No, who is it?"

"General Starvation, by damn."

J.B. Leighton took the hint, and when the transfer boat returned, it carried in addition to the coffee barter, a big chunk of pork and a lot of hard-tack.

So the days passed and the rainy season of the year arrived. The belief that there would be no winter campaign gained credence, and we settled down to the every-day life of the soldier as though we knew we were to remain in our camp during the remainder of the winter. But this was not to be.

CHAPTER III

Defeat At Fredericksburg

December 1862. *The army under General Ambrose E. Burnside had been organized by him into three "grand" divisions and formed in the attack on Fredericksburg, the right, left and centre, commanded respectively by Major-Generals Sumner, Franklin and Hooker. The Centre Grand Division was composed of the Third and Fifth Corps. The 12th New Hampshire regiment was an independent command taking the place of a brigade and part of the Third Corps. All were under the command of General Amiel W. Whipple.*

One thing was evident: Franklin must succeed or Burnside would be defeated; but delays had made General Burnside's original plan (to occupy Fredericksburg by the 20th of November) hazardous. The pontoons and bridges were plenty but the opportunity to successfully use them had long past. But with more persistency than discretion, he determined to carry out his original plan.

On the 10th of December, just as the sun was setting, orders came to Colonel Potter to move in light marching order.

J.P. Fahey

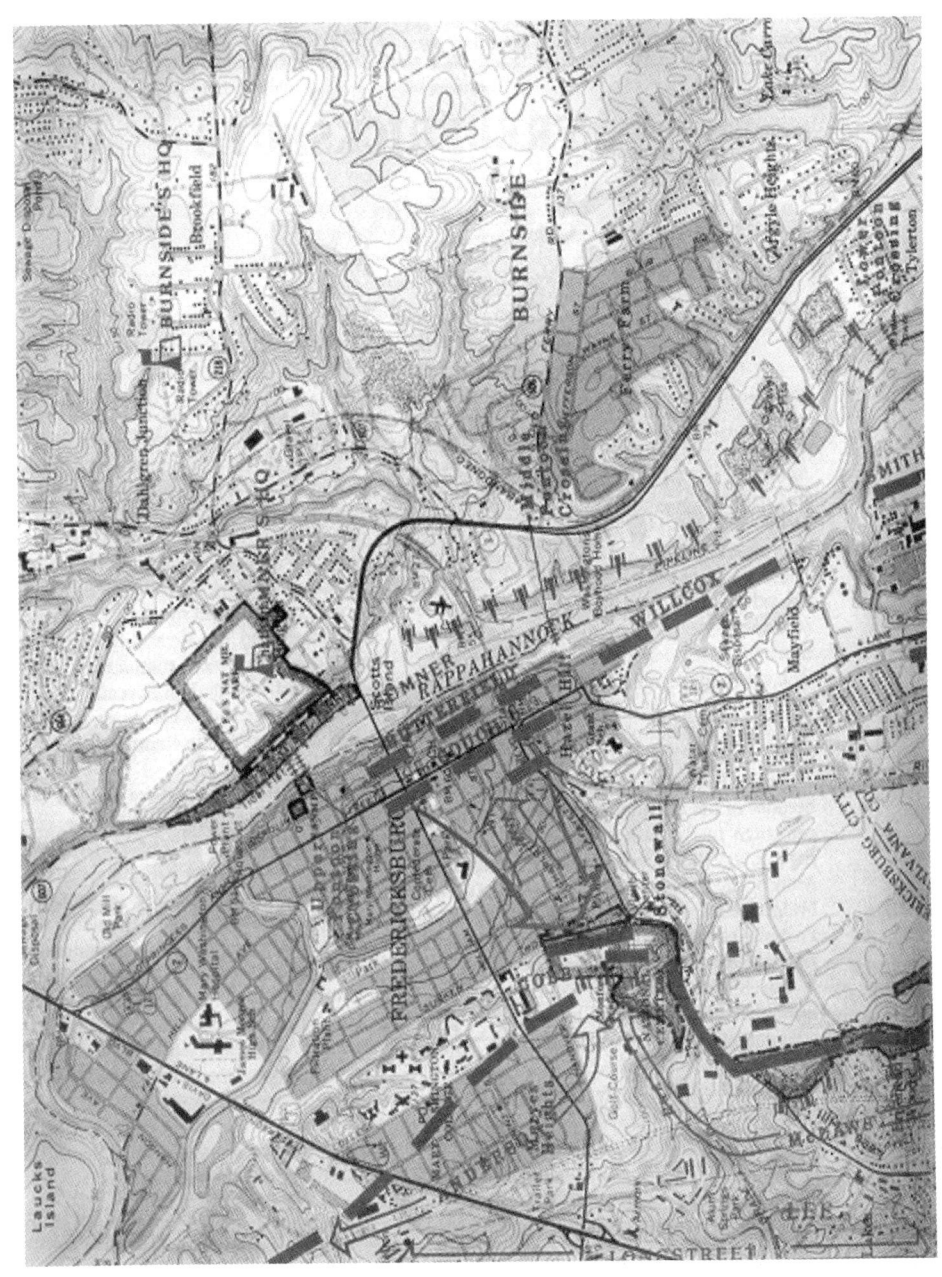

FREDERICKSBURG

December 11-13, 1862

MUSTERED!

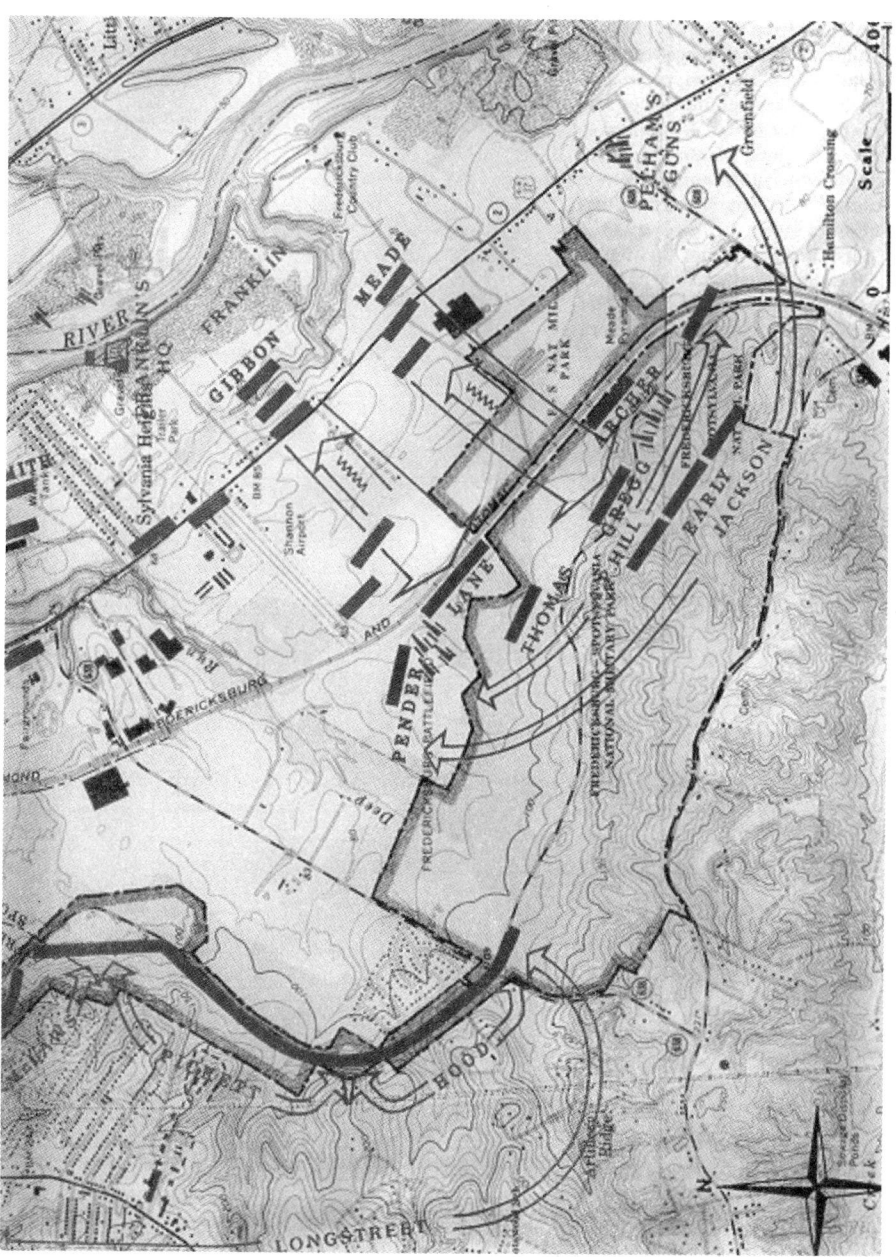

COMBAT STRENGTH
Union: *120,000*
Confederacy: *78,000*

CASUALTIES
Union: *12,600*
Confederacy: *5,300*

Our orders on Wednesday, December 10th, were to be ready to march with four days' rations and sixty rounds of ammunition and to leave our knapsacks and all extra clothing in our quarters. This indicated business, and the boys shuddered as much at the thought of exposure that might come as at the prospect of a battle, for the weather was severe and the nights cold.

This order to leave a part of our clothing in camp, which was given several times, was a mystery to all. When troops leave a given locality, they are never sure of returning—unless the commanding general is sure of being defeated and therefore obliged to return.

The next morning at five o'clock we were ordered to prepare to march. We hastily donned our overcoats, slung our arms and equipments, and placed our blankets in rolls to throw over our shoulders. While these preparations were being made, firing from the direction of Fredericksburg was distinctly heard, vivid reminders of the work ahead. We remained ready to fall in till eleven o'clock when the orders finally came to move, and we commenced our march to the music of the booming guns. After marching two or three miles, we halted and there remained the rest of the day.

From our position, the view was an inspiring one. The plain between us and Fredericksburg was covered with the army of the Potomac in battle array. The engineer corps was endeavoring to lay pontoons on the river, and the artillery on the high ground opposite the city kept up a constant cannonade all day long to protect the men at their work. For hours the roar of artillery shook the earth under our feet, though we were more than a mile from the battle scene. We bivouacked for the night near the 9th Regiment,

MUSTERED!

New Hampshire Volunteers. That evening there was another reunion of former Tilton students in that regiment and those from the same school in the Twelfth, of whom I was one. Home, the seminary and the coming battle were the topics of conversation, and all were hopeful of the result of the coming conflict. Appleton Huntoon treated the party to fried potatoes and a great luxury they were.

On Friday morning, December 12, after a cold, uncomfortable bivouac on the frozen ground, Whipple's division, of which our regiment was part, was ordered to advance to the head of the centre bridge in front of the city. We resumed the march towards Fredericksburg and halted on the bluffs opposite the city near the Lacey house. Six pontoons spanned the Rappahannock, three some distance below the city and three between the city and the bluffs where we were. West of the city on St. Marye's heights, the enemy was strongly entrenched. General Franklin had crossed south of the city and had already engaged the enemy, and General Sumner's forces had crossed on the bridges opposite the Lacey house, and occupied the city. Soon after noon, Colonel Potter received orders for the 12th Regiment to cross the river on the north bridge and take its place in the division column. In marching to this bridge, just as the regiment appeared on the bluff, it came within range of the batteries on St. Marye's heights, and three shells in rapid succession were thrown at us. The first went over our heads, the second fell short, but the third struck in Companies B and K, and eight men fell. Colonel Potter, with rare presence of mind, gave the command, "Right oblique, double quick march!" The regiment rapidly swung to the left into a ravine out of sight of the Rebel gunners. Colonel Potter later said that the cool and steady manner of the men was most commendable and that although he was not leading veteran regulars, he now knew he had the material from which they could soon be made and upon which in the hour of coming trial, he could safely rely.

Eight men were wounded: Lieutenant Charles Marsh and Everett Jenkins of Company B; Lieutenant William Dame, Samuel Eaton, Benjamin Ellsworth, Cyrus Philbrick, Homer Eames and James Tibbetts, of Company K. Of the eight, the last two died of their wounds a day or two later; and Jenkins, lying at the point of death for a long time, was left a suffering cripple for life. All the rest were permanently disabled. Just before this, where we were resting near the Lacey house, men had been at work for weeks preparing wood for the army and there were immense piles there. One man had left a small ax without any helve, and it occurred to me that it would be a fine thing to use in camp, so into my haversack it went along with my food. When the shells made their visit into our ranks and the run commenced for the ravine, this ax suddenly grew heavy. Indeed, it seemed to weigh a ton, and I acted on the impulse of the moment and let it go. Had it remained in my haversack, its weight would have slowed me down, and I probably would have been among the wounded.

So many troops crowded the bridge that the 12th Regiment remained on the east bank of the river till nightfall, when it marched back nearly a mile and there bivouacked on the soft, wet, cold ground, and we passed a most uncomfortable night.

During the night, eleven men from our regiment deserted. Among the number was Jed Hubbard of Company C. A comrade of his had recently received a pair of new boots from home, and that evening all were bemoaning the want of wood with which to build a fire when Jed said to his comrade, "You lend me your boots and I will get some wood if I have to go to New Hampshire for it." The boots were loaned, and Hubbard went to New Hampshire and did not return until he was brought back many months later under arrest for desertion.

First Scenes of War

On the morning of the 13th, we again started for the city and crossed the river on the upper bridge. The battle was raging in all its fury, the very ground trembling under our feet from the shock. There was a constant crash of musketry and thunder of artillery; solid shot and shells were flying over our heads, both from the heights occupied by the Confederates and from the Union guns on the east bank of the river. After reaching the city, we remained some time on the west bank of the river in mud so deep it was almost impossible to move. The city had been hastily deserted by the inhabitants when the bombardment commenced; nearly every building had been pierced with shot or shell, and many buildings, especially at the north end, had been destroyed by shot or fire.

While standing here in the mud and water, there commenced to arrive from the battlefield stragglers and skulkers pale with fright, wounded men, some with wounds that would seem to make it impossible for them to walk, and ambulances filled with the wounded — all pressing for the pontoons to pass to the eastern side of the river. Soldiers on stretchers were carried by, bleeding, groaning and dying as they passed; the faces of some of the regiment were nearly as pale as the poor sufferers, as they looked for the first time upon the horrors of the battlefield. It was not a scene to make new troops feel eager to participate in the deadly strife into which our silent men expected in a few moments to be led.

About two o'clock in the afternoon, after waiting here in anxious suspense for nearly two hours, an orderly, bare-headed and covered with blood and mud, dashed down the street followed by screeching shells and handed a paper to Colonel Potter. He had hardly done this when there was a *w-o-o-o-i-s-h* and a thud and the orderly's horse lay dead beneath his rider. The colonel called, "Attention, forward march," vaulted into his saddle, and the regiment advanced on the double-quick up Amelia street to Princess Anne street, the third from the river, and then filed to the left.

The march up the street, although lasting but a few moments, was by no means a quiet nor a safe one. One shell struck and exploded near the head of the battalion, throwing the mud in all directions and bespattering the colonel who called out, "Steady!" to his men as he coolly took off his spectacles and wiped them with his handkerchief; another shell killed an artillery horse close behind Company F, while a third left an officer mounted for an instant on a headless horse as he was crossing the street a few rods in advance. Most of the regiment filed in column to the left upon reaching Princess Anne street, but the shells and solid shot (some in ricochet order) came so thick and fast that two or three of the rear companies cleared the street by the left flank and thus narrowly escaped the sweeping volley that would otherwise have torn through their ranks.

When we halted, Company D happened to be in front of a very fine residence and took the lawn for a resting place. While there, I, along with others, took a stroll through the house. It had evidently been the abode of wealth and refinement but was now deserted and was trembling to its foundation with the shock of battle. While passing through the elegantly furnished drawing room, one man near me shouted, "Yes! It was the men who lived in such houses as this that brought on this war!" and in his indignation he took a chair and with it struck the keyboard of a fine piano, a blow that made kindling wood of the chair and badly damaged the instrument. It was a shameful act by one of our own.

At 4:00 p.m. we again moved, this time to Prince Edward street, the upper street of the city. We expected that the next order would be to advance in line of battle to the relief of the troops engaged, but we filed into another street while the shells, grape-shot, and bullets whistled over our heads and about our ears every moment we were marching.

On the way, we passed a church that was being cleared for use as a hospital, the pews being thrown out of the windows. The belfry was at that time in use as a signal station. At this point the screeching of shot and shell was constant. One shell passed over Company D near our heads, struck in the street near us, and exploded. Fortunately, the shell was moving from us when it exploded and the pieces were thus carried by its momentum in the same direction, and none of the boys were hit. But this close call was naturally a stunner and caused the column to break, and the boys for the moment lost all semblance of an organization. As the smallest corporal in the company, I was at the foot, or left, and when this occurred, I simply did my duty and endeavored to hurry the men back into the ranks. This was noticed by Captain J. W. Lang, who was at the head of Company I, the next in line. He reported the incident to Colonel Marsh, and I was later promoted to fill the first vacancy in the company as sergeant.

All this time, the battle had been raging furiously, and the slaughter of the Union troops in the vain effort to carry the well fortified heights of the enemy had been fearful and all for naught. Refugees from the front all told the same story of unavailing sacrifice; and while we tried to find some consolation in arguing that these men were giving the dark side of the picture, still we could not but inwardly feel that the reports were probably true, as they proved to be.

As we neared Prince Edward street, the crash of musketry was heavier than at any time previously. We could almost see the flash from the guns of the opposing armies through the smoke of battle and the gathering shades of evening. This proved to be the final assault of the day, when General Humphreys' division made the last desperate, but unavailing, effort to carry the enemy's works. Then the firing gradually ceased.

We remained in Prince Edward street during the night, but there was little sleep for us, though the night was comparatively quiet. I tore a board from a fence and used it as a bed thereby preventing my body from sinking into the soft ground.

Near the Front

The next morning, December 14, found the regiment in plain view of the frowning batteries of the enemy from which a morning salute was momentarily expected. Our position was now as important as it was critical, and the order that placed us there directed that it be held at whatever cost until relief should come.

Should there be another effort made to drive the enemy from his intrenchments, the Twelfth now occupied the front line; its situation critical. Yet on this Sunday morning General Burnside was not inclined to renew the fight of the day before, and General Lee could well afford to remain where he was—behind his works on the heights.

As daylight came, the boys began to look about them. In a yard close by, we found several cows which the owners, being absent from the city, had neglected for several days. These were given prompt attention, and the milk they furnished was greatly enjoyed. A house nearby was evidently vacated in a hurry, and in the basement was found everything needed for preparing food. Active operations were at once resumed. A dozen were promptly mixing flour for fritters, and the stove and range were surrounded by as many cooks. If the fritters turned out were not light, they were at least palatable to hungry soldiers and disappeared with amazing rapidity.

As the day advanced and the air cleared, we could plainly see the enemy's batteries on the heights which seemed but a short distance away; but we were told that the distance was nearly a mile.

The day passed uneventfully, and as night drew near, it became apparent that we would remain where we were during the night. There were comfortable beds in every house, but as we could not scatter and occupy the beds where they were, we concluded the beds must come to us; so mattresses and feather beds and fine bedding were laid on the sidewalks, and weary soldiers with clothing and shoes on retired early to rest.

At midnight I was called to draw rations for the company. A half hour later I again lay down, leaving the rations to be distributed in the morning. Two hours later there was a discharge of musketry at the front near us when all hustled from bed in double quick time and marched to the support of a battery just outside the city. Here we were ordered to lie down and remain perfectly quiet. Our position was a bleak one; a cold wind was blowing, and we keenly felt the exchange of our warm beds for the cold ground. From this position I made two trips with two men back to Prince Edward street for the rations I had drawn there, and then distributed them to the boys as they lay on the ground. When we first arrived at the battery, I heard one of the gunners ask another what regiment had come to their support. "It's a New Hampshire regiment. I don't know which," he replied. "Well, we are all right then," said the first speaker, "The New Hampshire men fight."

After a few hours supporting the battery, we marched to the north part of the city where we lay for a while in the open field; then we returned to the city to General Whipple's headquarters. The north part of the city had felt the blighting effect of the battle more than the rest. A large number of extensive buildings, which appeared to be manufactories, had been destroyed by fire. Those that remained were shattered with shot and shell, and the wind whistled dismally through the ruins. Nearly every building in the city was wholly or partially destroyed, and it was evident that the fire of the enemy in its efforts to dislodge the Union troops had been more destructive than the bombardment of the Union army. All the churches, halls, and many of the dwellings that had escaped destruction were used as hospitals.

The situation was now becoming critical: To advance was impossible, to remain invited ruin, and to retreat was too hazardous. General Burnside was determined to renew the attack regardless of the chances, while General Lee at a council on the 15th was advised by General Jackson to "drive the Yankees into the river." It is now known that one listened to his advisers and the other did not.

Monday, December 15, was a day of inactivity. In the morning we returned to Prince Edward street where we passed the day, and at dark returned to the support of the battery. During the early part of the night there was some picket firing and some musketry. The night was a horrible one. A cold wind pierced the heaviest clothing and rendered sleep impossible.

An Eerie Evening

About nine o'clock, a startling volley of musketry a little to the left broke the stillness of the night; and a strange, mysterious commotion was cast upon the city. The wooden shutters with which nearly all of the houses were provided began constantly slamming; every dog in the city continued for hours a most dismal howling and even the hogs joined in the chorus; the bellowing of cattle was occasionally heard above all. I find penned in my journal these words: "It seems as if all the hosts of hell were let loose in the city."

In addition to the howling of wind and dogs, there was also the sound of song and music — more sound than symphony. "Yankee Doodle," "Old John Brown," "Red White and Blue," "Rally Round the Flag," "When Johnny Goes Marching Home," and many other amusing or patriotic songs were sung with violin and piano accompaniment, while others equally as fond of music but less able to produce it, would undertake to interpret the "Devil's Dream" by the spirit-prompted taps and raps of the toe and heel.

Soon after two o'clock (Tuesday morning, the 16th) rain began to fall in true Virginia style, and we were ordered to march on what proved to be the retreat of the army, though we did not realize this fact till we neared the pontoon bridges. It was with no light hearts that we recrossed the bridges, for this was an admission that the battle of Fredericksburg had been lost and that the fearful sacrifice of thousands of brave men had been in vain. At this moment commenced the deep gloom that rested so long on the Army of the Potomac.

Left Behind

Colonel Potter had received orders to occupy the ground between the reservoir and the Kenmore house and to establish pickets from that house to unite with the pickets of Carroll's brigade. For this purpose, Companies F and C, under the direction of Colonel Marsh, were detached to hold that position, while the remainder of the regiment marched back into the city and formed a line on Princess Anne street, in front of General Whipple's headquarters near the place it occupied on Saturday afternoon. The rain poured down in torrents, washing away the earth from under the men as they lay silent and watchful.

At the time the march to the pontoons commenced, Companies F and C were on picket duty, and either through an oversight or design to keep the picket line intact and thus deceive the enemy as to the movement being made, no orders were given for their withdrawal. After the 12th Regiment had crossed the pontoons,

MUSTERED!

Lieutenant Colonel Marsh went back to the west shore and withdrew these companies, but so great was his haste that he forgot the men posted on the picket line. Sergeant Randolph, in charge of the pickets from these companies, discovered the true situation a few minutes later, and they proceeded on the double quick to the river which they reached just as the last planks were being removed from the pontoons.

Here is the account of the rescue mission as recorded in the history of the regiment:

> At five o'clock the regiment left its position in the city and retreated across the river. But Companies F and C, where were they? Alas, they had been left without notice or warning of their danger and were still in the face of the enemy, anxiously intent to discover any movement in their front, while all unconscious of the movements, more important to them, that were silently going on in their rear.
>
> Yet they were not forgotten by Colonel Marsh who asked permission of General Whipple to go back and take them off, but was refused for fear the attempt at so late an hour would hazard the safety of all the troops not yet across the river . . . but the Colonel was not the man to let possible contingencies deter him from what he now considered a present duty. His resolution was fixed; yet before he could act, he must obey the direct command of his superior to cross the river with his regiment.
>
> No sooner were his horse's feet on the opposite shore than he turned his head toward the city. [But] Colonel Potter remonstrated. "I posted the men there, and I shall take them off or be taken with them,"

replied Colonel Marsh. He put spurs to his horse and dashed back across the river, ordering the men who had already commenced to take up the bridge to desist until he could bring down the troops that had been left.

Riding out as far as he dared without attracting the attention of the Rebel pickets, for it was now daylight, he dismounted, and hitching his horse, hurried forward on foot until near enough to whisper his orders to Captain Langley of Company F and all followed him as quickly and quietly as possible to the river. It was now a race, instead of a march, until the Rappahannock was once more between them and the foe.

Yet in the unexpected call and hurry to obey, the vedettes had been forgotten. One of the men as he lay on the ground thought he heard some movement of men behind them and reported it to Sergeant Randolph who sent Corporal Osgood to the reserve to ascertain the cause . . . and it took the Corporal but a few minutes to discover that their reserve and battery had left. Sergeant Randolph understood the full meaning of this and lost no time in taking his squad, 'single file, trail arms, double-quick' to the river, just in time to cross before the bridge was taken up, section after section being swung into the stream, close behind them.

Someone Had Blundered

The battle of Fredericksburg will probably go down in history as perhaps the most stupendous blunder of the war. The one extenuating feature was that General Burnside knew he was not capable of commanding the

Army of the Potomac and shrank from the responsibility of the position. General Lee's army held St. Marye's heights a mile back from Fredericksburg, and here he had had months in which to add to the natural strength of the position. All this time, General Burnside's army, vastly superior in numbers to that of Lee's, had occupied the plain on the north side of the Rappahannock, opposite Fredericksburg. The time had been occupied in drills and perfecting the army for the coming struggle, but one essential for success seems to have been overlooked: General Burnside failed to inform himself concerning the nature of the ground he would have to pass over in making an attack. He refused to believe that a canal existed, (which ran parallel with the river between the city and the heights) though informed by competent authority. But when the supreme moment came, it was found to be there and greatly retarded the advance of the assailants.

General Burnside sent across the river 113 men under able corps commanders while he remained at his headquarters at the Phillips mansion, a mile from the river on the east side but in full view of the scene of action.

An attempt was made to carry the heights by a direct assault at various points, but every attempt was a failure. It could not be otherwise, for behind the stone wall and earthworks on St. Marye's heights were massed the infantry and artillery of the Southern army. Lead and iron were poured in a continuous stream into the ranks of the Union army, and thousands went down. It closed up its ranks and pressed on, or retired and reformed and renewed the attack, only to meet with the same result— failure. General Longstreet of the Confederate army later said that six assaults were made in front of his position and every one repulsed, that the field was covered with the dead and wounded, that the dead were piled sometimes three deep; and that after the third assault, the dead and wounded seriously impeded the advance of the assailants.

This condition existed all along the line. The most desperate valor was displayed by the Northern soldiers even though the humblest private was fully convinced that the attack could not succeed.

Much has been said of Pickett's charge at Gettysburg later in the war, but in that charge there was some hope that the 15,000 men hurled against one point of the Union line might succeed, yet here there was none, and brave men faced almost certain death without any expectation of success. Tennyson has sung of the *Charge of the Light Brigade,* and said "someone had blundered." That charge cost but fifty lives, but the ground at Fredericksburg was covered with thousands because one had blundered.

General Hooker, seeing the hopelessness of continuing the struggle, sent an aid to Burnside to express his views and finally went in person to protest, but all to no avail; so the struggle went on. When night put an end to the struggle, 1,200 gallant men were with the dead and ten times that number had been wounded or were among the missing.

Strange as it may seem, General Burnside was resolved to renew the struggle the next day and to lead the assault in person. He issued orders to this effect and was only deterred from his resolution by the united protest of all his corps commanders.

It did not take long for the army to realize that a stupendous blunder had been committed, and it is not surprising that the morale of the army rapidly sank to a low point. The idea was openly expressed that the South could not be whipped, certainly not unless a great general could be found capable of leading the Union army. Yet Burnside was retained as the commander of the Army of the Potomac and was to add the dismal Mud March to his record before he was removed.

After fifty years of thinking and reading, I have failed to see or find a single reason why the common soldier in the ranks was not right when his judgment told him it was simply an awful, useless sacrifice of life for General Burnside to hurl his devoted army against a strongly entrenched foe on the heights of St. Marye; and the wonder has grown during all these years that the authorities at Washington should have permitted it. During all the war, at least up to the time when Grant took the supreme command, the authorities at Washington knew in advance every contemplated move of the army, but in this case, the manner of assault could not have been known.

J.P. Fahey

CHAPTER IV

Camp and Hospital

December 1862. *After marching through the mud and rain till eight o'clock on Tuesday, the 16th, the regiment entered its old camp and took possession of its old quarters.*

Upon returning to their quarters, it became known to the officers and men that another blunder had been made in their absence. It seems that on the second day after the regiment had left, an officer rode into camp where the sick and wounded lay and ordered that every man who could walk and carry a gun should report to Fredericksburg at once. After marching as fast as they could – half of them nearly falling out by the way – they were ordered back to their quarters where their presence and condition was made known. Yet no one seemed to know who authorized or who brought the order.

On arriving in camp, rounds of cheers were given for Colonel Potter and Lieutenant Colonel Marsh. Our regiment had passed through a battle where the losses had been appalling and had suffered but little. Different portions of the corps had been detached from time to time to strengthen weak points or repel expected attacks; and in every case its officers had obeyed orders. But in the minds of the masses, it was Colonel Potter's superior judgment that had saved them; and the same lack of reason that had failed to see any good in him up to this time because he was not their chosen leader, now gave him the credit for their good fortune.

The Twelfth had continued to be an independent command, a brigade by itself, not subject to orders from any single-starred general unless acting as major-general commanding the division, as General Whipple was at this time. Because of this fact being taken advantage of by Colonel Potter, the regiment was probably saved from sacrifice at Fredericksburg. One of the brigade commanders who had been ordered to assault the enemy's works requested, more as a command than an invitation, that Colonel Potter join him with his "New Hampshire Mountaineers." The Colonel sternly replied, "I take my orders from General Whipple, sir; and I don't propose to needlessly sacrifice my men while I have the power to avoid it." His reply was overheard and did much to change his men's feelings from apprehensive endorsement to apologetic endearment. Thus, when the regiment reached Falmouth, the men presented Colonel Potter with gifts manifesting their change of heart.

The officers made the colonel the present of a fine horse costing $200, and the enlisted men, not to be outdone, contributed $230. They sent a sergeant to Washington and had a saddle and bridle made to order. Both were formally presented to the colonel, who was deeply affected by this sign of good will.

The horse was led out, all bridled and saddled, and the colonel was lifted into his seat and requested to show himself. The horse, thus richly caparisoned, proudly bore his grateful rider up and down the parade-ground, his bright silver trimmings reflecting the rays of the setting sun as he pranced to the loud cheers of the men. It was a picture which, could it have a life-like reproduction, the observers of that hour would go a long way to see once more.

This change of feeling of the men of the regiment towards its commander was extended to the governor of the state, for his appointment had proven wise and so they were willing to forgive the past, and the governor was invited to visit the regiment. He gladly accepted the invitation. General Whipple held a review of his division, and in the evening there was a notable gathering of distinguished officers, in the 12th Regiment's quarters where speeches were made by General Bowman, the governor, and Lieutenant John Durgin.

Life in camp resumed in much the same order as before the battle, and we soon came to the conclusion that no other move would be made that winter. With this in view, most of the tents were rebuilt on a larger scale. My tent was enlarged to seven by nine feet and the walls made four feet high; it was seven feet to the ridge pole, which enabled one to stand upright in the center.

While in camp at Falmouth, the making of baker's bread was commenced for the Third Corps near our quarters. The leveled ground constituted the bottom of the ovens and on this, large concave sheets of iron which constituted the tops were placed, thus forming large ovens. The tops were covered with earth and the heat from the fires made inside was thus retained for a long time. Here most excellent bread was baked by a corps of bakers, and we enjoyed the luxury of a soft bread ration.

MUSTERED!

Near the end of the year a visit by Hon. John P. Hale was received in the camps of all the New Hampshire regiments. The men recalled a time when Hale stood alone in the national senate chamber in his valiant fight for "free men and free soil," when the Senate, House of Representatives, Supreme Court, executive patronage and public opinion were united strongly against him. Now Hale had the approval of every branch of the Government and was being defended by more than a quarter million men in the field.

Sunday morning, January 11, Reverend John Chamberlain of Canterbury, state agent to look after the New Hampshire soldiers, preached to the men of the Twelfth. As he was preparing to sing a closing original selection entitled *The Railroad Hymn*, Lieutenant Colonel Marsh interrupted him saying he wished to dismiss the regiment because he feared the men would take cold owing to the damp weather. He directed the chaplain to close the services with prayer. Mr. Chamberlain felt insulted at this action and declined to preach in the afternoon.

At this time many were sick and the regimental hospital was crowded to capacity. Fever was the prevailing sickness, but much sickness was caused by homesickness. Scores died pining for home. On Monday morning, January 12, the remains of six who had died during the night were removed from the hospital tent and laid on the bare ground outside. Among the number was Milo Fogg of Company D. When Comrade Weeks had been buried on November 27, Fogg had been asked to fall in with the rest of the company to attend the burial, but declined; to the remark that he might need to be followed to the grave some day, Fogg had replied that he did not care whether anyone followed him to the grave or not. It seemed a little singular to me that comrade Fogg should be the next to need these services from Company D, but such was the case. During the next twenty-four hours, death claimed seven more of the regiment.

On the 14th of January, Samuel Page came to visit the boys from Bristol. His chief business was to visit John Chase of Company D who was sick in a Georgetown hospital. The next day I went with Mr. Page to visit the Bristol boys in the 9th Regiment. From there we went a little farther, from which point we could view the entrenchments of the enemy on the west side of the Rappahannock. On our way back to camp we saw a long pontoon train moving up the river, which clearly indicated a move of the army in the near future. On our return, the report of this movement and its significance was being discussed by the entire regiment.

Our surmises were verified, and the next day, Friday, January 16, the first order was received by the 12th Regiment, putting in operation the movement known in history as the Mud March. General Burnside was determined to cross the Rappahannock and flank the Confederate Army still entrenched at Fredericksburg. The crossing was to be at United States ford, twelve miles above Fredericksburg, but this plan changed to Banks ford, four miles nearer Fredericksburg.

Mud March

The first order for the Mud March notified the army to be ready to march at daylight with three days' rations and sixty rounds of ammunition. When the morning came, the order was countermanded and the time of marching was set for one o'clock on the 18th. Before this hour arrived, the order was again changed. On the 19th, the hour was again postponed for another twenty-four hours.

About noon on Tuesday, January 20, we started, but after going about one hundred rods, stacked arms and there stood till sometime after dark, a cold wind blowing all the time. About five o'clock it commenced to rain. Finally Col. Potter took the responsibility to march his regiment back to its old quarters.

When we reached our quarters, we found that sick soldiers from another regiment had taken possession of the 12th Regiment encampment and had pitched their tents on our old frameworks. In my tent were two from Company B, 124th New York Regiment. These men were attracted to our quarters by the reputation our regiment had gained throughout the corps for building superior, comfortable quarters. It was the first we had heard of this, and it encouraged us to continue to make such a contribution until our service together came to an end. We could not have the heart to turn these poor men out in the cold and rain, so we went to work to improve the situation. We built a fire, though there were now too many of us to lie down, and yet we got some sleep. All night long the rain fell in torrents.

At four o'clock the next morning Lieutenant Morrill came round and notified our company to be ready to move in one hour. When we looked out that morning, the face of the country was strangely changed. The entire countryside was thickly covered with the tents of the Army of the Potomac where it had halted the evening before. Even our own parade ground was covered. Previous to this move, there had been no other troops in our immediate vicinity.

About noon on Thursday, January 22, contrary to general expectation, the advance movement was again commenced amid a storm of the elements as well as a storm of curses from officers and men. All that afternoon we struggled on through mud more than ankle deep and went into camp after covering only about three miles.

No pen can properly describe that march. It was through a sea of mud. Roads were obliterated and no attempt was made to follow them. Artillery and baggage trains were so deeply mired that a dozen horses or mules could hardly move one piece. Many of the men, exhausted in trying to drag their weary limbs through the clay-like mud, and in utter disregard of what would be their necessity when night came, threw away their blankets and overcoats, and they soon disappeared in the mud beneath the feet of the men.

From sheer inability to move farther, the army went into camp on the second day in woods about five miles from our old quarters. During our march the rain continued to fall, and every hour added to the seriousness of the situation. That it would be impossible to continue the march and accomplish the object of the move was apparent to the humblest private in the ranks.

During the next day, there was no attempt made to move, but rumors of a return to our old quarters were rife. On the morning of the 23[d], the whole army was set to work with all the tools available building corduroy roads, and these roads led back to camp instead of in the direction of the enemy.

About four o'clock that day, we started our march back cheered by the warm rays of a shining sun. On arriving at our old quarters, a gill of whiskey was issued to each man.

Fighting Joe Hooker

At this time the morale of the army was at a low ebb. The whole history of the Army of the Potomac was not such as to inspire confidence, and under the command of General Burnside had come the Fredericksburg disaster and now the folly of the Mud March. The men in the ranks could reason, and judging the future by the past, some thought it useless to continue the struggle. Nearly all looked into the future with many misgivings.

The authorities at Washington finally grasped the situation, and on the 25th of January General Burnside was relieved and General Hooker placed in command of the army.

Great things were expected of "Fighting Joe Hooker," and instantly there was a change for the better. One of the first orders issued by General Hooker was one allowing one or two men in each hundred a fifteen-day furlough. This order alone wonderfully revived the spirits of the men. Some of the men thus favored failed to return, and the result was that after the first installment, few furloughs were granted. I had been informed by the company officers that I would probably be the next choice from Company D, but no more furloughs were granted from our regiment.

On Saturday, the 31st day of January 1863, the Twelfth was detailed for picket duty, and after this, we were regularly detailed for this duty. Our position was usually near the banks of the Rappahannock from three to five miles from camp, and our term of service was three or four days. On one occasion we were on the east bank of the river and could plainly see the enemy's pickets on the other side and talked with them. Their pickets rigged up a board-plank with a sail and loaded on it some tobacco and a southern paper, and we agreed to send back some delicacy and a northern paper, in return. The craft was put in motion and sailed straight for our shore, but when nearly across, it was capsized by a sudden squall, and their efforts came to naught. At other times the exchange of compliments between the pickets was successful and far more agreeable than exchanges of bullets under other circumstances.

On another occasion, I was one of the provost guards that scoured the country outside our lines for suspicious characters. We made several arrests, and I was sent back to camp with one man who was on horseback, but the fact that he was mounted was about all that could be proved against him, so he was released.

During the winter we were made very uncomfortable by heavy snowfalls, and the weight of the snow broke down the cloth roofs of our quarters.

The 12th Regiment still had not been brigaded, but had been in the Third Division of the Third Army Corps, commanded by General Stoneman. On the 8th of February, orders announced the resignation of General Stoneman. General Sickles succeeded him in the command of the Third Corps, and on February 19, the 12th Regiment was brigaded with the 1st and 2d Regiments U.S. Sharpshooters and the 110 Pennsylvania Volunteers.

MUSTERED!

On the 6th of March, the regiment was in line preparatory to marching to the picket line, when there was an exhibition of the impetuous temper of Lieutenant Colonel Marsh. Sergeant Frank Darling of Company C did not put in an appearance on account of illness. Colonel Marsh called him from his quarters and cut the stripes from his arms in the presence of the regiment. Dr. Fowler appeared about this time and swore Darling was not able to go on picket and should not go. The surgeon could excuse a man from duty in spite of the commanding officer, but he could not prevent Darling from being reduced to the ranks and so he had to suffer unjustly.

On Wednesday, March 11, after battalion drill, the regiment was formed en masse and thirteen prisoners, members of the regiment, were brought up and the sentences of a general court martial read. Most of these were men who had deserted before Fredericksburg. One member of my company had been tried for desertion at the time the regiment started on the Mud March. He was sentenced to forfeit ten dollars per month of his pay for the remainder of his term of service and to be kept at hard labor at the Rip Raps. The hard labor part of the sentence was remitted, and the man continued with his company and fought valiantly at Chancellorsville a few weeks later, dying from the effects of wounds there received.

On the 17th the monotony of camp life was broken by the sound of heavy cannonading up the river. The day before, a large force of our cavalry crossed the river to return a call made by the rebel cavalry a short time before, and this morning a sharp engagement ensued but without material results. The same day an order was read at dress parade making me a sergeant. This promotion elated me more than any other advancement or honor conferred upon me in the army or in civil life. It carried an increase in pay of only two dollars a month, so money was not thought of in this connection, but I had been promoted for doing my part, my duty, at Fredericksburg, and that was of great moment to me. A day or two later, a large number of express boxes—two army wagon loads—were received from home by the boys. I was one of the favored ones and in my box was a quart of popping corn. I popped the whole of that corn for a treat. Its fragrance drew many comrades to my tent. Thus, all the boys were on hand, and as soon as the treat was ready, they fell into line and each received a portion. It was a choice morsel and a vivid reminder of other days around the home circle.

Lincoln Reviews the Army

On the 6th of April, we witnessed a grand review of the cavalry and artillery of the Army of the Potomac by President Lincoln, on the plain about a mile from our encampment. There were 15,000 to 20,000 horsemen and many batteries. It was a most impressive exhibition. Two hours were occupied in passing the President, and the tramp of the horses over the soft ground sounded like a distant waterfall.

The next day President Lincoln visited the various encampments, and our regiment was drawn up in line to receive him. He was accompanied by a large number of generals and their staffs with a regiment of Lancers following behind as a body guard. President Lincoln wore a tall black hat, his feet nearly reached to the ground, and his great height, clothed in civilian's dress as he was, was in striking contrast to the rest of the company. As he passed along the front of our line, the regiment presented arms, the drum corps played and the boys all joined in giving lusty cheers. President Lincoln returned the salute by raising his hat.

This visit was preceded by a humorous event which occurred as the President and retinue passed through the regimental street to reach the parade ground. In this street a limb of a tree projected over the street, high enough for the ordinary man mounted, wearing a military hat, to pass under; but the tall hat which Lincoln wore came in contact with that limb, and the hat fell to the ground. An orderly promptly handed the hat to the owner, who replaced it on his head. This was in plain view of the regiment and a smile passed along the line as a result.

The following day President Lincoln reviewed the infantry of the Army of the Potomac. Although each battalion marched in close order by division, three hours were consumed in passing the reviewing stand. In general orders issued after the review, the 12th Regiment was commended for its "good appearance" and "worthy of special praise". The sight was a grand one, but would have been enjoyed more by all had it not been for the fact that a cold piercing wind blew all day, and we had several hours of waiting to do in heavy marching order before our turn came. Then, too, came the thought that this great army was only assembled to meet another great army, each bent on the destruction of the other.

CHANCELLORSVILLE May 1-3, 1863

COMBAT STRENGTH CASUALTIES
Confederacy 60,000   *Confederacy* 12,800
Union   130,000   *Union*   17,000

CHAPTER V

Chancellorsville

> *Alas! In how many homes of the North today is carefully preserved the last missive of love and affection from a father, brother, husband, or son, postmarked Falmouth, Virginia.*
>
> History of the Twelfth Regiment

April 1863. By the middle of April came signs that the great campaign of 1863 was about to open. The fifteenth of the month brought with it the greatest downpour of rain of the season. The same day came orders to be ready to march with three days' rations in the haversack and five in the knapsack. We were to take rubber blankets and shelter tents but no woolen blankets and no extra clothing except overcoats.

But no movement was made till two o'clock in the afternoon of April 28, when orders came to strike tents. Soon the regiment was forming in line, while the drum corps, at the suggestion of the sergeant-major, played the tune *The Girl I Left Behind Me*, for leaving Falmouth seemed like leaving home. The colonel, riding to the centre-front, gave the command: "Shoulder arms; right face; right-shoulder-shift arms; forward, route step, march."

"We are off for Richmond or the grave," expressed some of the boys, all in remarkably good spirits considering the possible work ahead. With Joe Hooker to lead or direct, all felt sure of success. We marched briskly for three or four hours without rest, then loitered along with frequent stops, but without orders to rest till after eleven o'clock p.m. when we bivouacked for the balance of the night. We laid our rubbers on the ground, put on our overcoats, spread shelter tents over us and, though cold, slept soundly.

The next morning we were awakened by the sound of musketry and cannon, and about seven o'clock we fell in and marched about a mile farther south to a place on the north bank of the Rappahannock below Fredericksburg. There we lay all day, which was a mystery to us then, but we later discovered that our march to this point was simply to blind the enemy as to the real purpose of Hooker.

Three corps, the First, Third, and Sixth, under General Sedgewick, had marched to this point below the city to give the enemy the idea that the real attack was to be made there, while Hooker, with the main army, was intending to attack the enemy on its left flank, above the city at Chancellorsville. A portion of these troops, about 12,000, had crossed the river on pontoons and had deployed in line of battle below the city. The Third Corps under Sickles, in which was the 12th Regiment, was held on the east bank but in plain view of the enemy in order to carry out the delusion. From the point where we spent the day, I could see on the other side of the river both armies drawn up in battle array, but neither side sought to bring on an engagement. A captive balloon high in the air above us was making observations.

We remained here over night, and the morning hours were wearing away when a courier dashed up and handed a paper to the adjutant. This was read at once to the regiment and was an order from General Hooker in which he said that the operations of the last three days had determined that the enemy must "either ingloriously fly or come out from behind his defenses and give us battle on our own ground where certain destruction awaits him." The men went wild with joy. Hats and caps went into the air, and they cheered as they never had cheered before. The same news was given to the other regiments, and cheering and martial music were heard in all directions. Whether there was sufficient ground for this exuberance of spirit on the part of the commanding general is a matter of doubt, but it served a good purpose and wonderfully sustained the men during the test of endurance that the later hours of the day were to call forth.

While this show of force was being made south of Fredericksburg, Hooker was crossing the Rappahannock above. The next move was for the Third Corps under Sickles to join Hooker, in the shortest time possible. Leaving Sedgewick with his two corps on the west bank of the river, the Third Corps started about one o'clock p.m. on a forced march for the right wing of the army. It made a long detour from the river, keeping in the ravines or out of sight as much as possible, hoping, though it would seem without reason, to keep this movement from the knowledge of the enemy. That General Lee knew of these movements and their object is a matter of history.

The day was intensely hot. The dry clay-like soil of Virginia was quickly transformed into dust by the marching men, horses and artillery, and the air was so heavily laden with the particles of earth that one could see but a few feet in any direction. Water was scarce, and the halts to find it or to rest were very few. On, on we pressed, much of the time on almost the double quick, until it seemed that each step must be the last. My feet were sore and blistered, but I was not as badly off as many others whose shoes had given out entirely. The route was strewn with blankets, overcoats and shelter tents thrown away by the men to lighten their loads.

Finally at about one o'clock that night, having reached a point near Hartwood church, eighteen or twenty miles from where we had started, a halt was called for the remainder of the night.

As soon as the order was given, a rush was made for a small sandy brook close by, and so anxious were the men for a drink or to secure water for coffee or their canteens, that they got into the stream like a herd of cattle and soon the water was thick with sand. Up to this time I had acted on a school boy notion that coffee was injurious, but this night I drank coffee for the first time, and though I strained it as well as I could through my lips to keep as much of the sand as possible from entering my mouth, I found it so refreshing that I was henceforth a great coffee drinker. Coffee and hardtack promptly disposed of, it was but the work of a minute to spread our blankets on the ground, and we were soon in blissful sleep.

At four o'clock in the morning reveille sounded, and we opened our eyes and arose from our beds sore and stiff from the over-exertions of the day before. As soon as a hasty breakfast had been swallowed, the march was resumed, but we did not march as fast or as far as the day before. We had evidently arrived within supporting distance of the right wing and so there was not the necessity for haste that existed then. We crossed the Rappahannock on pontoons at United States ford, and our march was practically over by noon. Within less than twenty-four hours from the time of starting the day before, we had covered nearly thirty miles. Considering that each man carried his musket, equipments, knapsack, haversack, and canteen—perhaps 40 pounds in all, besides extra rations for five days—the march was a great feat.

Soon after crossing the ford, we entered extensive woods on the south side of the river, and we could hear firing occasionally a little way in advance. This continued for some hours. At four o'clock, by command of the colonel, every man snapped a cap on the tube of his musket to clear it, loaded his piece, and then fell in, in light marching order, one man of each company being left to guard the packs. We marched toward the front about two miles and formed in line of battle, where we remained till half past ten o'clock.

While waiting here for further orders (between 4:00 p.m. and 10:30 p.m.), the advance of General Jackson's Rebel troops were silently but swiftly marching past the right flank within less than half a mile. Jackson's men later reported that some of the 12th Regiment's men, who had gone into the woods in search of water, were discovered by Jackson's flankers and only saved from death or capture by Jackson's fear of making known their near approach and thereby imperiling their own safety.

A Rebel prisoner taken the following night reported to Lieutenant Morrill that "General Jackson was for a few moments a prisoner in your hands but you didn't know it." Sergeant Tilton, who was thrown out on picket that night, reported that a Rebel general, whom he believed to have been General Jackson, rode out of the woods a few rods, took a quick survey of the open field in front and then rode back into the woods. Tilton lay silent and unseen in the sedge grass within a hundred feet of where the general halted; but in the dusk of the evening he could not distinguish with certainty, and having orders not to fire but to fall back at any advance of the enemy, he dared not take action.

After sunset the air was very chilly, and we gladly obeyed the command to return to the place where we had left our packs, where we bivouacked for four hours, and then again fell in, taking all our belongings with us.

Cheering reports continued to encourage the men. One reported that General Hooker had the rebel army surrounded and would hold them with a fast grip till they surrendered. Another reported the enemy in rapid retreat. Some were ready to cheer at each favorable report, others expressed their doubts, while others hoped for the best and waited.

The theory of a retreat was believed by many as it was in keeping with the information given by General Hooker, but I noticed that many who had seen long service in the Army of the Potomac shook their heads in derision when such an idea was advanced. To the repeated expressions that "Hooker's got 'em"; "the Johnnies conclude to 'ingloriously fly' rather than fight us on our own ground"; "there is no stone wall butting, stuck-in-the-mud nonsense this time" could be heard the ready rejoinders of the old veterans: "Never crow till you're out of the woods"; "You'll find out before you know it that Old Lee is neither a fool nor a coward"; "his men can fight equally well whether behind stone walls or pine trees"; and often heard:

> "Go Slow, Joe
> and let your hair grow
> for don't you know
> that 'taint all so?"

In order to understand the part played by the 12th Regiment, a brief account of the general situation at Chancellorsville is here given.

General Lee still held the Confederate army on Marye's heights back of Fredericksburg, in a strong position behind entrenchments. General Hooker was in command of the Federal forces and had a superb army of 130,000 enthusiastic, well-disciplined troops who had unbounded faith in their leader, despite the reverses that had attended their efforts under other leadership. Lee had an army of only about 60,000. Hooker's battle plan has always been considered a wise one. It was to attack the Confederates in their rear, and thus force them to meet him in the open, where his superiority in numbers would count. With this end in view, he sent General Sedgwick in command of three army corps, the First, Third and Sixth, to make a demonstration below Fredericksburg which would give the impression that the main attack was to be at this point. With the main body of the army, he marched twenty-seven miles up the east bank of the Rappahannock, crossed the river at Kelley's ford, then came down the river to Chancellorsville, a few miles above Fredericksburg, and there halted and, strange as it may seem, at once assumed the offensive.

This gave General Lee an immense advantage. He hurled the larger part of his force on weak points on Hooker's line and then hurled the same men against

General Sedgwick, who was advancing from the south with 22,000 men, and defeated him.

General Hooker had marched his army through the thick woods on the south side of the river, in which no army could be maneuvered to advantage, and reached the open country north of Fredericksburg where his superiority in numbers would have counted—the very spot that he seemingly intended to reach—and there halted. Here he seemed to have experienced a mental collapse and in every respect was unequal to the occasion. The enigma of the battle of Chancellorsville has not been solved and perhaps never will be. The charge of drunkenness on the part of Hooker, largely believed by the army after the battle, was disproved by a court of inquiry. If the findings of the court were correct, the contentions of his friends may also be correct, and that was that General Hooker resolved to be in his normal condition at this time and therefore took no stimulants, and his mind, therefore, accustomed as it was to daily draughts of intoxicants, failed to act with its usual vigor—in fact, that he collapsed from the want of stimulants. Whichever point of view is taken, one sees in the result a temperance lesson. There is another view taken on the condition of General Hooker, and that is that the long and severe strain on his nerves in planning the campaign and executing the first part of it had resulted of itself in a collapse of his mental capacity and that his mind ceased to act. He had been unable to rise to the supreme importance of the hour when his full vigor was most needed. The same has occurred in the history of other great generals, and even in Napoleon, when, after long continued strain, the mind refused to work till rested. Psychologists tell us that these transitions are frequently of lightning-like suddenness, and so here may have been a cause for which Hooker was not responsible.

After having reached the open country, and with victory almost in his grasp, he ordered his advance back into the woods, and then assumed the defensive. The point vacated was near Banksford, less than three miles above Fredericksburg, where a junction was expected with Sedgewick, who was fighting his way up from below the city. On the north side of the river at this ford was massed a large artillery force, ammunition and army trains, which were to join the main army.

This order was such a surprise to the commanding officers that General Couch sought to have it recalled, but to no effect, and it was reluctantly obeyed. When falling back, the order was countermanded, but it was too late; the enemy had already occupied the position vacated. This move sealed the fate of the battle. General Lee at once occupied the ground abandoned by the Union troops and was able to whip the Union army in detail.

Saturday afternoon, on the second day of the fight, a large body of Confederates was seen moving west along the front of the Union army. General Hooker deluded himself that these troops were retreating, but they proved to be General Jackson's force of 35,000 men marching seventeen miles to attack the army on the left flank and rear. The Eleventh Corps, under General Howard, occupied the extreme left, facing south and was in no position to meet an attack from the west and rear. General Schurz, who commanded a division of this corps, asserts that he was convinced — and so were many other officers of his division — that the troops seen were not retreating but marching to gain a position at their right and rear, and so reported repeatedly to General Howard, but he shared the opinion of Gen. Hooker so strongly as to the retreat that no new alignment of the corps was made to meet the assault of General Jackson. Towards night, the assault came with terrific force, and the disastrous rout of the Eleventh Corps occurred, threatening the safety of the entire army. This corps was composed largely of Germans, and for a long time these loyal Germans rested under the stigma of being cowards, when the responsibility for their defeat rested largely on the shoulders of General Howard. But the attack under Jackson on the Eleventh Corps was dearly bought, for its intrepid leader, while reconnoitering late in the evening, was severely wounded by his own men and died a few days later; and the Confederate army lost its most valuable leader, next to Lee.

On the third day of the fight, when the 12th Regiment suffered so severely, had Hooker thrown his reserve into action, victory might even then have been won, for 35,000 troops under Meade had not fired a gun. Unfortunately, on this day, during the fiercest of the fight, General Hooker was incapacitated by a shot which struck a pillar at the Chancellorsville house against which he was leaning, and he was rendered unconscious; he remained so for an hour or two and no one stepped into his place.

On the fifth day the army retreated, and imbecility even in retreat was shown by General Hooker. He and his staff crossed the river at United States ford and left the army to follow. A great rain raised the river to the danger point, and one of the three bridges was used to strengthen the other two. Here on the west bank of the river waiting to cross were massed from 7,000 to 8,000 troops. A single shell thrown into this mass of humanity might have caused a panic that would have been fearful to contemplate, but fortunately for the Union army, General Lee was willing that they should depart without making any effort to impede their movement.

May 2, 1863

The first gun of the day was fired about five o'clock, and desultory firing was now kept up almost continuously by troops in advance of us.

It was Saturday morning, May 2d, and one of those beautiful mornings that come to Virginia at this season of the year, but beneath her skies were gathered two mighty armies of kinsmen, with all the modern appliances of war, determined to destroy each other.

Just before we moved that morning, "The Fighting Parson," Lieutenant Rev. John Durgin, mounted a rotting pine stump pulpit and gave a patriotic talk. He reminded his listeners that the hour of action had come and expected all to do their duty like men worthy to bear the name "New Hampshire Mountaineers" and to prove themselves on the coming field of battle heroically true to their country and their God. Never a more attentive audience listened to a speaker than those who caught his words in the wilderness of Chancellorsville. The next day "The Fighting Parson" was left for dead on the field.

As Lieutenant Durgin lay dying on the battlefield from a minie ball which passed directly through him, he gave the Masonic sign of distress to a Confederate officer, who brought water and saved his life. Within six months of being reported dead, Durgin reported for duty at Point Lookout.

J.P. Fahey

B. B. L. 5–11½.
CAPT. JOHN M. DURGIN.

After falling in, we marched to the Fredericksburg plank road, and passed the Chancellorsville house, a large two-story, brick, plantation house where Hooker had established his headquarters. A short distance beyond, we turned to the left and followed a narrow path through a piece of woods, and then turned to the right, where we halted for two or three hours. Here were signs that fighting had taken place before our arrival. Rails from the fences had been piled up and covered with green boughs, evidently to shield sharp shooters. Our artillery, on elevated ground a little in our advance, was playing into the enemy's trains, and it was said that the enemy was retreating. Later it was found that the troops in front were those of Jackson marching to gain a position in the rear of the Eleventh Corps.

From this position we advanced in line of battle. In making this movement we came under musketry fire, but an order to lie down was instantly obeyed, and only one or two were wounded. Resuming the advance, we waded a brook nearly waist deep and then halted. Companies F and G, the extreme left companies, were advanced beyond the rest of the regiment as an advanced guard or to cover a retreat. As the left general guide of the regiment, my place in action was with the left company, so I was with Company F at this time.

Left Behind Again

It was while we were here the latter part of the afternoon that the disaster to the 11th Corps occurred, and the 12th Regiment was hastily withdrawn. But Companies G and F were given no orders to withdraw

The Twelfth had not proceeded far when Colonel Marsh came riding back and found, as he feared, that Companies F and G had been left down in the meadow – by order of Colonel Bowman, commanding the brigade – to cover Bowman's retreat and were still awaiting orders a half-mile in the rear – where in a few moments they would be marching to the rear of the Rebel army as prisoners of war.

Ordering the sergeant-major to run toward the front of the column and get orders from Colonel Bowman to take the companies off, Colonel Marsh rode back over the hill and waited with them for a reply to his message. He was welcomed with almost tears of gladness by the men, who expected every moment to be surrounded by the Rebels who were already moving to cut off their retreat.

Anxiously waiting, we finally heard the words "Bring them up." We marched, or double quicked, for nearly half a mile through the woods with Johnnies on either flank, all unconscious of our presence or we of theirs. The sergeant-major, exhausted by his long hard run, sat down and rested, waiting to accompany his comrades in the little rear guard that was coming. Soon he heard the double-quick tramp and then the labored breathing from our hurry up the hill, and then he was with us in our rapid march to catch up with the regiment.

Jackson's Advance

The Eleventh Corps, occupying a position at our right, had been stampeded by an unexpected onslaught of Stonewall Jackson's division of the Rebel army. This was nothing less than a disaster and seriously threatened the safety of the whole army. It appears that all this might have been avoided had the commanding officer of the Eleventh Corps, General Howard, listened to frequent reports that the enemy were making movements at the right, which indicated an attack from that direction in the rear of the Eleventh Corps.

While the panic stricken Eleventh Corps was rushing headlong to the rear followed by Jackson's victorious troops, Major Keenan and his four hundred cavalrymen were hurling themselves against the advancing foe and cutting their way through the Rebel ranks with their sabers. Berry's division of the Third Corps along with Sickles and Pleasanter came to their aid with twenty-five cannon which, double-shotted with grape and canister, covered the ground with Rebel dead and stayed the advance of the enemy.

It was just at this time that our regiment arrived to support the batteries. Company F was sent forward and deployed near the edge of the woods into which the Rebels had been driven. The Third Corps was now bunched up on cleared ground almost surrounded by the Rebels, who had already paralyzed the effectiveness of one corps and now threatened the safety of another.

We rested during the night on the ground fiercely fought over during the latter part of the day. The boys, with clothes still wet from fording the deep brooks, suffered much, lying with chilled limbs and shivering bodies uncovered upon the cold ground with no chance to warm or scarcely to move. Few, if any, closed their eyes in sleep. The events of the day, the situation of the night, and the unavoidable strife awaiting the coming morrow, the memory of home and loved ones whom all felt they should never see again, combined to give serious reflection.

Nearby the surgeons were operating on the wounded, and wet clothes and chilly winds were not the only cause of our inability to sleep as we lay on our arms that night, for the groans of the unfortunates pierced the night air. The heart-piercing cries of one poor fellow, continuing until death came to his relief, are still sounding through memory's half-deserted halls.

Besides these terrifying sounds, there occasionally reached our ears the exultant cheers of the Rebel hosts as the news of the victory of the afternoon spread from one part of the Confederate army to the other.

About midnight General Birney made an attack on the enemy within full view of our position, drove them back a short distance and recaptured a part of the Eleventh Corps guns. This brilliant charge was made just to the right of our own position and, lighted up by the flash and blaze of the enemy's artillery and musketry along the dark edge of the dense forest for a background, was a scene that no one who saw will fail to recall.

With the dawn of day our forces began to fall back and make new alignments. The Confederates followed with a spirited firing, when the Union army faced about and returned the fire.

May 3, 1863

On Sunday morning, General Sickles received orders to withdraw from his perilous position and unite with the main army – not an easy order to comply with under enemy fire.

Whipple's Division, being farthest from the woods, was first to move.

Down through a narrow valley of swampland, regiment after regiment followed each other as Hazel Grove was abandoned to the surrounding line of "butternut and gray" who were pushing forward on three sides. Passing beside a fence, every man was ordered to shoulder a rail to fill up a miry creek for the artillery to be hauled across.

After marching about half a mile eastward on a line nearly at right angles with the plank road, on either side of which the Confederates were savagely pushing, the 12th Regiment was halted. They were faced into line of battle and ordered to lie down just in front of a couple of batteries that had taken position on the crest of a low sand ridge and which now opened a rapid fire upon the woods in front.

The 12th Regiment was in the second line of battle. Our position was along a brook, where we were commanded to lie down. Perhaps forty rods in front, the first line engaged the enemy and sought to stay his advance. In our rear, batteries were placed so near us that the heat from the guns as they were discharged obliged us to stop our ears and cover our faces to keep from being stunned and scorched as shot and shells screeched past and over us.

From the woods in front came a continuous roll of musketry. On the right and left the sounds of deadly conflict came to our ears in startling detonations like the waves of a mighty tempest. A few rods to the rear a score or more of brass and iron twelve-pounders were sending twenty shells a minute over our heads. From the woods in front and from Hazel Grove elevation on the left, the

Rebels were answering back and sending their bursting shells all around us.

Between a little stream and the darker line of the forest—half a gunshot beyond—there was an open space of ground ascending gradually toward the woods through which the Rebels were cutting their way into our prostrate ranks, lying face to the ground and head to the foe.

This was our position on the early morning of the third day of May, 1863.

While lying there, close to my side were Henry and Uriah Kidder, brothers, both from Bristol. Uriah turned to me and said, "Richard, Henry is dead." I looked and saw a ball had struck him on the top of his head and passed out near his right eye. He did not move after being struck. He was one of three killed while we lay at the brook, but many more were wounded. Charles Gilman and Winsor Huntress were both struck in the head by musket balls and instantly killed.

The non-commissioned officers were provided with tourniquets made of metal and an elastic band for use in case of need in action. I had one, and during the fight placed it around the leg of comrade George Swain next to me, who was badly wounded in the leg. It checked the flow of blood, but the poor fellow died of his wounds the same day.

Nothing but smoke could be seen as regiments, torn and shattered, were retreating on the right and left. Some in Zouave uniform with apparently full ranks were falling back from the enemy before having hardly engaged him. The other two regiments of the brigade—84th and 110th Pennsylvania—were no longer to be seen upon the left, having advanced obliquely in that direction into the fight, followed by Colonel Bowman, who left the 12th New Hampshire to look after itself.

Along the open space in front, staff officers dashed swiftly to and fro, and riderless horses ran wild, while wounded men in constantly increasing numbers were coming; here and there irregular squads – mostly of Blue, but some in Gray – were hastily retreating.

On the right front, about midway between the brook and the woods, was another regiment, half-hidden in the tall grass awaiting, like the 12th, orders to advance.

How long the regiment lay in this position, forced to receive but unable to return the enemy's fire, no one can tell or will ever know. It was long enough to make many vacant places in the ranks of our regiment.

Until the Last Man Falls

Suddenly a staff officer rode up to Colonel Potter with another order informing him that the regiment at our right front was to advance first and the 12th Regiment to follow and support it. The order, direct from General Whipple, commander of our division, stated: "You are ordered, Colonel Potter, to immediately advance your regiment into the woods, engage the enemy there, and hold him in check until the last man falls."

Although the regiment at our right front received similar orders, no efforts of their officers could induce those men to breast the fierce fire ahead. Be that as it may, they did not advance... But the 12th New Hampshire did.

Colonel Potter, seeing the vain attempt to get the regiment at our right started, called upon his own; and all of the Twelfth, save the dead and dying, immediately arose and moved forward to the edge of the woods.

MUSTERED!

Such an order was enough to make the heart quail. Obedience to it meant that upon one single regiment of less than six hundred men – now for the first time under musketry fire – must fall the weight of at least three times their number. The powder-stained veterans of Stonewall Jackson, whose fall the night before they had sworn to avenge, were at that very moment pressing forward to complete a victory which they confidently and correctly believed was already within their grasp.

General Whipple, as he stood upon the top of the hill in the rear of his batteries, could see how wide was the breach that the Twelfth was now left alone to fill. But it must be filled, or his division would soon be cut in two, and all his batteries in the enemy's possession. "Hold him in check" were the words that implied all, and more than could be expected from any single regiment.

Our regiment stood isolated and alone, and the real work of the day for us commenced. Directly in front there was a lull, portentous of the fury of the quick recurring blast, whose coming was heralded by that savage-like screech so well known to every old soldier as the Rebel Yell. With nothing confronting them, they cheered their success and rushed onward to meet and defeat the next Yankee line that dared oppose them. Indeed, from the very start after reaching the woods, it was for the Twelfth a forlorn hope. Yet the men, no less than the officers, understood and realized their duties and dangers, and were ready and willing to meet them.

We reached a position on a knoll near the edge of the woods. The Rebels were further in the woods on lower ground and on the other side of a hill beyond, and thus they could see us better than we could see them.

We gained the crest of the hill in double quick and sent a volley of buck and ball, flanked by rifle minies, into the close advancing lines of our foes. Reaching the crest, Colonel Potter, having already exceeded his instructions, halted the men, more by the motion of his extended arms than a verbal order, and pointing with his sword to the enemy's line in the woods beyond said, "There the devils are! Give 'em hell!" The simultaneous volley that instantly followed reminded us that the battlefield is about as near that woeful place as any other spot on this sphere.

We poured a deadly fire into their ranks and prevented for a time a further advance of this part of their line. Here we held our ground till all the Union troops on our left and right had retreated and the Rebels had advanced to our rear on both flanks. At one time a Zouave regiment came to our aid at our left, but after firing one volley, retreated in double quick time. They were old fighters and perhaps took in the real situation quicker than we did, for this was our first musketry engagement, and we did not know enough to retreat.

The right companies had no sooner given their first volley to the front than a large battalion of the enemy marched obliquely past them, as if intending to outflank their position and attack them in reverse. Companies C, K, and B half-faced to the right and opened fire upon their flank. At the same time, one battery, on or near the plank road, gave them such a grape and canister reminder of their temerity, that they went back over the hill quicker than they came.

The musketry duel that now ensued between the foot soldiers of the 12th New Hampshire and the Virginia Cavalry opposed to them was "one of the most desperate and destructive

MUSTERED!

for the time and number engaged that ever was fought on any battlefield of the war." [History of the 12th Regiment]

We opened a brisk fire upon the Johnnies and received as effective fire from them in return. Our men fell rapidly. We neither retreated nor advanced, and it was not long before one-half our men lay dead or wounded in a long windrow along our line.

So hot was the fire upon the centre that the color bearers were both wounded. Colonel Potter sprang forward and urged his men to stand firm, but there was no attempt to retreat or purpose to yield any ground to the enemy, for every man standing still faced the foe straight up.

A moment later Colonel Potter was wounded, followed by Sergeant McDuffee, severely wounded, but still holding fast to the State colors that he had up-borne in advance of the line. The national colors were still waving defiantly in their place on the battle-line by the brave-hearted, but severely wounded, Sergeant Tasker; Lieutenant Bedee had received a blood-signed, bullet-sealed pass to the rear but refused, preferring to stay and fight with the few men left on the field.

Soon the tall, commanding form of Major Savage was no longer seen standing firm and resolute in the midst of battle; his brother, Captain Savage was breathing his last beside the stream; Captain Durgin had been shot through the body and lay dying at the foot of a tree; Lieutenant Cram, just promoted from the ranks, was lying lifeless among his dead comrades.

B. BK. L. 6–2.
LIEUT. COL. GEORGE D. SAVAGE.

B. S. L. 6–0.
CAPT. MOSES H. SAVAGE.

G. B. L. 5–11½.
LIEUT. GEORGE S. CRAM.

Captain Orlando Keyes, commander of Company D, was shot through the heart as he stood close by my side, defiantly waving his sword in the face of the foe. When struck, he sprang into the air, then dropped dead at my feet. He had been wounded while we were at the brook, but refused to retire.

B. S. L. 6–0.
CAPT. ORLANDO W. KEYES.

All the field officers were wounded, and all but two of the line officers were among the dead or wounded. Of the fifty men and officers that were taken prisoners in this battle, all had been wounded and captured as far back as the brook and sand hill directly in the rear of where the regiment was then fighting.

Yet the battle, so desperately begun, went on, the fire of the enemy seeming to increase as that of the regiment diminished. From the hot-barreled muskets of our men, round ball, buck-shot and minie-bullets were still being hurled against the foe.

Our men had sixty rounds of ammunition when we went into the fight, and we stood in our tracks for nearly two hours and expended all our ammunition, and then hastily gathered more from the cartridge boxes of the dead and from the hands of the wounded. Those muskets remaining whole became so foul that the cartridges could only be driven down their barrels by punching the ramrods against a rock or tree.

Finally, after all had fallen or retired but a handful of less than twenty-five men, Lieutenant Bedee, who had just been informed that he was the only ranking officer left on the field, aroused himself, though wounded, to the full sense of the responsibility so unexpectedly thrown upon him. Remembering that the order to Colonel Potter was to hold the ground to the last moment, he determined to continue the fight until he could assess the situation. Swiftly he surveyed the field and concluded that unless something was at once done, there would be none left for either capture or retreat. Quickly he gave the command to load and lie down. The boys hesitated to obey, and Bedee, seeing the Johnnies advancing, gave the order, "Rally round the flag, boys, and get out of this." Thinking, by the first part of the order, that the lieutenant could see one of the flags somewhere, there was a moment's delay, for there were no flags remaining on the battlefield. But we understood that retreat had been already too long delayed, and that it was our legs and not our muskets that must now save us.

On the right, the Confederates had advanced along the plank road and had captured a part of a battery on Fairview and were already engaging the rallying line of the Third Corps near the Chancellor House; while on the left, the Confederate force had taken and held the whole of the ground from Hazel Grove, where the fight first commenced in the morning, to the western slope of the Chancellorsville plateau.

The Twelfth for some time had been fighting and desperately trying to hold its ground in the midst of the enemy. It had fought for at least two hours and held in check for that time a much larger force of the enemy. From their advance into the woods up to this time, they had breasted the battle-storm alone, no other regiment having been seen that wore Blue.

The 12th New Hampshire was over half a mile in advance of the nearest organized Union force anywhere in that part of the field. They had become separated from the rest of the division and engaged in their own private war entirely alone, blocking the enemy's path long enough to suffer 325 casualties — more than any other regiment on the battlefield, Blue or Gray.

Yet they did not know that the door to the narrow and only avenue of escape was swiftly swinging to its close, for they would soon be caught between the advancing enemy and General Sickles' line of fire.

While on the retreat, the Johnnies were close at our heels and in advance of us on the right and the left, far beyond the position held by us before that position was abandoned. Several of our few survivors fell. One of my comrades who was running at my right—I did not know who—fell with a piercing cry of pain and terror. About the same time, a ball struck the stock of my musket and knocked it from my hand, numbing my fingers. I kept on without waiting to pick up my musket.

From the woods to the Chancellor house, a distance of perhaps half a mile, was an open field, and over this we had to pass; yet it seems a wonder that any man could pass through the storm of shot and shell that swept this field and live. The air was full of flying missiles and the ground was plowed up in all directions.

At my left, as I fell back, there was posted a battery to check the advance of the Confederates. The guns were evidently charged with grape and canister. The Rebels charged on these guns with closed ranks, and the fire swept the ground mowing great gaps in the ranks. We learned later that three charges were made by these men. Whether the guns were taken to the rear or captured, I know not, but the Rebels were soon in possession of this part of the field.

The plain over which we passed was thickly strewn with the dead and wounded, and many a harrowing scene presented itself. One that I recall still stands in vivid colors in my memory. A fellow from our regiment, assisted by two comrades, was making his way to the Chancellor house. He had the flesh so torn away from his hips that I could see the joints work in their sockets as he traveled.

While crossing this plain a new danger confronted the survivors of the regiment. General Sickles was trying to form a new line of battle near the Chancellorsville house, and his gunners were about to fire on the advancing enemy without observing the small squad of survivors from the 12th Regiment between.

As the remnants of the 12th New Hampshire emerged from the ravine on the lower side of Fairview, the quick eye of General Sickles caught sight of a small pocket of blue among the gray, and spurring his horse to the front of his guns, shouted out in frantic tones to his gunners about to pull the lanyards, "Hold on there! Hold your fire! Those are my men in front!"

On arriving safely at the new line of battle, Lieut. Bedee was met by General Sickles, who, amid the cheers of his men, rode forward to meet us, and a brief conversation took place between General Sickles and Lieutenant Bedee:

"What regiment, and where's the rest of it?"

"Twelfth New Hampshire, Sir, and here's what's left of it."

"Then fall in, my brave men, and help us hold this line."

"But we're all out of ammunition, General."

"Then pass to the rear with your gallant men, and give my guns a chance."

And we passed through his lines close to the Chancellorsville house and the woods beyond.

Scarcely had Lieutenant Bedee taken us through the lines before he was hit in the head by a piece of shell, which crazed him for a time, and Lieutenant French, wearing straps without a single bar, had now the honor of commanding the regiment. From colonel to a second lieutenant—twenty-eight officers reduced to two—and only about a score of soldiers left out of nearly six hundred enlisted men and officers that went into the fight. That is the sad but accurate picture of the 12th New Hampshire as it fell back beyond the reach of Rebel bullets at Chancellorsville.

MUSTERED!

B. D. L. 5-10½.
LIEUT. HENRY A. L. FRENCH.

Captain Hall of Whipple's staff had been for some time hunting for the 12th Regiment and found the few surviving members and conducted them back out of range of the enemy's shells. Up to this time, nothing had been known of the position or condition of the regiment by either Colonel Bowman or General Whipple.

There we rested for a few hours. I lay down on the ground and, thoroughly exhausted, at once fell asleep. As I awoke, I was told that two women who had been rescued from the cellar of the Chancellorsville house had just been conducted by. As we passed this house, the bricks were being scattered by shot and shell and the house soon took fire. The house, used as a hospital at the time, was hastily cleared, and at the last moment, an officer visited the cellar and there found these women who had taken refuge there when the battle began. Their rescue from the burning building was widely heralded in the papers a few days later.

Near the Chancellorsville house was a well that supplied the house with water. A large number of men, famishing for water, crowded about this well regardless of the flying missiles of death, and here some were wounded and killed. My first impulse was to obtain water here myself, but I quickly took in the situation and concluded to move on.

After we had rested in the woods a short time, we gathered around those few already found, forming a rallying nucleus for those still hunting for the regiment. Toward night, led by Colonel Berdan of the sharpshooters, we, with others that had come in, were ordered back to the Rappahannock, where we had crossed on our advance.

In a short time, I overtook John Moores, a comrade of my company. He had been badly wounded in one foot and was making his way to the rear as best he could. I gave him assistance, and after proceeding perhaps a mile and twice trying in vain to persuade a surgeon to dress his wounds, we were overtaken by a mounted man, and I induced him to dismount and give Moores a ride to the hospital near the river.

Hospital and Wounded

The headquarters of this hospital was a large, two-story house occupied a short time before by a Virginia planter. Every room in the house was filled with the wounded, and many, perhaps a thousand, were lying on the grass outside, and a few physicians were at work giving temporary assistance and forwarding the men to the hospitals on the east side of the river.

While in the woods in the hottest of the fight, the centre band of my musket had been carried away by a piece of shell or bullet. I picked up another musket and had used it but a little while when I noticed by a private mark upon it that it belonged to Louis Rowe, my tent-mate. I had glanced over the dead and wounded near me but did not find its owner and was satisfied that he had been wounded and had gone to the rear. Therefore, as soon as I arrived at this house, I commenced a search for him. After going through every room in the house and spending a long time hunting among those on the ground outside, I found him. While in the act of firing, a minie ball had ploughed a furrow along the back of his left hand and then entered his right breast, making a wound from which he died nineteen years later. He dropped his gun and slipped his knapsack from his back, and then walked the three miles to the river. I made the poor fellow a cup of tea, and, as he was chilly and had lost his overcoat with his knapsack, I covered him with my own. I obtained a stretcher and saw him started across the river, and then I rejoined the few remaining in the regiment, who had rendezvoused near by.

The giving of my overcoat to my tent-mate was a great privation to me as I had no blanket, but it was the means of saving it, for if I had selfishly kept it, I should have lost it the next day as will appear later. The overcoat was returned to me when Louis returned to the regiment at Point Lookout the next fall, and I still have it, a valued relic of the war, stained with the blood of my comrade as it is.

Division hospital at Falmouth was crowded with wounded soldiers after the battle. Here many of the brave boys died from sheer neglect, for the doctor in charge and his assistants were staggering around drunk while the light was going out of the eyes of some who would be among the living could they have had proper care and attention.

Doctor Fowler, having properly cared for all the cases under his immediate charge, went over and offered his services to the many yet uncared for in the division hospital. His offer being insultingly refused, he turned around to leave, when his quick eye caught sight of a hand moving to attract his attention on one of the cots near by. Approaching, he found one of the most pitiable cases of mangled and suffering humanity he had ever seen. Nothing more was needed to bring his temper, naturally quick and already started, to a white heat. Stripping off his coat and drawing his revolver, he threw the doctor in charge and his assistant into a chair, the latter on top, and with an oath, bade defiance to rank or rum while he dressed the wounds of the poor fellow, who as a last hope, had besought his aid. Needless to say, he was not molested by anyone during the operation.

On another occasion, while assisting in the same hospital and attending to one of his own men who was lying in a very critical condition, General Sickles and staff suddenly came in with quite a number of attendants bustling and clanking along behind. This was too much for the doctor and turning upon the General, whom he recognized, said: "If I were in charge here, I would not allow you to come in!"

"Why, sir, what do you mean?"

"Mean? I mean you are doing more harm here in five minutes than can be undone this side of eternity. Look at that man!" (pointing to a man whose eyes were wild with delirium, just balancing on the dividing line between life and death). "See for yourself what I mean!"

The General saw his error at once, and ordering his followers back, he quickly and noiselessly exited the ward.

MUSTERED!

B. B. L. 6–0.
SURG. HADLEY B. FOWLER.

Wise, defiant and noble, this beloved doctor was mustered in with his father, Capt. Blake Fowler, and his 14-year old son, George. His grandfather, David Fowler, who was a soldier of the Revolution, signed up also but was too old (over 70) so hired a substitute to take his place, giving a representation of four generations in the same regiment.. At Chancellorsville and Gettysburg he was chief surgeon at the brigade field hospital where he became known as the "Life & Limb Saver" because of his skill and courage. In the Winter of 1864, General Butler ordered him to build and take charge of a hospital for the Army of the James at Point of Rocks, Virginia. After the war, he returned to Bristol where he practiced his profession as he had before the war.

G. G. L. 5–7.
CAPT. BLAKE FOWLER.   GEORGE H. FOWLER.

Captain Blake Fowler, *father of surgeon Fowler, enlisted at 58 years old. He fought in every battle.* **George Fowler,** *grandson of Captain Fowler and son of Doctor Fowler, acted as his father's private orderly during the war. He was 14 years old, and the adopted son of the regiment. After the war, he became the town apothecary.*

General Whipple, our division commander, fell at the hands of one of these Rebel sharp shooters soon after our arrival at the front. While being carried from the field, he uttered to his officers his last wish—that he should live long enough to give Colonel Potter and his brave men a just report.

That he did not is greatly to be regretted, for no official report was ever made of the part the 12th Regiment bore in the battle of Chancellorsville. General Whipple knew better than any other general officer of the difficult, almost impossible task when, in want of any other troops present, he ordered the Twelfth to hold the ground of a whole brigade.

Colonel Bowman, commanding the brigade, knew little or nothing of what the regiment did, or even of its position after he left it alone at the brook in the early morning, and thus could not, and did not, make a report of it. Colonel Potter was severely wounded and sent to Washington and never returned to the Regiment, but was later made brigadier-general. For his neglect in not making a report and giving the men of the 12th New Hampshire the credit that solely belonged to them, there is no justification.

Two unofficial recordings of the regiment's heroic part in the Chancellorsville battle have been found: A letter from Colonel Daniel Hall, Captain on General Whipple's staff at Chancellorsville, and a testimony given by General Sickles after the war at the Third Corps reunion in Boston.

From Colonel Hall's Letter:

> I well remember the 12th New Hampshire and when it was posted in the edge of the woods below the Chancellor House. It got separated, by some chance, pretty essentially from the rest of the division. I rather think its separation was brought about by its fighting better and more doggedly maintaining its position. Part of the division was on the right and part on the left of the

plank road, and not closely connected. The Pennsylvania regiments brigaded with the Twelfth were not ranged with it on the line of battle, but . . . were posted in reserve or to guard its flanks and were dispersed or driven back before the Twelfth was. General Whipple and his staff were attending rather more to the rest of the division, because, as I remember perfectly well, he had full confidence in the Twelfth . . . and believed it would hold its ground as long as possible.

After our line was broken almost everywhere and the army was practically driven from its position, and a retreat . . . was imminent, the 12th New Hampshire Regiment was still maintaining itself and had not given up its ground. Then, when the whole line had retreated toward the Chancellor House, the situation of the Twelfth began to be a matter of inquiry, and steps were taken by General Whipple to save whatever might be left of it. I cannot say that I carried any order to the regiment, for it was fighting alone and not under the orders of any immediate superior. Colonel Bowman, commanding the brigade, had lost connection with it; but I remember finding the remnant left of it after it had got back as far as the Chancellor House, and of taking it off the field . . . under orders of General Whipple to find and save the regiment, if I could. This was toward or about noon. At two o'clock, or thereabouts, the whole army fell back into a new line of entrenchments toward the river.

Of the remarkable gallantry and stubbornness of the 12th New Hampshire that day there is no question. It was a matter of common talk among us, and General Whipple, after he was wounded by a Rebel sharpshooter and knew that his wound was mortal, spoke of praise of that

Regiment and of Colonel Potter, wishing that he might live long enough to do these brave men justice.

Though not a field officer was left, and scarcely a line officer, and nearly three-fifths of its entire number were killed or wounded, the 12th New Hampshire came up the slope to the Chancellor House in fair order amid the fire and shouts of the exultant Rebels swarming out of the woods.

Colonel Bowman gave no direction to the Twelfth that day after the first formation in the early morning, and it was not under his eye at any time after during the battle. I also remember what a magnificently large regiment of stalwart men it was when it first came to the front . . . over six hundred that went into the fight. . . . I wish I might help by my testimony to do the justice to the gallant 12th New Hampshire which my lamented friend, General Whipple, did not live to do.

From General Sickles' testimony at the Third Corps reunion in Boston:

"I know that the 12th New Hampshire was the last regiment that left the field that day. When I had formed my last line near the Chancellor House, and my artillery was just about to open on the Rebel lines that came pressing out of the woods at the foot of Fairview, I noticed a little squad of blue emerge in sight over the hill on our left front; and putting spurs to my horse, I rode in front of my batteries and ordered the gunners to hold their fire as there were some of my men between us and the Rebels. I was interested to know what regiment the men belonged to, as I supposed all my troops had fallen back some time before that, and when they came up, I found they belonged to the Twelfth New Hampshire Volunteers."

MUSTERED!

[General Sickles was then told that his statement explained what some of the Twelfth men who were in that squad had said about him at the time.]

"What was that?" inquired the general.

"They said, Sir, that you were riding up and down in front of your line, bare-headed and swinging your hat, and crying out: 'Hold on there, gunners! Hold your fire! Those are MY men!'"

The general laughingly replied: "That little squad — for as I remember it there wasn't much more than a baker's dozen left of them, was there? — sprang into sight all at once and entirely unexpected to me. And if I hadn't seen them just as I did, there wouldn't have been anything left of them. Oh, yes, I certainly know and shall never forget so much about the 12th New Hampshire at Chancellorsville!"

Reports from Colonel Bowman and Assistant Adjutant-General Dalton, both of whom knew and saw little of the position or action of the regiment after it had taken its position in the morning – and as late as seven days after the battle – do not touch upon the Twelfth at all, other than stating that its "position was a critical one, the troops on either flank having fallen back and the batteries having been withdrawn."

Bartlett's history of the regiment states: "If that position was a critical one, as indeed it was, what shall be said of the position of the Twelfth more than two hours afterward when it stood fighting at least seventy-five rods in advance of its first line of battle with both its flanks firmly held by Rebel troops?"

While this sketch is simply a narrative of the personal experience and observation of a foot soldier, and in no sense a history of the battle, one cannot help but allude to the fact that through all the awful carnage of that Sabbath morning, 35,000 Union troops, ready and anxious to sweep back the victorious hordes of the Confederacy, were allowed to remain inactive in the woods within supporting distance, without being ordered to fire a shot.

Thus all in vain are thousands slain,
For want of a little nerve and brain.

    Our regiment went into the fight Sunday morning, May 3, with 25 commissioned officers and 549 enlisted men. Six officers and sixty-nine enlisted men had been killed, and three of the field and staff officers and 250 company officers and enlisted men had been wounded; a total loss of 325.

    Company D went into the fight with a total of fifty-eight and of these six were killed, twenty-five wounded and five were missing, so that we had in arriving at camp only twenty-two left.

    The losses of the Union army are given in official records as 1,082 killed; 6,839 wounded; 4,214 captured or missing; a total of 12,145. [The above statistics given by Musgrove were from War Department records prior to his death in 1914.]

    When Musgrove penned the above, he could not have known that his own regiment's losses at Chancellorsville would fill unwanted space among the official records, for the 12th New Hampshire would go down in history as suffering the greatest number of casualties in any regiment, North or South.

    Up to the time of rejoining my comrades, I had been so engrossed with the scenes of the day that no thought of home or friends had entered my mind, but as I then sat down to rest, my mind flashed to far-away home, and as I thought of the sad news that must be borne them, tears came freely, and I realized more than ever before that the immediate actors of the war were not the only sufferers in this great conflict. But the men were too tired for serious reflections, and as soon as our shelter-tents could be spread as a roof over water-soaked quarters, we lay down in wet blankets.

As evening came, and no sound of fife or bugle reached our ears, the camp took on the silent gloom of a graveyard with every tenantless and dismantled quarter, its walls and chimney standing as left, like a tombstone. And when at the close of day, the drum corps, for the first time after its return, played the "retreat," it sounded like a funeral dirge.

I had a piece of shelter tent, and joining that with a piece carried by a comrade, we erected a shelter but having no overcoat or blanket, I shivered with the cold in my sleep. About two o'clock in the morning, heavy firing on the picket line at the south of our position caused all to fall into line and stand ready for action. No movement was made, but there was no further sleep that night. The next morning the same solemn, death-like gloom reigned.

Those who were there will never forget that first roll-call after the battle With tearful eyes and choked utterances, those few present remembered their loved comrades and tent-mates among the absent as their names were called, with no response — as, ever so softly, the living responded to their own.

Dark clouds gathered and burst into a torrential rain around noon. One man likened it to "an aerial volcano from which came not only a deluge of water, but toads, frogs, snakes and fish, which were found on the ground after the shower." Yet the drenching seemed God-sent to the wounded and dying lying unprotected on the field. It soothed inflamed wounds and checked burning fevers, relieving many and saving some.

    To those who watched, it appeared as if a heaven-shed curtain of tears was falling upon the closing scene of battle, in the tragedy of Chancellorsville.

CHAPTER VI

After the Battle

May 1863. The day and the following night passed without any general engagement or movement by our army, but it is now known that at midnight a council of war was held in the tent of the commander-in-chief. General Hooker, with three-to-two of his corps commanders against him, decided to retreat without further effort from the battlefield of Chancellorsville.

As was to be expected, the news of our losses carried great sorrow to New Hampshire. Letters from home stated there was great excitement as well as sorrow at Bristol. One of my letters was opened at the post office and read to the crowd in waiting before it was allowed to go to the parties to whom it was addressed. The first news that reached Bristol was simply rumors as gathered by one and another, and consequently very unreliable. Several were reported dead who later were found alive, and some time elapsed before the exact truth was known.

Battle Reflections

Although I had been with Company F when it came near being captured on Saturday night, when the battle of Sunday morning commenced and the men began to fall, I wanted to be with my own company, beside friends from home, in case I should fall. So I took my place with my company comrades, three of whom were the Nelson brothers.

Corporal Albert Nelson was wounded from a piece of shell striking him in the head. His brother, Dan, went to his aid, and while helping him from the field, brother Major was found, also wounded, but not so badly but that he lent a helping hand in assisting Albert. A few minutes later Dan received his death wound. A ball struck him in the back, penetrated his bowels and protruded in front. The enemy was close upon them, and Dan begged his brothers to leave him to his fate rather than that they all be captured, and so he was left to die in the hands of the enemy.

B. D. L. 5-4½.
CORP. ALBERT D. NELSON.

B. D. L. 5-4½.
DAN P. NELSON.

B. D. L. 5-6½.
MAJOR J. NELSON.

Stephen Nelson made a trip to Washington to learn the fate of his boys, two of whom he found were wounded, but of Dan nothing more was ever learned later other than reported by myself and his brothers.

An effort was made to secure the remains of Captain Orlando Keyes and some others who fell in action on the 3d of May, and First Sergeant Hall of our company was sent over the river with a flag of truce for this purpose. But he returned without effecting his purpose.

It could hardly be said that the dead on the field had been buried. Loose earth only had been thrown over the remains, and they were not in a condition to be removed. Sergeant Hall reported the stench on the battlefield to be terrible.

It was not strange that at such a time wild rumors were in constant circulation. We were informed that Chaplain Ambrose was killed and that Colonel Potter, who was wounded, perished in the Chancellor House.

The first Sunday the chaplain of Berdan's Sharp Shooters preached to us and eulogized our late chaplain. A few days later, however, both the chaplain and Colonel Potter returned. The colonel was wounded and unable to travel and was therefore captured, while the chaplain, true to his nature, continued to minister to the wounded till he, too, was captured. Both had now been paroled. The colonel continued on his way to Washington and did not return to duty with the regiment, but was later made brigadier general. The chaplain resumed his work of love among the men and so continued to expose himself to the enemy for the relief of the men in the trenches. Such devotion as his was rare even among the men of his cloth in the army.

B. LB. L. 5–8.
CHAPLAIN THOMAS L. AMBROSE.

Battlefield Humor

Amusing scenes are enacted even on the battlefield. Near me was a man from another company who skulked behind a tree. The colonel grabbed him by the collar and struck him with his sword. The man jumped to avoid the blow, and they went round in a circle two or three times, the colonel hitting him a blow at every jump.

A sergeant skulked behind a tree and was seen by William Martin, who, himself, had twice attempted to desert. He went to a lieutenant and said in an authoritative manner, "Lieutenant Morrill, you order that man from behind that tree." The order was promptly obeyed. A minute later Martin was struck in the arm by a minie-ball, and, dropping his gun, he bounded like a deer to the rear. The wound was not considered a very serious one, but it caused his death a week later. While in the hospital, he said to a visiting comrade, "Now I have something that will take me out of the service." It did, but not in the way in which he had planned.

THE GRUMBLER

One man in our regiment was nick-named "the grumbler" because "he would grumble at the right as well as the wrong, at good luck as well as bad." When retreating from the woods at Chancellorsville where he had been knocked senseless by a minie ball that had grazed his scalp, he was overtaken by one of his comrades, who later recalled his sputterings — while the minies were flying thickly around him and great streams of blood were running down his face and clothes: *"This's about what I expected . . . Joe Hooker might have known better than come over here . . . but now he's got here, I don't see why in thunder he don't stay and fight, instead of backin' out this way . . . can't see any sense in fighting until you're most all killed and then quit . . . If I'm gonna fight, I wanna fight and git the thing over and done with it."*

SHAKESPEARE ON THE BATTLEFIELD

On the blood-drenched field of Chancellorsville, when the battle was at its height and the boys of the Twelfth were falling on the right and left, one of the "actors" in this tragedy, thinking to act a double part, embellished his role with a line of Shakespeare.

All at once he dropped his gun, raised his hands in a theatrical motion and while a comrade nearby looked on expecting to see him fall from a shot in some vital part, loudly voiced Mercutio: "Ask for me to-morrow and you shall find a grave man." Then coolly picking up his gun, he went on with his main role until the close of the dreadful scene.

Near the close of the battle, an officer belonging to another brigade, who came up to the right of the Twelfth, had the following encounter with Sergeant Piper:

QUICK CHANGE OFFICER

He [the officer] walked for a little distance along the battle-line of the regiment and exclaimed: "My God! Look at this line of death! Whoever saw dead men on dress parade before?" He was seen by several of those who were still fighting on the right of the regimental line, and seemed to be cool and self-possessed, as if there were not the zip of a bullet or sound of a gun to be heard. As Sergeant Piper was the highest officer left in command of the company, he came up to him while he was battling to survive:

"What regiment *IS* this, and how long have you been fighting here?"

"Twelfth New Hampshire; can't tell how long."

"Where are all your officers?"

"Haven't seen any lately."

"Well, hold your ground a little while longer if you can, brave man, and I will –"

The remainder of his sentence was not completed as he started for the rear, but Sergeant Piper understood him to mean that he would look after us. But in a few minutes he came running back, not so cool, and when within hearing distance shouted: "Fall back at once! They are coming down upon you ten deep!"

In the middle of the battle, the same Sergeant Piper, a man of few words, was told on the battlefield that he would have to take command of Company C as he was the ranking officer left. Piper replied, "Well, I'll do the best I can," as he vigorously rammed another cartridge down his gun barrel. He kept his word.

B. H. L. 6-¾.
SERGT. JOHN L. PIPER.

Roll-call came early on May 4th, at which ninety-seven enlisted men and four officers responded to their names. These were organized into four companies with a commissioned officer to each, and Colonel Bowman, with the fragments of his brigade, started for the front. Arriving there, we found immense breastworks constructed of logs and earth had been erected and behind these, we felt confident that the Union forces would be able to hold their ground. But it was evident that the army was in no condition to make an advance. Behind these works the men were allowed to break ranks and pass the time as they saw fit, and many, to while away the time, engaged in gambling, using gun carriages for tables. During the day, the enemy's sharp shooters, perched in trees, were engaged in picking off our officers.

On Tuesday, a little before noon, nearly all the enlisted men of our regiment were detailed for fatigue duty, under the command of Lieutenant Fernald and Captain Smith. By a blunder on the part of someone, we were ordered to leave our arms, knapsacks and haversacks. We marched a mile or more through the woods to the rear and right, and were set to work throwing up entrenchments to prevent a flanking movement by the enemy. An officer in charge swore roundly when he saw what condition we were in, but added that he was not responsible, and we must stand it, rations or no rations, as the work must be completed to the river by morning.

Knee Deep in Mud

Towards night it rained again as it rains only in Virginia, and soon the trenches were half full of water, but still the boys toiled on. About eight o'clock that evening, an order came for us to return to where we had left our arms and knapsacks. We tramped back through the dark woods, and finally reached the road between the pontoons and the front. Here it was easy to see that the army was on the retreat, for the artillery was going to the river with all possible speed. Instantly the officers of our detail lost control of their men, and there rose a wrangle between the officers and the men. Some contended that there was no evidence that the infantry had moved, and that we should return to where our arms and knapsacks were; others were in favor of striking at once for the river. The officers were unequal to the occasion, and their command rapidly disappeared, every man striking out for himself. Comrade Jewett and I, with a few others, decided to stick together and to return to the front for our effects. When we reached there the greatest confusion prevailed. The infantry had moved, but we had seen none. Where our brigade had gone no one knew. Large parties were engaged in destroying everything that could be of value to the enemy. Knapsacks were rifled and then burned, and muskets were heated and bent by a blow against a tree. I picked up a knapsack that had not yet reached the flames and found a haversack containing some food, which we devoured, but none of our arms or equipments were found.

There was nothing for us to do but to strike out for the pontoons, over which the infantry must go, and so we set out. But such a road! The artillery had churned the earth through the woods, in the roads and on both sides into a sea of mud knee deep through which it seemed impossible to make our way. At one point I slipped and fell and I have often, since the war, questioned whether I could have rallied from that mudhole had Comrade Jewett not come to my aid. Our experience that night has been recalled at nearly every meeting of our comrades since the war.

MUSTERED!

B. B. L. 5-4½.
LIEUT. ALONZO W. JEWETT.

About midnight we came to a clearing near the river and struck the line of march of the infantry. Here some soldiers had a fire of fence rails, and here we passed about four hours, trying to dry our clothes, nodding over the fire and watching for our place in the moving column. The Third Corps came along about four o'clock, and finding our brigade, we fell in and crossed the river. A march of ten miles by short stages brought us towards night to our old camp, more dead than alive. On this march, some of the mounted officers (who were not conspicuous in action) were impatient and occasionally swore because the men did not keep well closed up.

It was late in the afternoon before the few of us who were strong enough to keep along with the colors ended our toilsome march. The scene of our late happy encampment, now silent, tent-less and disconsolate, made us sad and solemn.

We built a fire in the old fireplace and made some coffee, which greatly revived us, but, oh! our hearts were sad and heavy, for more than half our number had fallen in battle. Not even the thought that we were still alive and in our old quarters was enough to sustain many of those who had not half recovered from the shock and strain of battle and who had been obliged to fall out all along the march, some within sight of their own company grounds.

Two or three days of complete rest were given the men after our return to camp, and then probably in part to divert the thoughts of the men from their losses, and possibly in part for sanitary reasons, orders were issued to level all the old quarters and build new. So the ground was cleared, new tent companies were formed, an effort was made to forget the past and look hopefully into the future, and before many days had elapsed, we had adapted ourselves somewhat to our changed conditions.

On the 12th of May we were in line for the first time after the fight. The division was paraded near division headquarters, and the death of General Jackson of the Confederate army was announced. Though an enemy, the division stood with uncovered heads as the order was read.

Gradually some of our boys who were missing or wounded returned to camp. One of the first to return was Warren Tucker of Alexandria, who joined us on the 15th. He was wounded, a ball passing through his shoulder under the shoulder blade. The wound had not received much attention and maggots were crawling out of it.

I.B. R. I., 5-7.
WARREN TUCKER.

MUSTERED!

Tucker, who was taken prisoner at Chancellorsville, said that a Confederate captain who fought in front of the regiment at the time of his being wounded, later inquired about the name and number of troops that so long and stubbornly held his brigade in check; and, after incredulously receiving the information that only one regiment was then and there opposed to them, said, "Well, if your regiment had advanced a few rods further it would have had a breast-work of our dead to fight behind." Tucker also reported that the Rebel officer told him that they never met infantry troops in battle before who fired grape and canister [referring to the buck and ball cartridges].

Joseph Young, reported dead, was alive, with a terrible wound through his thighs. Levi B. Laney and Benjamin Saunders are both still living, though both were badly wounded.

Among those who were killed was a dear classmate at Tilton, Henry Whitten of Company G. It was only a few days before the fight that we were talking of old times and our chances of returning to school. He was a young man of high purpose and ambition, a noble fellow. He felt confident that he should return to school, but he was cut down in the promise of his early manhood.

Wild rumors were in constant circulation. The most persistent one was to the effect that we were to be sent home on a furlough to enlist men to refill our depleted ranks; or that we were to be sent to some fort. But the most disquieting rumor of all was to the effect that our regimental organization was to be blotted out entirely on account of our reduced numbers and the men distributed into other organizations where needed. One rumor even assigned us to an organization outside the state, the 84th

Pennsylvania Volunteers. Some foundations for these rumors existed in the fact that one day twenty-three men were taken for duty, temporarily, in a New York battery, and a little later twenty men were taken for provost duty at General Sickles' headquarters.

May 30th our regiment again went out on picket. Our station was near the place we had previously been posted. A few hours' work made comfortable quarters and then some of the boys went to work on a brook near by. Some built a dam, others a miniature sawmill and soon there were in operation here six water wheels which carried three upright saws, a cross-cut and a circular saw, a trip hammer, and a churn. A man in the mill had a saw in one hand and a jug in the other, and a woman stood at the churn. When the thing was in full operation, Colonel Berdan, a New England boy himself, came along and laughed heartily at the exhibition and flattered the boys by remarking that none but New Hampshire men could put such an establishment in operation and that he hoped they would someday be running larger establishments of this kind in the same country.

The men at this time were in pretty good spirits owing largely to cheering news from near Vicksburg. It was said that General Grant had been successful in five successive battles, and had captured 10,000 Rebels and ninety guns, and that his army was in possession of all the outer works of the city.

While here one morning there were discovered indications that the enemy had planted a battery on the south side of the river and erected earthworks. The same morning a lieutenant came from camp and brought the intelligence that Private Patrick Hickey had died in hospital of wounds received at Chancellorsville and that my tent-mate, William Straw, of Hill, was dangerously sick of fever in the regimental hospital.

On June 5, I visited him for the last time, made him as comfortable as I could, and then penned a letter to his wife for him. The next day he was sent to the Division hospital and I did not see him again. He died at Alexandria, June 20, 1863. Another tentmate, Rev. Asa Witham, was sent to the division hospital at the same time, being unable to travel on account of rheumatism. Thus the last of those who shared my tent before the battle of Chancellorsville had left me. They were kindred spirits, and as there was no prospect of either of them ever returning for duty I was greatly depressed at their departure.

About this time, the wife of Charles G. Smith arrived from Bristol expecting to find her husband alive and hoping to take him home, but he had died at Aquia Creek of his wounds on June 6.

B. D0. L. 5–8½.
CORP. CHARLES G. SMITH.

Returning to camp, there were rumors in the air of moves on the part of the Rebel army and our own. A captive balloon near us was making observations of the movements of the Rebel army, but information gathered thereby went to headquarters instead of to the men in the ranks. The conclusions arrived at from what was seen and heard at these times and many others were sometimes correct and sometimes not.

Later the balloon moved up the river, and it was concluded that the object it was observing was moving in that direction. This conclusion was correct, for soon it was known that the Rebel army was moving north, and soon the invasion of the north was effected and we were making movements that culminated in the battle of Gettysburg, where the backbone of the Confederacy was broken.

CHAPTER VII

Marching North

June 1863. The first orders to move on the Gettysburg campaign came June 6, in the evening. We were directed to be ready to move at daybreak the next morning. During the day there had been heavy firing in the direction of Fredericksburg, so we naturally expected to move in that direction and concluded there might be warm work for us on the morrow, but no orders to move came.

On Thursday, June 11, we learned that as our old Third Division had been decimated in battle and its commander killed; the remaining fragments would be distributed to the other two divisions. We received orders to move, as we supposed, to be nearer the headquarters of our new division, the Second. Accordingly, we packed up everything we could muster strength to carry, that we might enjoy them in our new camp, but after marching about two miles towards our supposed new quarters we observed that the entire army was on the move, and we made haste to dispose of everything that was not absolutely necessary for the march.

We joined our new division near division headquarters and then countermarched towards our old encampment. Some could not help asking the question, why we did not remain where we were and join our new command as it passed instead of making an unnecessary march, and some attempted to answer, but the reason was not complimentary to the division commander, and it might not have been correct. The day was hot, but we pressed on, hour after hour, and finally halted near Hartwood church on the Warrenton road, seventeen miles from our starting point.

The next morning reveille sounded at four o'clock and we were soon again on the move. As the day advanced, the heat became intense and the road was strewn with blankets, overcoats, shelter tents and clothing of every description. I determined to hold on to mine, but towards noon my blanket was dropped to lighten my load. The roads were dry and the passing army beat the ground into fine dust several inches deep while every twig and leaf was laden with dust, and the air was so thick with the flying particles that one could see but a little way ahead. We made a brief halt at noon and then the march was resumed towards Kelley's ford which we passed about five p.m. At dark we crossed the Alexandria and Orange Railroad, where it crossed the north branch of the Rappahannock, and a mile beyond stacked arms, as we supposed, for the night. We had covered about twenty-six miles, and if ever the poor boys were thankful for a rest it was then. I started with others for water, but before we found any, we heard the command given to fall in. Hurrying back, we again took our place in the ranks, and then we traveled almost at a double quick two miles further, but which seemed to be five. The men were continually falling out, and when we finally came to a place to bivouac, of twenty-six men in my company only six were in line, and I was one of those. Perhaps I may as well confess that I did not dare to stop to rest for fear I should not be able to resume the march that night. We had halted at Beverly ford, where a cavalry fight had taken place a few days before.

The next day was the Sabbath, June 14, 1863, and it proved to be a veritable day of rest, an uncommon thing in the army. This was necessary, in part, at least, to give the stragglers an opportunity to reach camp and they were coming in all day. There was much speculation at this point among the men as to whether we were on a retreat or on a race after the Johnnies, but we soon learned that General Lee was even then moving by rapid marches to the north, and our forced marches were absolutely necessary to follow him.

At six o'clock that evening the army again resumed the march and continued on the road all night, reaching Catlett's Station at seven o'clock in the morning. There we rested till 2:00 p.m. when we resumed the march, and continued with brief halts till midnight. Then we were allowed to bivouac. Between the two bivouacs we had covered from thirty to thirty-five miles. This was even a harder march than the Saturday before and was indeed the hardest march of my army experience. The same conditions prevailed as on the Saturday before. The heat was intense, the dust blinding, many fell out and some died of exhaustion on the road.

We had halted this time at Manassas Junction, and on every hand were seen the marks of the hand of war — buildings and bridges and trains of cars destroyed, and other marks of the contests between two hostile armies. In one place was a pile of thousands of muskets and carbines, all destroyed by burning.

Tuesday, the 16th, we marched only about two miles and then again went into camp, where there were better facilities to obtain water, and rested for the remainder of the day.

Here we received news that General Lee had already entered Pennsylvania. This news was received with general satisfaction by the army because the opinion was that the farther he entered that state the less likely he would be to return.

The next morning, Wednesday, June 17th, we marched to within two miles of Centerville. On the way we crossed Bull Run and a portion of the battlefield that took the name of this stream. A halt on the way gave the men an opportunity to bathe in its waters, which was gladly embraced. Here we had a chance to mail letters, but, as only half an hour was given for writing, our communications were short.

On Friday, the 19th, we marched to Gum Springs, which place we reached about dusk. A cold rain prevailed, and during the night we felt the need of the blankets we threw away just one week before. The shelter tents, which we still had, sheltered us from the rain, and the rubber blankets were needed to protect us from the wet ground, but we had no covering besides the clothes we had on.

We remained at Gum Springs till the Thursday following (the 25th).

Gum Springs was a dreary, dismal, swamp-like place to stop in, and the woods around were filled with guerrillas. Several soldiers who had straggled from the line of encampment were found lying dead in the woods with a bullet hole through their heads or bodies, or hanging from the limbs of trees. Had they never been found, they would have been recorded as "absent without leave," and their children and relatives would always have had to bear the stigma of their being deserters.

Expected attacks from the Rebel cavalry and other alarms came daily, and occasionally our field pieces would play into this or that piece of woods to drive out an imaginary or real foe. While here, gambling with cards was indulged in more freely than I had observed in any other place. The moral tone of the Second Division was not as high as the old Third Division, and gambling was the order of the day most of the time. This was one of the diversions of the boys and was practiced rather from a lack of a better way in which to pass the time than from depraved nature, or a desire to make money easily. The stakes were usually small.

We were ready for a start at 9:00 a.m. on Thursday, and the corps commenced to move at that time and for more than two hours continued to file out to the road. Then came the baggage train which, when in columns, extended five or six miles. We got under full march about 10:00 a.m., going northerly. We reached Edwards Ferry at 5:00 p.m., having covered fifteen miles, and here we hoped to spend the night; but we did not even stop to make coffee. We crossed the Potomac on a pontoon bridge, and then took the tow path of the Ohio and Chesapeake canal and continued the march toward Harper's Ferry. At this point, rain commenced, and in some respects this march was even harder than the famous march of Saturday, June 13. For twelve miles we continued on the tow path, the night was dark, the rain fell in torrents, the tow path was narrow, so that each was compelled to walk in the steps of his file leader, thereby churning the earth into deep mud. There were many bad places in the path which checked the head of the column, causing very uneven marching to those far in the rear, and making long waits followed by double quicks to close up, even though many pounds of mud adhered to the feet. These long waits were of no relief, however, for there were no opportunities to sit or lie down. This was more tiresome than the ordinary march. There was no opportunity to straggle, but the narrow path did not prevent large numbers from falling out, and nearly half the men were scattered far to the rear when the colors halted about midnight near the mouth of the Monocacy.

The "tow-path march" followed the Ohio and Chesapeake canal. The foot soldiers marched all day with no rest or food, and the march continued into the darkness, hour after hour, through rain and mud. Many slipped, stumbled and fell into the canal. Two or three of the Twelfth lighted the pathway for their comrades with pieces of candle they had saved from their haversacks. When one soldier was forced to stop, his comrade or tent-mate, rather than leave him alone and uncared for, would stop with him; soon others nearby, at the point of giving up themselves, began to stop with their comrades. So, at first by twos and fours, and then by tens and scores, the men fell out and found a resting place for the remainder of the night.

Still General Humphreys and his staff rode on unmindful of his suffering followers on foot until he halted about midnight at the mouth of the Monocacy. No division of the Army of the Potomac ever made so long a march in so short a time under such adverse conditions.

"Where is the regiment?" asked one of the Twelfth boys, who had fallen in the rear, of Captain Langley, about eleven o'clock on that never-to-be-forgotten night. The captain, who was

MUSTERED!

riding back to find out the same thing, replied, "The colors and a dozen or so of the boys have halted a few rods ahead, but most are somewhere in the rear."

The tow-path march from Falmouth to Gettysburg was enough to test not only the pluck but the endurance of the bravest and strongest; and toward the close of one of the longest and hardest day's marches on the slippery tow-path, fifteen-year-old James Marshall got so "wearisomely sad" that he thought he could not go on. At this, the smallest and youngest of his comrades, fourteen-year-old Orrin Colby, walked up to James and slapping him on the shoulder exclaimed: "Cheer up here, and give us a smile for a tear. We shall live to tell our grandchildren of this yet."

R. L. L. 5-4½.   Bk. LB. L. 5-4½.
CORP. ORRIN G. COLBY.   CORP. JAMES F. MARSHALL.

Orrin Colby and **James Marshall** *were two of the youngest in the 12th. They fought side-by-side in every battle the regiment was engaged in, both being wounded at Cold Harbor; neither was ever on detached duty or ever asked for an excuse or a pass. When the regimental history was written in 1897 both were not yet fifty years old. But both "boys" were grandfathers.*

For the first time in my army experience, I was with those who fell out. Finding a grass plot near the path, four of us buttoned our shelter cloth together, pitched it as a tent, and then lay down. I chanced to be one of the outside fellows, and a part of the time at least my body was crowded out under the tent and I received the full benefit of the rain as it fell in torrents all night long.

Wet as I was, I got some sound sleep. Upon waking in the morning, we discovered an abandoned negro hut near by which we took possession of, built a rousing fire by using a portion of the hut for fuel, and partially dried our clothes and made coffee. Then we started to overtake the colors. We were with the majority that day, and the crowd marched on without officers in command, though there were officers in the company of stragglers. It was a go-as-you-please march, and we did not overtake the head of the column till five o'clock in the afternoon at Point of Rocks.

We were informed that only about a dozen men of the 12th Regiment were with the colors when the final halt was made the night before. Even General Humphreys in his report said the march was more exhausting to officers and men than the march of the 14th and 15th. If, as was reported, he chose to march on the tow-path to prevent straggling, he made a great mistake.

We started from Point of Rocks early the next morning and marched seven miles to Jefferson, where some, expecting on the strength of a rumor to remain over night, pitched tents. After an hour's rest the order came to fall in and we again took up the line of march and did not make a general halt till we arrived at Burkettsville, Maryland, ten miles from our noonday halt. There we turned into a field, pitched tents a second time and prepared to spend the night, when again came the command to pack up and fall in. This march took us to the top of Cedar Mountain, and we halted at Campton's Gap, the spot where the battle of South Mountain commenced. As an evidence of the struggle here a citizen pointed to the places where twenty or thirty Rebels were buried in one grave. After a short stay here we again moved on but only for a short distance to where we passed the night, thankful for any opportunity to sleep.

The morrow, Sunday, was pleasant and cool, and, in spite of the presence of large bodies of troops, the church bell in the small hamlet rang to call worshipers together. This was the first time such a joyous sound had greeted our ears for many months, and some of us proposed to attend service, but instead we fell in and took up the line of march. The First Brigade moved out first, and the Twelfth, being on the right of the brigade, led the division.

Since crossing the Potomac into Maryland, we noticed immediately that we were among friends. The majority of the people were without doubt Unionists, and those who were not wisely kept in the shade. Where before we saw only desolated fields and many ruins, now we saw prosperous farms and growing crops.

At Burkettsville we were greeted with a Union flag in the hands of a young lady on the balcony of a residence. The effect was magical; the boys cheered, the regimental flag was unfurled and the brigade band played. We halted for the night near Frederick City, Maryland, having marched about twenty miles that day.

At twelve o'clock the supply train arrived and I got up to draw rations; then divided them up and distributed them to the men. At four o'clock the reveille sounded and the column soon moved and I had only time to finish my work and then fall in, having had but little sleep and no breakfast.

It is much easier to march at the head of the column than at any other point, especially the rear, so the several divisions of a corps alternate in taking the advance. The same rule holds true in the several brigades and with the regiments of the brigades. By fortunate changes, under this rule, the day we left Frederick City, the 12th Regiment led the Corps. I say fortunate, for it was not only easier marching at the head of the column, but our regiment, being there, was taken for provost duty at Taneytown, Maryland, where we passed the night. Ordinarily this extra duty would have been considered a hardship, but not so here, as will appear later on.

We marched twenty-three miles that day, and, notwithstanding our favored position, all the boys were exceedingly tired as we were getting well worn out. I remember as a halt was called just outside the village, I sank down to rest by the side of the road, and a few minutes later I saw on the opposite side of the road at a farm house, several women bringing from the house pans of milk, doughnuts and pies, which they placed on the doorsteps for the soldiers. I helped dispose of those refreshments and instantly felt like a new man. And then these women poured out such love for the Union that we retired not only refreshed, but with a fresh inspiration for the cause.

On reaching the center of the village, our regiment filed into a side street and then stacked arms. Guards were placed and then the rest were at liberty to roam through the town. The corps passed through the town while the 12th Regiment remained for guard duty.

MUSTERED!

The whole town was out to welcome us, and the boys did not need introductions to the girls. My eyes caught sight of two very pretty and intelligent young ladies and we were soon engaged in an animated conversation—such a treat for one who had been deprived of all female society since we left home. Our newly made acquaintances proved to be the daughters of the Presbyterian minister of the town. Some of the young ladies were particularly demonstrative. One I remember, even now. She stationed herself on the sidewalk near the main body of troops, and with flag in hand, as each officer passed, whether he was a general or a line officer, on foot or mounted, she sang out, "Hurrah for the Lieutenant." To her a lieutenant was as big a man as a general. In fact, she knew no difference. All were friends of the soldiers at sight, and every house was open to serve meals for the boys who were always hungry when there were good things to eat. That night my duties and recreation kept me up till late, and then I spread my rubber blanket on the flat slate stone sidewalk, and, with my knapsack for a pillow, I slept soundly till reveille sounded in the morning.

We were on guard duty during our stay in Taneytown, and our chief duty was to prevent soldiers who had no passes from entering the town.

Tuesday till noon, the Twelfth Army Corps was passing through the town, and as soon as they had passed, we withdrew from the town and went into camp about three miles out on the Emmitsburg road.

General Sickles received no order on Tuesday and so advanced his corps as far as Emmitsburg during the forenoon, where he received orders to move toward Middleburg. General Meade had decided to meet and defeat the Confederate army, under Lee, between Emmitsburg and Manchester on the line of Pike's creek.

But before Sickles could move, he received a dispatch from General Howard stating that his corps and the First Corps had been attacked in full force by the enemy at Gettysburg and calling urgently for assistance. Knowing that under the rules of war it was discretionary for him to obey the order or the call, Sickles promptly decided on the latter, leaving one brigade and battery to guard the wagon train. In less than an hour his whole command was marching toward Gettysburg.

MUSTERED!

COMBAT STRENGTH
Confederacy   75,000
Union   95,000

GETTYSBURG

July 1, 1863

CASUALTIES
Confederacy 28,000
Union   23,000

CHAPTER VIII

Gettysburg

July 1863. Wednesday, the first day of July, occurred the first day's fight at Gettysburg. Two or three days before, General Hooker had been relieved of the command of the Army of the Potomac and General Meade had succeeded him. The Confederate army under General Lee was in Pennsylvania. Harrisburg and even Washington were threatened, and the greatest excitement prevailed throughout the North. Under these circumstances, the wisdom of a change in the head of the army was questioned, and this step had a depressing effect on the army. Officers and men in whispers discussed the situation and silently shook their heads as though fearful of the coming of another disaster.

That Wednesday morning we passed through Emmitsburg with the buildings of many streets in ashes, the result of the hand of war, and pressed on towards Gettysburg. I remember as we passed through the town, the rain was falling heavily, and the men did not present a very cheerful aspect. At one door stood an aged woman, and just as I passed her door, I heard her say, "Oh, men, don't look so down-hearted." There was no doubt as to that woman's loyalty.

As the day advanced, the rain ceased and we hastened our steps.

In the morning, General Reynolds had met a portion of the Rebel army at Gettysburg and a sharp fight had occurred, resulting in the death of Reynolds and the defeat of the Union arms. The Union forces under General Howard were pressed back and took possession of the range of hills known as Cemetery Ridge. This defeat on Wednesday may have been a blessing in disguise, for these same hills to which the Union forces were driven were occupied by the several Union corps as they arrived later and constituted the invulnerable position held by the Army of the Potomac in the succeeding days of the battle.

All that afternoon we pressed forward, stimulated by the roar of battle at Gettysburg that reached our ears. Staff officers and couriers dashed to and fro bearing dispatches or giving orders preparatory to the coming conflict. The shades of evening came, and the roar of cannon gave place to the stillness of night, but on we pressed. Though weary from a long march, there was no need of orders to hasten our steps, for all were making the best time possible, fully realizing the importance of the hour.

At 1 o'clock in the morning of Thursday, July 2, the Twelfth reached Gettysburg and bivouacked with its division at the left and rear of Cemetery Hill, the only ground then held by the Union forces. At the same hour, General Meade arrived from Taneytown and made a moonlight inspection of his lines. Generals Howard and Hancock informed him of the enemy's position and the general outline of the field.

The Third Corps would have been in position before midnight, but for its leading brigade running into the enemy's lines.

About midnight we reached the vicinity of Gettysburg. We were marching with rank well closed up, ready for action, when we halted and a command was passed down the line to lie down on both sides of the road as noiselessly as possible. By a strange mistake or a lack of information as to where the enemy was, we were marching directly into his lines. When we halted, his cannon planted in the road ahead of us could be dimly seen. In column as we were, his cannon would have reaped a rich harvest of death had he opened on us. Why he did not, we never knew.

Instantly the order to lie down was obeyed. The rattle of tin dippers and canteens was suppressed and the men dropped to the ground beside the highway. The commander of the brigade, his staff and servants passed to the rear. As they were passing, some wag near me said in a voice loud enough to be heard by many, "Officers and niggers to rear, march." This "shot" was received with suppressed laughter by all who heard it.

The men arose in their places noiselessly, countermarched, and when out of range, the column struck out across the country from the Emmitsburg road, where we were, to the Taneytown road, making a circuit of the Round Tops. About one o'clock in the morning, we reached a position north of these hills and bivouacked for the remainder of the night, after a march of nearly twenty-five miles.

GETTYSBURG
July 2, 1863

Extending south of Gettysburg on the west is a long ridge known as Seminary Ridge because on it near the city stands the Lutheran seminary. A little less than a mile to the east and nearly parallel with it is Cemetery Ridge, extending from the city two miles or more to the Round Tops. It was on this latter ridge that the Union army took position after the fight of the first day, while the Confederate army took position on Seminary Ridge. It was the ground between these two ridges that was fought over in the battles of the second and third of July, and a large portion of the field could be covered by the eye at a glance.

On the morning of the second day, the Confederate army was posted the entire length of Seminary Ridge from a point opposite Round Top, facing east to the city. Near the city, this line made a sharp bend to the east, extending in this direction nearly a mile, and then made another bend to the south-east of Cemetery Ridge. Its entire length was nearly five miles and in shape like that of a fishhook. As the different corps of the Union army arrived, they took positions facing this line. Their formations were like that of the Confederates, in two or three lines of battle.

At the extreme right of the Confederates, opposite Round Top, were posted the veteran troops of its army under General Longstreet. Opposite these troops, General Sickles took position with the Third Corps, the 12th Regiment being in the first line of battle at the extreme right of the corps.

It was expected that the Rebel army would follow up the advantages of the first day's fight with an early attack on our lines, and therefore the Union army was astir and making coffee with the early dawn; but the greater part of the day passed and not a gun was fired except by the pickets and an occasional shot from a battery.

A little past twelve o'clock General Humphreys advanced his command toward the front and formed his full division for action with his First Brigade in the front line, which when deployed with the 71st New York, Second Brigade on its left, just filled the space allotted to his division by General Sickles.

The Second and Third Brigades were massed in the rear at intervals of about two hundred yards. Then General Carr ordered the 1st Massachussetts to deploy as skirmishers and cover his front. The division remained in this formation until just after four o'clock, when it was ordered by General Sickles to move forward to the Emmitsburg road and connect with the First Division – General Birney's – on the left.

This brought the left of the leading brigade close to an old log house by the road. At the rear of the house was an apple orchard where Seeley's battery was posted, just to the left of the house. The Twelfth was placed there to support it.

One hundred men from the 16th Massachusetts were ordered to occupy the house and make holes between the logs to shoot through. This regiment was on the right of the 12th New Hampshire, and the 11th New Jersey was on its left.

The Emmitsburg road ran along the crest of a ridge, so that Humphreys' advance to it was seen by the enemy, and opened upon by two batteries – one at the left and one almost directly in front. The latter was silenced by the shots from Seeley's guns; but, until this was accomplished, the Twelfth occupied a dangerous position in which the artillery duel between the two batteries brought the regiment in direct range of Rebel shots.

Finally General Sickles brought on an engagement by opening fire with his artillery on his extreme left. This engagement spread north and soon the whole line was engaged in mortal strife, the ferocity of which has seldom been seen on the battlefields of the world. The contestants numbered nearly 180,000 men.

The hardest fighting of the day was on the left, held at first by the Third Corps alone, for here was the weak spot in the whole line—since called "the bloody angle". General Sickles had made this angle by swinging the left of his line to the rear in order to protect his flank. Here were massed during the second day nearly one-third of the entire Confederate army. The other attacks along the line, though desperate, were largely to prevent assistance being sent to the left.

In this part of the battle, General Meade and his associates claimed that General Sickles made unwise choices of alignment, positioning and engagement, which not only uselessly endangered the Third Corps' destruction, but also hazarded the safety of the whole army.

General Sickles and his followers, on the other hand, asserted that if it were not for Sickles' decisive action to take the advance position and engage the enemy when and where he did, the first day's battle would have been the last because General Meade was already contemplating a retreat; if the Confederates had attacked before he had a chance to fall back, Little Round Top, the key to the position of the Union, would certainly have been lost. General Sickles also claimed that the position he took complied with Meade's orders.

Whether by or against General Meade's orders, the position was a dangerous one, inviting attack upon both sides of the exposed angle at the orchard, while supported upon neither.

It is not our purpose to enter into a discussion, extending to the present day as it does, as to whether the alignment of General Sickles or his acts in bringing on an engagement at this time were wise or contrary to the science of war, or whether the sulkiness of General Longstreet in declining to bring on a general engagement in the early part of the day, as ordered, contributed to the general result of this battle. It is a fact that General Sickles by commencing the engagement, prevented the withdrawal of the Union army by General Meade, as it is claimed was his intention; and that the heroism of the men in the ranks in both armies made the battle the stupendous one it was. Even after the exhausting fight of three days, had it been left to the men in the ranks of the Union army to dictate a line of action, the northern army would have thrown itself between the Potomac river and Lee's retreating army or crushed him while attempting to cross the river and thus perhaps have ended the rebellion then and there.

When Sickles opened fire with his artillery, the enemy replied, doing much execution, extending to the position held by the 12th Regiment; and here some of our men fell. We were then ordered to advance and lie down in an apple orchard. Cannonading increased. and the shot and shell from both sides passed over us, making the very air hot with the flying missiles. Fortunately this was mainly an artillery duel between batteries posted on higher ground, and we suffered but little.

The regiment remained in the orchard for an hour or more, when it moved obliquely to the right a few rods and took position on the road just to the right of what is now known as the Smith house. The battle was raging with increasing fury on the left, where Birney was vainly trying to hold his own, assisted and encouraged by General Sickles, who was giving his whole attention to what, as yet, was the most exposed and hardest pressed part of his line.

After lying in this position nearly an hour, the infantry at our extreme left became engaged. The roll and roar of musketry as the two armies came together was appalling. Gradually it came nearer like a mighty thunder storm, not rapidly but with tremendous force and deafening roar — one continuous crash. Nearer and nearer the roar of the carnage came, drowning even the screeching of the shot and shell over our heads. As we lay together waiting for our call to battle, we wondered about the unknown and unseen: *Is there no force of the enemy on our front? Have they received a check on our left? Or are they getting ready to attack our flank? Have we got to fight here? Or shall we be ordered to fall back before we are surrounded?*

While this fighting was going on at our left, our part of the line advanced to the Emmitsburg road, driving the enemy before us. Indeed, the right of our regiment crossed this road, thus giving it the most advanced position held by the corps that day. The correctness of this assertion is verified by official maps and the history of the battle published since the war, and by the side of this road now stands the 12th Regiment monument marking its most advanced position on that day.

But this was not a position that could long be held. The heavy fighting at our left was the result of a desperate effort to crush our line at the bloody angle. Then the enemy dealt desperate blows and partially succeeded.

The line of the Third Corps was rolled back upon itself and the safety of the entire army threatened. A battery was planted by the enemy that raked the position held by the 12th Regiment by the left flank, and this, in connection with the musketry and artillery fire in front rendered our position such as no troops could withstand, and then, too, our advanced position rendered our capture certain by the oncoming host if we remained where we were. Fortunately, a retreat was ordered.

While retreating, the guns of the Sixth Corps, posted on high ground in reserve, played over our heads into the ranks of the enemy and helped to check their advance, but, while at the Emmitsburg road and while retreating, the men of the Twelfth suffered their greatest loss.

Lieutenant French, while giving an order, fell dead. Here, by my side, fell comrades Horace Plaisted, John Taylor and Frank Knowlton, who had his right hip carried away by a shell. As he fell, he uttered a piercing cry, stretched out his hand to me imploring aid, and expired.

After we opened fire upon Wright's attacking columns, the 12th New Hampshire was ordered to execute a movement known in army tactics as "changing fronts to the rear." To face danger and death from the enemy is one thing, but to turn your back to the enemy while executing such a difficult movement is another matter. In this case the changing of front was to the left. Troops can take hard blows when like blows can be given in return, but here, in making this movement, no reply could be made to the enemy though our men were still falling.

While breasting the full blast of battle in our front as well as a staggering assault upon our flanks, we were successful in executing the movement and remaining intact. The men of our brigade, somewhat broken, fell into line with the Sixth Corps, advancing to our relief, checked the advance of the enemy and then drove them pell mell in the opposite direction.

Colonel J.B. Bachelder, Gettysburg historian, describes the regiment's perilous position on the afternoon of the second day:

The Twelfth New Hampshire was at that time attached to the Second Division, third Corps, commanded by Major General Humphreys. It formed a portion of Carr's brigade, of which the 1ST, 11TH, and 16TH Massachusetts, the 26TH Pennsylvania, and the 11TH New Jersey Volunteers were the remaining regiments—a brigade sustaining a record second to none in the Army of the Potomac. This brigade held the extreme right of the Third Corps, and was formed along the Emmitsburg road, slightly on the posterior slope of a ridge supported by the New York Excelsior brigade. Graham's brigade of Birney's division lay on its left and held the salient of the line at the Peach Orchard, against which General Longstreet made a furious assault with Barksdale's and Wilcox's brigades, breaking the infantry lines, forcing the artillery to retire, and carrying the position, thus threatening General Humphreys' left, and compelling him "to change front to the rear." During the execution of this, Longstreet's victorious troops continued to advance, their attack seriously embarrassing the movements of Humphreys' division, and at the same time Perry's and Bright's brigades, which had advanced under cover of the ridge, attacked Humphreys' right.

It was a fearful moment and will be remembered by every participant as one of the most trying, thrilling, and exciting scenes of their experience. General Humphreys could readily have withdrawn his command, but such an act would have endangered the success of the battle; and he instantly decided to hold the enemy in check, even at the sacrifice of his own life and his whole command, until a new line could be formed in his rear, which was subsequently done and brought up by General Meade in person.

General Humphreys, placing himself in the midst of his command, was everywhere present, sustaining and encouraging his men. His officers fell thick and fast about him. Captain Chester of his staff was seen to spring with a convulsive start. Turning to his commander he said, "General, I'm shot." General Humphreys sprang to his assistance, clasped him in his arms, and sustained him in the saddle until Captain Humphreys, his son, could take him in charge. An orderly took the horse to lead him from the field, when at that instant a round shot killed the horse and carried away the orderly's head.

At this moment General Humphreys' horse, bleeding from seven bullet wounds, was struck by a shell and springing convulsively into the air, threw his rider violently to the ground, without seriously injuring him. Just then Captain Humphreys was shot through the arm, and General Carr and Captains McClellan and Cavada each had their horses killed.

A portion of the guns of Turnbull's battery retired through the infantry with a prolonged firing as they went. Others were drawn off by members of the Sixteenth Massachusetts Regiment and some were captured. It was then that General Barksdale fell mortally wounded.

In the very centre of this terrible conflict stood the Twelfth New Hampshire Regiment, while thick and fast fell its brave and gallant members.
[Excerpts from *Twelfth New Hampshire Regiment 1862-1865* by Capt. A.W. Bartlett, Concord, N.H: 1897]}

The Twelfth, in the attempt of the brigade to avoid the coming cyclone by changing front, and then to extricate itself, was caught and hurled into the vortex of the battle, where helpless (like the rest of the brigade) to either withstand or defend, it was so shattered and scattered that little more than a sergeant's squad of it was left when it again faced the foe and was left to unite with other regimental fragments of the brigade to help retake the ground that had been yielded.

But the work of the day was not over. The enemy reformed and massed its troops for another supreme effort. The scene changed with great rapidity and power. Longstreet's massed artillery played into the Union ranks with terrible effect, and his infantry, strengthened with fresh troops, made a desperate attempt to break the Union lines and capture the Union guns in the rear of the Peach Orchard— just as desperate efforts were made further to the left to obtain possession of the Round Tops. Few realize the importance of the action at this time. The result of the battle and perhaps the destiny of the nation hung in the balance. The Union troops, veterans as they were, instead of flying from the scene as did the raw troops at Bull Run, held their ground, and a hand-to-hand fight ensued.

Then on the double quick came the Second and Twelfth Corps to their assistance. They swung into line under a murderous fire and checked the advance of a victorious foe.

In the struggle at this point the 5th New Hampshire covered itself with glory. Here its gallant leader, Colonel Cross, fell, in trying to stem the tide, and here fell General Sickles with the loss of a leg.

The advance of the enemy thus checked, the Third Corps was ordered to fall to the rear.

When this order came, night was falling on the scene. Two thousand men of our division had fallen, and of the brave men who composed the 12th Regiment at noon of that day, one-half had been left dead or wounded on the field, while a few had fallen into the hands of the enemy as prisoners of war.

Lieutenant French, commanding Company F, was shot through the head just as he was receiving from Captain Shackford the order to change front, and fell at the captain's feet.

About the same time, both the state and national colors went down; and soon all the color guards were either killed or wounded. Within a radius of a few rods from where the colors went down in blood, there were more men of the regiment left dead and wounded than were now left to defend them.

Saving the Colors

Sergeant Sylvester Howe, carrying the State colors, fell spiraling to his death. But so firmly were his fingers closed upon the fabric of his flag that when Corporal Davis snatched the colors from the dead sergeant's grasp, he left in Sergeant Howe's death-clenched hand a piece about one foot wide and fifteen inches long.

B. D. L. 5-10¾.
LIEUT. HENRY A. L. FRENCH.

DB. Bk. L. 5-11.
SYLVESTER D. HOWE.

Sergeant Luther Parker of Hill, carrying the United States. flag, fell with a thud. Corporal Samuel Brown, reached out to grasp the flag as Sergeant Parker fell, and in this brave act, he himself fell dead, still holding the flag up high as he fell. But even as death grasped him, Brown would not allow the proud emblem of our national sovereignty to trail in the dusty or touch the ground, for it served as a covering sheet atop that brave guard, who lay beneath its folds.

LB. Bk. L. 5-9½.
SERGT. LUTHER H. PARKER.

B. B. D. 6-⅛.
CORP. SAMUEL BROWN.

Sergeant Charles Emery and Corporal John Davis were the last to save the flags from capture by the enemy by snatching them from the dead, while the Rebels and danger of death were pressing heavily upon them. They carried them until they caught up with the regiment, just as it halted to re-form its line for another advance. Here they gave the colors to Adjutant Heath, who carried the national and state colors back to where the brigade halted.

D. B. L. 5–6¼.
LIEUT. ALBERT W. BACHELER.

Private Albert Bacheler, carrying a wounded comrade on the retreat, was the last to leave the battleground; while doing so, he noticed the piece of flag left in the grip of Sergeant Howe's fist, which he attempted, unsuccessfully, to snatch away as he hurried to catch up with the regiment. Not being willing that so much as a shred of the flag should fall into the enemy's hands, he stopped, under a most destructive fire. With his wounded comrade on his back and his own front to the enemy, he stooped down and unclinched the dead sergeant's fingers, one by one, and thus saved the precious fragment which he kept and still has in his possession.

With all the other officers in the regiment dead or wounded, Lieutenant Fernal was left alone in command of the few men of the regiment remaining on the field.

Under these conditions, Lieutenant Fernal would have been justified in leading his men to the rear, instead of the front, but stung with madness at the wretched work of giving away so much ground at such a sacrifice, he shook his sword defiantly toward the enemy, and then waving it over his head as a beckoning sign to his men, he shouted, "Come on!" and led his little band straight back over the field upon which they had been defeated, increasing his command with released prisoners as he advanced, to drive the Rebels as quickly from the battlefield as they had taken it.

B. L. I.. 5-11.
CAPT. WILLIAM H. H. FERNAL.

It is not known if any other regiments of the brigade rallied and retraced their steps back nearly to the positions they had first held, but if so, none did it quicker or with less number of officers and men than the 12th New Hampshire. Yet neither the first nor second counterattacks would have been successful on this part of the line had not the Rebel forces become broken and disorganized themselves by their impetuous pursuit.

When reaching a point beyond the range of the enemy's guns, the men of the Third Corps prepared to spend the night as best they could. There was no pitching of even shelter tents, and the comrades of different organizations fraternized in groups as most convenient and built the ever needed camp-fire and made coffee.

Many were short of rations, myself among the number. My haversack contained some coffee and that was all, but in falling back, I passed a place where hardtack had been issued and the crumbs from the boxes lay upon the ground. They had absorbed moisture from the ground, but hungry as I was, I gathered what I could into my haversack for my supper. That evening the men about the camp-fires divided rations so that all had a little. In our party were several Johnnies, who had nothing to eat. We shared with them our meager supply and were soon on as good terms with them as though through the day we had fought side by side.

The men around the camp-fires that night were not in a talkative mood. They were worn out and weary with the excessive marches of the last few days and the hard fighting of the last few hours. Their hearts were sad, once more, that so many of their comrades had fallen. And then there was a general feeling that our arms, as a whole, had not been successful during the day, and many a veteran as he lay upon the ground that night was unable to sleep because of fears that the fearful losses of the day had been of no avail. He recalled to mind the terrible carnage at Chancellorsville, just two months before, and its disheartening effect, and feared another disaster was to be added to the cause of the Union. We judged the battle as a whole by what we had seen in our immediate vicinity, when fortunately, the battle was not a disaster, though not as yet a sweeping victory for the Union.

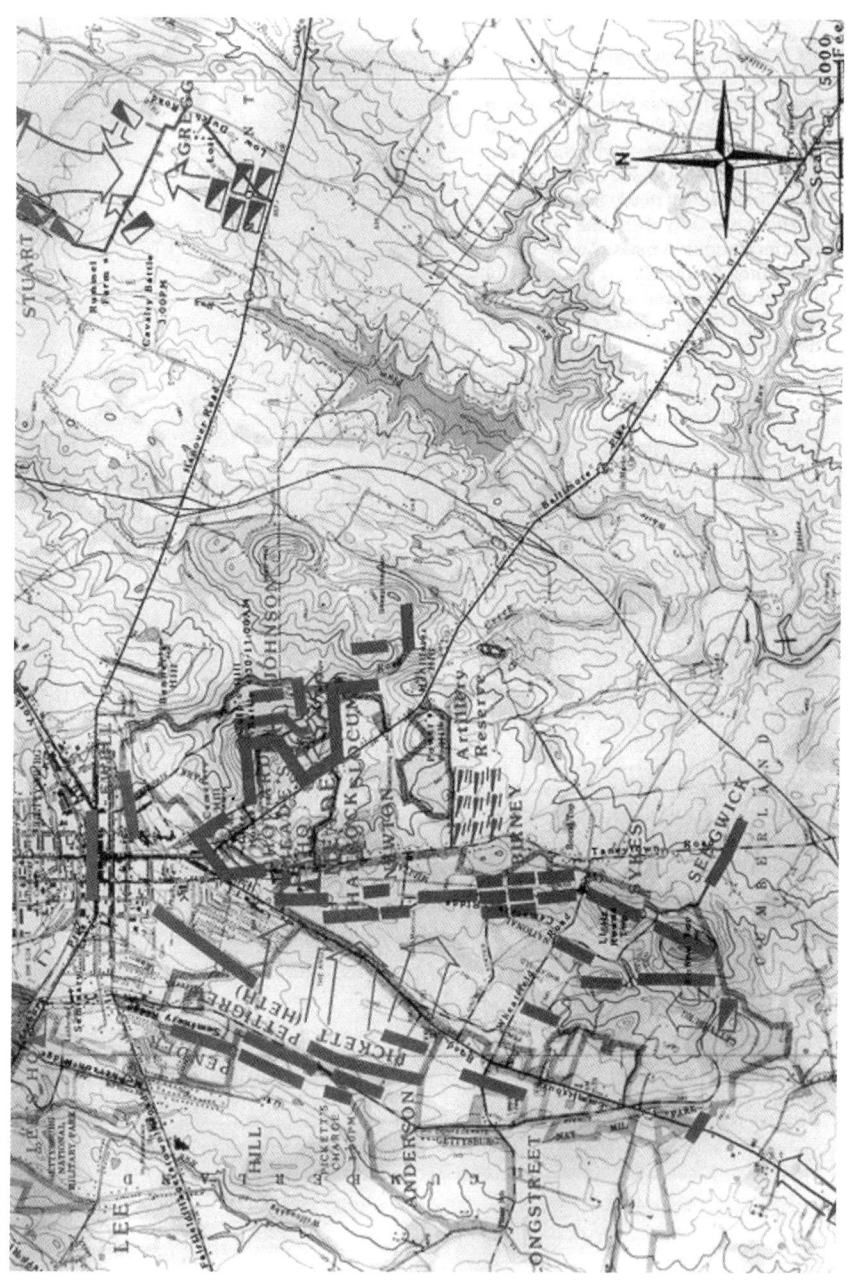

GETTYSBURG
July 3, 1863

MUSTERED!

Light had hardly dawned the morning of the third day at Gettysburg when we awoke to a reveille of booming cannon on the right, where the Twelfth Corps had commenced the work of retaking the ground that they had been obliged to yield to Ewell's forces the night before. In reorganizing, I took the State flag and carried it that day and for a few weeks afterward.

The boys of the Twelfth left for duty—in all only about fifty—gathered around the flag, some standing, some sitting on the ground, and the following anxious conversation (recorded in a number of our journals) took place:

"Turn out here, boys; don't you hear the partridges drumming? Early birds catch the worms, don't you know."

"Catch the Devil you mean," comes the reply from one who is more cross than polite.

"Well, I guess *he's* catching *them*, by the sound over there; he'll have us all before night, or the Johnnies, will."

"That's what I'm beginning to think, comrades," chimes in a third.

"Yesterday they got 'way round our left, and after they finished up the job with us, they attacked our right, where they'r' at it again this early; before noon they'll have both our wings clipped so we can neither fight nor fly, and then the last one of us'll be bagged."

"Begins to look as if you'r more'n half right, Bill, by thunder," breaks in a new voice, "and when this army goes *up* the Union goes *down*."

"Like Lucifer, never to rise again," suggests a young officer who has been listening. "Let me tell you, boys, it's now or never. If we can't win on our own soil, we never can. This is the beginning of the end. This battlefield is the turn point; and this day's struggle will decide the battle."

"Don't you think, lieutenant, that our army is getting the worst of it so far, from all appearances?"

"Well, I must confess, so far as we can see, that indications are not very favorable; but it's very little we know of the actual condition of things or the strength and positions of the two armies. If all our forces are united here, I don't believe Lee has got men enough to defeat us, if General Meade half knows his business, and dares let his army perform it."

"Yes," remarks another officer; "but that fatal IF has so many times defeated this army in other battles, I almost tremble for the result. Meade's appointment just on the eve of battle has not improved its spirit. What has Meade ever done to bring him to the front in such a crisis as this?!"

"Nothing," comes the quick response from half a dozen at once. To this there was no dissenting voice, though by this time quite a crowd had gathered.

The young officer who had first spoken, now slowly and reflectively speaks again:

"Well, boys, that all may be, and this very day prove your words prophetic, but none of us desire it. Blunder or no blunder, our trust and our duty is the same. If our leaders are wanting, we must not be; if others let loose, we must all the firmer hold on. Though this Army of the Potomac has been often defeated, it has never yet been destroyed, but is here in force and power today to perform its great work and mission of saving this republic for the light and hope of centuries yet to come."

There is a slight delay, and then a smattering of cheers is begun, spurning the young lieutenant to continue:

"If this nation is to go down in blood into oblivion, neither Meade nor Hooker, nor all the military strategy of the world can save it. But if it is to rise triumphant, as God in his mercy and wisdom has we trust decreed, then read your hymn book covers, boys: 'To doubt would be disloyalty, to falter is a sin.'"

He continues: "Before yon rising sun shall set, the Southern Cross will be broken, and the Southern Confederacy receive a blow from which it will never recover."

The young lieutenant, in his patriotic fervor, had become earnestly eloquent; and what had begun in joke ended so seriously impressive that it needed only the chaplain's *amen* to fitly close the morning exercises.

The young lieutenant who spoke prophetically in the dawn's early light of July 3d at Gettysburg was Lieutenant Asa Bartlett.

CAPT. ASA W. BARTLETT.

Artillery firing succeeded that of the pickets and later the infantry became engaged, and thus the great fight of the third day at Gettysburg came on and culminated in victory to the Union army, and the high-water mark of the Southern Confederacy was passed.

During the artillery firing of the morning, our regiment lost a few men from shells, but in making the alignments for the day fresh troops formed the first line of battle, and the remnant of the Twelfth was assigned to the support of a battery posted on the crest of a hill, and we constituted a part of the third line of battle on that part of the field which met the fury of Pickett's charge later in the day.

The morning passed with intermittent fighting, brisk artillery duels, the crash of infantry and in some cases the bayonet charge, and the enemy was driven back at all points. The ground lost the preceding day was recovered. The actions of the morning were Union victories.

Noon came and General Lee, after surveying the field from the cupola of the College building on Seminary Ridge, determined to seek to retrieve the disasters of the morning by making a supreme effort to pierce the Union centre and thus destroy the Union army.

On Seminary Ridge, opposite our position, were massed the fresh troops of General Pickett's division, which had arrived during the night before and which was to be nearly annihilated that day and gain immortal renown in the greatest onslaught of modern warfare. His division, largely increased by re-enforcements from other commands, numbered about 15,000 men.

When Lee issued his orders for the supreme work of the day to commence, 115 of his guns, massed, opened fire on our center. As many or more guns from the Union lines from Round Top to the city responded, and for two hours the greatest artillery duel of the war continued. The ground shook and trembled beneath us and the air was full of screeching shot and shell, and many a brave man on both sides got his passport to eternity.

Pickett's Charge

Finally there was a lull in the artillery fire and Pickett's division moved en masse with bayonets fixed toward the Union lines, about one mile distant. The Union guns, which Lee hoped he had silenced, opened on the advancing hosts. Huge gaps were plowed in their ranks, and their path was strewn with the dead and wounded, but still they pressed on; then grape and canister decimated their ranks and finally, as they came within close range, musketry fire added to the awful slaughter; but still undaunted, they closed up their ranks and pressed on until the Union lines were reached, and then a desperate hand-to-hand contest ensued. But this was not a contest that could long be continued, and an order to retreat was sounded, which a few were able to obey, but the larger part of the assailing party that survived threw down their arms and became prisoners of war. The high-water mark of the Confederacy had spent its fury on the rocks of the Union lines and the Southern cause from this hour was doomed. But along the path traveled by these devoted men lay nearly a thousand Confederate dead and many times that number of wounded.

During this charge the awful carnage was going on in our immediate front. Our orders were to lie down and we were very willing to obey, but we saw enough and heard enough to know that the existence of a nation may have rested on the work of the hour, and as standing erect even for a moment might mean the end of our earthly career, we were left to judge the progress of the fight mainly by hearing.

As we lay in support of the battery, there was one gun on the Confederate side that gave us particular anxiety. It was of large calibre and was posted a long distance away in our front. At regular but very brief intervals it threw a shell directly in line with our position. Upon starting from the muzzle on its mission of death, the shell left a small trail of smoke in its rear. As it neared us, it fell lower and lower, and we were certain it would strike by the time it reached us and annihilate the whole regiment, but each one passed over us almost within reach of the hand and crashed into a ledge a little at our rear. As it struck, scattering the rocks in all directions, each man took a long breath, and then turned to look for the next comer, each time with the same result.

The Wounded

As at Chancellorsville, our regiment lost heavily during the two days of our engagement. On the morning of July 2, there were 222 men in line and during that day and the following, 20 were killed on the field and 73 wounded, of whom six died of their wounds. The total losses to the Union army in the three days were 3,070 killed, 14,497 wounded, and 5,434 taken prisoners, a total of over 23,000 men.

Of my immediate comrades who suffered in this fight, besides those already named, was Charles N. Drake. He had passed through the slaughters at Fredericksburg and Chancellorsville unscathed, but here his right leg was shattered with a grape shot. He crawled a few rods to the rear and took shelter behind a large rock. While lying here, the Union line fell back bringing his position between the two lines, and here a minie ball from the Union army passed through his left lung very near his heart. At night he was carried from the field and in the afternoon of the following day his leg was amputated and, strange as it may seem, he recovered and lived thirty-two years, able to do a fair day's work as a carpenter.

B. B. D. 5-7½.
CHARLES N. DRAKE.

Henry Fellows was wounded in the arm and had several ribs broken, but he walked twenty miles to the rear and died of his wounds six weeks later.

Adna Hall was wounded in the early part of the fight in the first day of our engagement. While in a stooping position a minie ball plowed a path down his back. He died of his wounds at Philadelphia.

Sylvester Swett had his knapsack and canteen shot from his person and a minie ball entered his ankle and was not removed till forty-eight hours later.

Sergt. Uriah Kidder was wounded and helped over a fence by a piece of shell striking his knapsack, and Daniel Bohonan, a Bristol boy serving on the quota of Danbury, was wounded.

Comrade Samuel Brown of Hebron was among the killed. Among the wounded were Frank Marshall of Hill, Lieutenant Merrill, Moses Gilman, Arthur Kimball, Hiram

Philbrick, and Jonathan E. Leavitt of Sanbornton; Samuel Robinson and Corporal Howard Taylor of New Hampton; William French and Stephen Gray of Alexandria; Samuel Adams of Danbury; while Charles Edgerly and George Drake were among the captured.

On Saturday morning, following the fight of Thursday afternoon, a soldier of another regiment called and inquired for me. He said that a comrade of mine, badly wounded, was at the Sixth Corps hospital and wanted to see me. I at once hastened to the place indicated and there on a stretcher I found Jonathan Leavitt, of Sanbornton, a tentmate, in a terrible condition. Both feet and ankles had been crushed by a cannon ball or shell. By mistake he had been carried to the Sixth Corps hospital, the stretcher placed under an apple tree. And there he had lain for forty hours unattended. His feet had turned black and were fast becoming a mass of corruption. Scores of surgeons not far off were operating on men of the Sixth Corps, but this poor man, desperately wounded as he was, had received no attention whatever.

Perhaps it was because the diamond on his cap indicated that he belonged to the Third Corps and there were men of their own corps just as much in need of assistance as was he. I say this may have been the case, so I will make no reflections. My first act was to give my comrade a drink of water and then I attempted to find some surgeon who would dress his wounds, but all were too busy even to hear my story.

I then hastened back to camp and called on Hiram Ferrin, Uriah Kidder and Orrin Colby to assist me, and together we carried Comrade Leavitt two miles to the Third Corps hospital where we found Dr. Fowler, who gave him immediate attention. Dr. Fowler administered ether at once and then placed the poor fellow on the amputation table, but before removing him from the stretcher he passed his knife through the mass of flesh and bones and left his feet and ankles on the stretcher. Dr. Fowler amputated both stumps and such was the demand for help that my offer to assist was gladly accepted, but young Leavitt died in the operation.

He was evidently aware of his critical condition, but anxious to live. On the road to the hospital we met a regiment of cavalry, and the surgeon stopped and looked at Leavitt's wounds: "Well, doctor," said Leavitt, "is there any chance for me?" "Yes; there may be," replied the surgeon slowly. The last words the poor fellow spoke, addressed to Dr. Fowler, were of the same tenor, "Shall I pull through, doctor?" "Oh yes, you are young," was the reply.

Having seen my comrade breathe his last, I looked about me before returning to my regiment. In one tent close by was comrade Drake and by his side Sergeant Parker, each having lost a leg on Thursday. The prospect for the recovery of Parker was much the brighter of the two, but a few days later the tying of one of the arteries gave way and he bled to death in a short time.

The scene about me was one never to be forgotten. Men were mutilated in all conceivable ways and piles of legs and arms told of the work of the surgeons. Many limbs had been buried in shallow trenches, and a brook close by, swollen to large proportions by the heavy rain that followed the battle, had uncovered many and these were exposed to view.

Years later in talking with Comrade Drake of these scenes, I asked him what disposition was made of his leg.

"The hogs ate it up," was his prompt reply. Then he explained that he felt the pain as the flesh was torn from the bones by the hogs just as plainly as though the leg had not been amputated. As many hogs roamed the battlefield and its vicinity, as I myself observed, I thought it quite probable that comrade Drake was correct.

Sleeping beside the dead was the experience of many a soldier during the war, but the following incident from the history of the regiment holds a touch of pathos:

Albert Jones and Christopher Joy, of Company A, were both mortally wounded at Gettysburg and died on the field, the former about midnight and the latter at two o'clock in the morning. Their comrade, Thomas Lawlor, as kind as he was brave, found them in the evening after the fight and remained with them until they died.

Jones suffered but little pain, and seemed resigned to his fate. After his death, Lawlor gave his whole attention to Joy, who was suffering much from wounds in the breast and back, desiring frequent change of position and requiring the constant effort of his faithful attendant to aid and comfort him. Two slow hours passed and the pains of his dying patriot ceased; and so kindly gentle was the approach of death, to release him from his suffering, that Lawlor thought he was going to sleep. But scarcely did his fingers on the pulseless wrist tell him that his comrade was dead, then he himself was soundly sleeping by the side of his dead comrades, to awake only when the loud roar of cannon sounded the reveille of another day – to end at last, in victory.

MUSTERED!

G. L. I. 5-9.
ALBERT D. JONES.

B. B. L. 5-8.
SERGT. THOMAS E. LAWLER.

B. D. L. 6-0.
CHRISTOPHER C. JOY.

So, side by side, there slept the brave,
The living with the dead.

After the Battle

On Monday, the 6th, in company with some of my comrades, I went over that portion of the field near us. Evidences of the fearful strife that had taken place were on every hand—broken caissons, disabled guns and gun carriages, small arms in profusion, knapsacks and canteens were lying about, dead horses not yet buried and wounded horses looking with almost human faces at one for relief. In all directions the earth had been plowed with shot and shell, trees were scarred and limbs cut from the trunks and small trees felled by the fierce iron storm.

At the base of Little Round Top a most ghastly sight presented itself. Burial parties had buried most of the dead on the field where they fell, but here the surface was thickly covered with rocks; graves were hard to dig and soil was difficult to find, or it may have been that this part of the field had been overlooked. At least none of the dead here had been buried. At the base of this hill, the Johnnies had charged at fearful cost at Hazlett's battery placed near the summit. The dead lay here so thick that it was with difficulty that we could walk without stepping on the lifeless forms. The features of all had turned black, and maggots were crawling in and out of the gaping wounds.

The boulders had protected the lower part of the victims and nearly all the death wounds were in the head or upper parts of the bodies. Nearly all of them had their pockets turned inside out showing that human ghouls had here robbed the dead. These scenes are still vivid on the page of my memory, causing a shudder of horror still.

The stench from the battlefield was terrible, and we were anxious to be on the move, especially as all the water that could be obtained was from brooks flowing over the field of battle.

Saturday night a fearful rainstorm came as usual after a battle. The men were unprepared for such a storm and suffered much during the night. In the morning we moved to higher ground, but it was impossible to obtain water, except we used the washings of the battle-field, and the stench grew worse rather than better.

On Sunday, July 5th, it was known that the Rebel army was on the retreat.

Shortly after noon the very windows of heaven seemed to have been opened. Rain fell in dashing torrents, and in a little while the whole face of the earth was covered with water. The meadows became small lakes, raging streams ran across the road in every depression of the ground.

General Imboden of the Confederate army had charge of the wounded sent south from the battlefield, and he has written that his train of wounded men was seventeen miles in length. About 4:00 p.m. the head of the column was put in motion to begin the ascent of the mountain. The train of Confederate wounded in our distant front was moving rapidly and from every wagon issued wails of agony. The storm increased in fury every moment. Canvas was no protection against it, and the bodies of the wounded lying upon the hard naked boards of the wagon were drenched by the cold rain. Horses and mules were blinded and maddened by the storm and became almost unmanageable. The roar of the winds and waters made it almost impossible to communicate orders; night was rapidly approaching and there was danger that in the darkness the confusion would become more confounded.

For four hours Captain Barker, on horseback, galloped along, passing to the front. In the wagons were Confederate soldiers wounded and mutilated in every conceivable way. Some had their legs shattered by a shell or minie ball; some were shot through their bodies; others had arms torn to shreds; some had received a ball in the face, or a jagged piece of shell had lacerated their heads. Scarcely one in a hundred had received adequate surgical aid; and many had been without food for thirty-six hours. Their ragged, dirty, and bloody clothes, all clotted and hardened with blood, were rasping the tender, inflamed edges of their gaping wounds. Very few of the wagons had even straw in them, and all were without springs. The road was rough and rocky. The jolting was enough to have killed strong, sound men. From nearly every wagon as the horses trotted along came cries and shrieks to our ears:

"O God! Why can't I die?"

"'My God! Will no one have mercy and kill me, and end my misery?"

"Oh! stop one minute, take me out and leave me by the roadside to die."

"'I am dying! Oh, my .poor wife and children! What will become of you?"

Some were praying, while others were uttering the most fearful oaths and imprecations that despair could wring from them in their agony. Occasionally a wagon would be passed from which only low, deep moans and groans could be heard. No help could be given to any of the sufferers—though we now saw them as our brothers in humanity, not our enemies in war.

The storm continued and the darkness was fearful. There was no time even to fill a canteen with water for a dying man; for except for the driver and guards, all were wounded in that vast train of human misery. No language can convey an idea of the horrors of that most horrible of all nights of our long and bloody war.

While here, the army heard the news of the fall of Vicksburg, and the rank and file were anxious to be led against the Rebel army in the hope that the work of crushing the rebellion might be finished then and there. Instead of this, however, came the news that the Confederate army was retreating. The greater part of our army was in pursuit. The next morning (Monday, July 6) an order was read that our cavalry had destroyed the enemy's pontoons. This was cheering, but we saw no indications later that the report was true, at least it resulted in no serious injury to the Rebel army.

South Again

At three o'clock Tuesday morning, July 7th, the Third Corps commenced its march southward. It halted at noon at Emmitsville, and then pressed on and bivouacked for the night near Mechanicstown, about eighteen miles from Gettysburg. Wednesday we reached Frederick City, Maryland, and Thursday night bivouacked at Foxes Gap, on South Mountain, northeast of Frederick City. Friday we marched to within five miles of Hagerstown, Maryland, still further to the northeast, reaching there about 7:00 p.m. Here we expected to remain for the night, but at ten o'clock the call to fall in was sounded and we tramped five miles more to Boonesboro, which we reached at 3:00 a.m. Saturday. We halted in a wheat field, and the newly cut grain made comfortable beds for the remainder of the night for the weary soldiers.

Now came several days of comparative inactivity. We were hanging about the Rebel army, apparently not daring to attack, and our movements were regulated by theirs. At one point we occupied strong entrenchments just vacated by the enemy. We were constantly under arms and were frequently drawn up in line of battle but apparently neither side dared bring on a general engagement.

On Wednesday, July 15, the reveille sounded at five o'clock, and we were told we would not have time to make coffee. After falling into line, we stood where we were for the entire Twelfth Corps to pass; then we struck almost into a double quick through Pleasanttown and reached Sharpsburg, where we halted ten minutes. Then we were told we were to march through the town and then rest a few hours. We resumed the march and on we rushed through the dust, under the hot sun, spurred on by the officers. It seemed that some great emergency must demand such hasty marching; and so the men did the best they could. But General Lee's army had crossed the river into Virginia two days before, and if there was any justification for this haste, the men in the ranks never found it out. There were many cases of sunstroke, and I saw several by the wayside who appeared to be dying.

Straggling was very general and finally all semblance of organization was lost, and the head of the column halted, and went into camp to allow the stragglers to catch up.

This day we passed over the Antietam battle ground, crossing the stream here on the stone bridge, which was one of the storm centers of that fight. There were many evidences of the severity of this engagement, chiefly on the trees, which had not yet outgrown the wounds they then received.

That afternoon we went into camp near where a sutler had just erected a large tent well stocked with supplies for the men. Not since the army had left camp near Falmouth had there been an opportunity to patronize a sutler and the crush was great. He had but few clerks and the officers must be served first so the men had to wait. Tired and hungry as all were, grumbling and threats soon commenced; then the high prices charged and the poor quality of the goods only exasperated them the more. My tent was but a little way off on higher ground in full view of the sutler's tent, and seeing trouble in the air, I retired to my tent to take observations. Only a short time elapsed when the excited men drew their jackknives and cut all the guy ropes of the tent. Then there was a grand rush for the sutler's goods, and the poor man's stock was rapidly disposed of at retail but at ruinous prices, and a thousand men were making tracks for their tents loaded with sutler's goods. By the time a guard arrived, there were no soldiers or supplies in the immediate vicinity. The goods were distributed with marvelous quickness. A box of tobacco, for instance, which started off on the shoulder of a man, was almost instantly distributed into the pockets of the men, and nothing but the box remained. Sutlers were in the army to make money. They generally made it, but got the ill will of the men by their extortion.

The sutler of the 12th Regiment, Woodbury Sanborn, was an exception to the rule. He was a firm friend of the boys and was respected and loved by them in turn. After the war as long as he lived, he was a leading spirit in our reunions.

WOODBURY SANBORN.

In our march through Maryland going south, as in going north in the pursuit of Lee, the people showed their loyalty in many ways, and this was recognized by the army in marching as though on parade, the drum beating or bands playing and the colors unfurled. In carrying the colors on the march rolled up as they usually were, it was but little more difficult than a musket, but in marching through Maryland, the colors were unfurled much of the time, and, especially if even a light wind blew, it required all my strength, light in stature and weight as I was, to carry them and keep in my place in the line. Each day the task became harder and I was finally obliged to ask the adjutant to relieve me of the flag. Sergeant Shepard succeeded me.

For a few days after being relieved of the colors, I felt played out. In fact, I was sick, and one morning I responded to the sick call, and Dr. Fowler promptly gave me an order for a ride in the ambulance. This was the only time that I was ever excused from the ranks while on the march; and this morning, when presenting myself at the ambulances, I found they were full, so, after giving my knapsack to one of the drivers, I trudged along on foot.

On Friday, July 17, we reached Harper's Ferry, and had a fine opportunity to see this world renowned place. We marched past the engine house where John Brown and his deluded followers made a brave defense, thence crossed the river into Virginia, and bivouacked on Boliver Heights.

The next morning early, we resumed the march and reached Hillsboro. Here we halted about an hour and then retraced our steps a half mile and went into camp. While resting beside the road in Hillsboro, I observed a spring house near a planter's residence, and so visited it to fill my canteen. On entering, I was agreeably surprised to find several pans and pails of sweet milk placed in the running water to keep them cool. It was a lucky find for a thirsty soldier. I took a liberal drink, filled my canteen and rejoined my comrades, telling them of my find; and a large number at once made a break for the spring house, and all the milk left promptly disappeared. Later in the day, I picked some blackberries, and the same day one of my comrades captured a chicken at a near-by farmhouse, which I broiled and assisted in eating, so that I fared pretty well that day. We were then in the same vicinity as in the previous fall, when we fared well by foraging.

We left Hillsboro early Sunday morning, July 19th, and marched ten miles, and the next day fifteen miles to Upperville, Virginia and encamped only a few rods from one of our camping places the fall before.

Wapping Heights

We left Upperville, marched about eight miles and bivouacked a mile beyond Piedmont Station. Early the next morning, we resumed the march, and leaving the Warrenton road, took the one that led through Manassas Gap to Front Royal.

As we pressed on towards Front Royal, there lay beside the road a dead Rebel. He was perhaps twenty-five years of age, tall and fine looking. He was well dressed, clean shaved and with curly hair that extended to his shoulders. He had evidently prided himself on his good looks and was quite likely the idol of some household, perhaps the centre of some fashionable family circle. The sight of this dead young man impressed me deeply, accustomed though I was at that time to scenes of death. Once again, I felt the troubling appearance of my enemy as my brother, and during the years that have since passed, I have frequently recalled that scene.

The road was up and down steep hills, over rocks and through brooks. The road hard and the day hot, we were glad to halt and stack arms about four miles from Front Royal. Here the cavalry men told us that the Rebels were but two or three miles in advance. Soon we saw a part of the Third Brigade advance as skirmishers and very soon open fire. They continued to advance and the reserve to follow up, with the remainder of the brigade in line of battle.

Our turn to move forward soon came. The enemy fell slowly back for about a mile, we following, when the firing commenced to grow warmer, and the enemy opened upon us with their artillery, but fell short of reaching us and did us but little harm.

We took quite a number of prisoners as we moved onward. Two Rebels, when they saw their captain fall in our lines, threw down their guns and ran and helped him to our rear, thus getting into our lines.

The engagement here was but little more than a skirmish, and the dead and wounded numbered but a hundred or two. The Rebel loss was perhaps as heavy in men who allowed themselves to be captured as by the dead and wounded.

Darkness coming on, we lay down to rest on the ground by our arms, with equipments all on, ready to spring into line at a moment's warning. We had no permission to sleep, even in that condition. But as the order was to rest, we soon fell asleep and did not wake up until morning, although we lay on rocks upon the side of a hill so steep that we had to get our heels against a stone to keep from sliding down.

We expected a renewal of the fight next day, but in the morning there were no Rebels to be found, and we advanced to within a mile of Front Royal, when a single shell sent over by the enemy caused us to halt, form a line of battle again, and in this way we moved forward upon ground perfectly awful to march over. When we got to the town, we halted, and a cavalry force was sent ahead but discovered no Rebels that side of the Shenandoah river. We then retraced our steps and marched back about eight miles where we camped for the night. That day we marched about sixteen miles, halting for the night within six miles of Warrenton, where our regiment did picket duty until starting again the next morning about five o'clock.

We supposed we were to have a rest at Warrenton, and draw some shoes and clothing, which we were really suffering for. My feet had been so sore for several days as to give me great pain every time I stepped. Instead of resting, we passed through the town toward Culpepper. It was hot and dusty, and we were so worn out that it seemed impossible to move any further. In this condition we were taking a short rest when the bugle sounded for us to fall in. Suddenly an order came for our regiment to proceed no further. We were detached from our brigade and ordered to report to General Marston. It was said we were going to Point Lookout to guard prisoners; and if ever news was gladly received by weary soldiers, this was by us. Yet we hardly dared to believe it true, but we were glad for a change of any kind that promised a little rest.

On Sunday, July 26, the regiment marched back to Warrenton, and I was detailed with eight men to guard the regimental property which was sent to the depot there. After posting my men, I made an individual boiled dinner in my tin cup. My haversack contributed the salt pork, and a southern gentleman's garden near by contributed the vegetables. I was anxious to make coffee in the same dipper, and so I presume I did not give the dinner a sufficient time to boil, but it was a good treat even if not quite done when eaten.

As may be imagined, the men were delighted at the prospect of a change. For forty-seven days they had been on the march or on the battle field; they were reduced in flesh and exhausted in body; the shoes had almost entirely disappeared from the feet of many; and the clothes of all were ragged and dirty. No wonder the boys went into camp with light hearts, waiting for the train to convey them to Washington, where they were to take the boat for Point Lookout.

The 2d and 5th New Hampshire regiments were equally fortunate, as they, too, were detached from the Army of the Potomac, and ordered to report to General Marston for duty at Point Lookout. On reaching Washington, the 5th New Hampshire was still further famed, for from there they were ordered to New Hampshire to recruit and did not reach Point Lookout till November following.

The several regiments composing General Marston's brigade and the prisoners we had captured at Front Royal left Warrenton, Virginia for Washington in three trains at 10:00 a.m., Monday, July 27, 1863, the 12th Regiment moving first. We arrived at Washington about midnight.

On our passage from Warrenton to Alexandria and Washington, the people gathered at the stations to see us pass. This was especially true at Alexandria, and the disloyalty of the people was shown in many ways. We had as one member of the Twelfth a man who was connected with the commissary or quartermaster's department. He was not therefore obliged to wear a regulation suit at all times. He had procured a butternut jacket and found he could get favors at the farmhouses when wearing it much better than when he wore a blue jacket, many supposing him a Johnnie. On this trip he wore this jacket and rode in the baggage car unarmed with the guard, and many of the people evidently thought he was, like others with us, a prisoner of war. He consequently received many favors from the people, among which were kisses thrown at him by the girls. Even in Washington, more favors were shown the prisoners than we received, showing that the secession element there was still prominent.

On arriving at Washington, we were given quarters in the soldiers' barracks. When in Washington ten months before we were a thousand strong, but at this time, there were just sixty-nine guns as they were stacked in the centre of our quarters.

Lieutenant-Colonel Marsh, who had not seen his regiment since he left the Twelfth on the field of Chancellorsville, upon seeing us exclaimed, "My God! Is this all that is left of the 12th New Hampshire?" and wept like a child. Captain May, when he saw our ragged and haggard condition – some not able to be outside the hospital and all without clothes or money – pulled out his pocket-book and said, "Here, boys, help yourselves," giving and loaning several hundred dollars.

For forty-seven consecutive days the regiment had been in active campaign service, on the road or battlefield, making many forced marches by day and night, and the condition of the men was one of actual destitution and suffering.

The first day here was devoted to rest and it was appreciated. In the afternoon I visited the new capitol near by, then in process of construction. Peddlers selling all kinds of pastry and fruit swarmed about our quarters all the time we were there, but, fortunately perhaps, we were short of money and could not indulge as freely as the appetite suggested. Our prisoners, who were quartered in adjoining barracks, did not need to purchase, for friends brought all they could consume.

On the night of the 28th an incident occurred that showed how easily even veterans may be stampeded when taken by surprise. During the day we learned that some cavalry regiments in the city were disgruntled about something and disposed to make trouble. At night we were told to have our arms and equipments ready for instant use, as we might be called during the night to help the authorities preserve order. The guns were stacked in the middle of the barracks, and the men slept on both sides of the stack. In the middle of the night a man got up in his sleep and butted over the first stack of guns. This struck the second stack and that went over. In turn the whole line went crashing to the floor. One of the first guns that fell struck a man on the foot and in pain or fright he cried out. The scream and the crash of arms made the men think the cavalry were among them cutting and slashing. The men sprang to their feet and rushed like mad men from the building, and by the time they were fairly awake, they found themselves in the middle of the street. It chanced that I was awake at the time the cause of the panic happened and saw it all, and as the men commenced to spring from the floor I yelled at the top of my voice that there was no cause for alarm, but not a man heard me. This episode was the cause of a hearty laugh when the men came to their senses.

Wednesday, July 29, Alonzo Jewett and I worked making out the payroll of our company for the previous two months.

On Friday, July 31, we were paid for four months' service, and the afternoon of the same day, about six o'clock, we went on board the steamer *John Brooks* at Seventh Street wharf.

At noon the next day, we landed at Point Lookout, Maryland.

CHAPTER IX

Point Lookout

August 1863. Point Lookout is a narrow arm of land one fourth mile wide, lying between the mouth of the Potomac River and Chesapeake Bay in Maryland. The Potomac there is three or four miles wide and its waters on the south wash the northern shores of Virginia; to the east is the broad expanse of the bay, while a mile or more to the north the land between these two bodies of water is contracted to a narrow strip, so that the Point is almost an island — an ideal place for a camp of prisoners of war, its surrounding waters being easily protected by gun boats along with the narrow strip guarded by a battery.

Previous to the war, the Point was a summer resort of some note for those days. One small hotel stood on the beach facing the bay, and long rows of barrack-like cottages, all connected, stood south of the hotel, one facing the bay and another the river.

At the time of our going there, the United States had a general hospital at the extreme point in buildings erected for the purpose, with a capacity of five hundred beds. At this time about one-half were filled. The hotel was appropriated by General Marston who was authorized to establish, and to take with him, the three New Hampshire regiments (Twelfth, Second and Fifth) that had suffered the most in the field.

To soldiers from the field, with the experience that had been ours during the year previous, the Point seemed almost a fairyland. Our shelter tents were discarded, and we drew new A-tents, one for every two men. The officers drew wall tents. These were pitched on a well laid-out ground on the Potomac shore. The 2^d Regiment encampment was just south of us on the same shore, while the camp for Rebel prisoners was located on the Chesapeake shore, east of our camp, and here were placed the prisoners we brought with us from the front.

The next day after our arrival, we drew new clothes throughout. This was indeed a luxury. For a long time what little we had, had been ragged, dirty and infested with vermin. For several weeks a daily exercise was taking off our clothes and hunting for "greybacks." Yet they continued so numerous that they were a constant annoyance, especially at night when they greatly disturbed our slumbers. Carrying our new clothes in a bundle at arms length so they would not come in contact with the old, we traveled to beyond the limits of the camp, where we shed the old ones, took a good bath, donned the new and traveled back to camp. If "clothes do not make the man," they certainly on this occasion made us feel more like men than we were before.

The Rebel prisoners were generally well satisfied with their lot. When they landed, I was one of the sergeants of the guard over them. Their presence attracted all the men and boys on the Point, who crowded the guard so closely that I was obliged to order them back. In doing this, I ordered one of the Johnnies, who was dressed in civilian clothes, to "get out from among those prisoners and let them alone." The fellow evidently did not care for an opportunity to escape and hesitated about obeying the order, and the other Johnnies joined in a laugh that told me the mistake I was making, and so I added, "I guess you may as well stay where you are."

Almost from the moment the regiment broke ranks on the Point, there was a grand rush of the boys for every scrap of board that could be utilized for a seat, a bunk or a table. Everything loose in sight was soon traveling towards camp, and then some made a descent on the board fence near the Hammond general hospital. The small guard at this point was entirely inadequate for its protection, and the surgeon in charge found that he could protect but a very small area at one time. A few days later not a board was left to his fence. Alonzo Jewett at this time was First Sergeant of Company D, and I was his tent-mate. In a little while we had a bunk in which to sleep and a table, though I do not now remember where or how we got the material of which they were composed.

One source of pleasure at the Point was the water, where we could bathe and sail and fish to our hearts' content. For a week or two no duty was required of the men except such as was absolutely necessary.

Under date of August 12, I find the following entered in my diary. "One year ago today, twelve of us Bristol boys enlisted. Of that number, Henry Kidder, Dan Nelson, Luther Parker, and Charles G. Smith are dead; five have been severely wounded; and only three, Alonzo (Lon) Jewett, Uriah Kidder and myself, remain for duty. As great a change has taken place throughout the regiment. Oh, how many hearts are bleeding for lost ones slain by the ruthless hand of war, and how many more are doomed, God only knows."

On the night of August 13, we were given a taste of Point Lookout weather. There was a very severe thunder storm accompanied by a gale that leveled scores of tents. The officers' quarters suffered most because their tents were the larger, and the wind struck them with greater force. The morning presented a ludicrous sight—many an officer drenched to the skin was walking the beach waiting for the day.

Soon after our arrival, Sergeant Fellows of Company H and I were detailed for permanent duty at the camp for the prisoners of war. I therefore had a fine opportunity to study these men, and I became well acquainted with many of them, some of whom I esteemed highly. Among the number were some brother Masons, and it was a pleasure to contribute to their comfort, and indeed to the comfort of all as well as I could.

These men were quartered in A-tents like our own, though they were older and as many as could lie down in them were assigned to each, usually six. The government allowed the same rations to prisoners of war as to its own soldiers, and at first there were no "savings" from their rations for any purpose, at least there was no systematic savings, and if these men did not receive all the law allowed, it was because there was a shrinkage as it passed through the hands of the commissary department. This food was prepared by cooks chosen by the men themselves, and at first, the men were satisfied with their allowances.

Their tents were arranged in streets with enough for one hundred men in a street. I was at first given charge of one street, but as the number of men increased by additional arrivals, the number under the command or charge of each sergeant was increased to five hundred, and so I finally was in command of five hundred Johnnies. As the new men arrived, it was our duty to make out a descriptive list of each, recording his name, age, birthplace, his company and regiment, and when and where captured. Their signatures were required, and it was surprising to a Northerner to find the large number who could not read or write.

Each day the men were called into line and responded to a roll call, and the policing and sanitary conditions of the grounds were looked after. After a little, a sergeant of their own number was selected to make a daily detail for police duty and who had some authority and was held responsible for the good order of his street. He also called the roll, and I simply counted the men as they stood in line to see that all were present.

Large wall tents were erected for the accommodation of their sick. The regimental surgeons visited this hospital at stated times, but the immediate care of the sick fell very properly upon nurses from their own ranks.

At first there was simply a guard around their camp day and night, but very soon a stockade of logs placed upright in the ground was made, the prisoners being compelled to do all the work. The number of prisoners continued to increase until they numbered ten thousand. Then a board fence, or stockade, was erected. To surround this large camp on three sides required a fence about one mile long; it was twelve feet high, the boards being square edged and placed close together. About two feet from the top was a walk on which the guard walked back and forth. The whole was made strong enough to withstand a rush of the men in the camp, if one should be made.

In place of cooking outdoors, ten cook houses and mess houses were erected, each to accommodate one thousand men. The cook houses were provided with large arch kettles in which to do the cooking for one thousand men. In the mess rooms there were four or five long tables at which the men stood and ate their meals.

In place of tents for the hospital spoken of above, wooden barracks were erected outside the stockade at the north, and a short distance to the south another stockade was erected for the confinement of commissioned officers of the Rebel army.

August 18th, another installment of five hundred Johnnies reached camp, and other sergeants were detailed for work in the prison, and the work of those already detailed largely increased.

Religious Rebels

Most of the newcomers were North Carolinians from General Jackson's old corps, and this may have accounted for the fact that they were a very religious set of men. Though gambling was the constant diversion of a large number, the religious element seemed to be stronger among these men than among other men of the Confederate army, and stronger than in our own army.

They said they used to have great revivals in their corps when Jackson was alive and mingled with them. No wonder that his soldiers followed him until they fell dead in their tracks on their forced marches around our right flank at Chancellorsville, or that they fought with such desperation in that battle to avenge his death.

MUSTERED!

Every evening prayer meetings were held between the tents and the cook houses and were attended by a large proportion of the men. The fervent prayers that were offered for the success of their arms and for the preservation of the men in the field fighting for the right as they saw it left little doubt that men ever fought with more devotion or a firmer belief in the justice of their cause than did these men of the Southern Confederacy.

One evening as the patriotic Confederate prisoners offered up an impressive petition to the God of Battles before retiring, Irish Ed Ryan, who had listened attentively in his own tent close by, was suddenly possessed by the spirit and began his own patriotic prayer in his true Irish strain of eloquence, his voice rising higher and higher as he concluded his fervent appeal for victory and peace for both friend and foe to hear: " O Lord, what we most desire and must have is the Union as it was, and the constitution as it is; we ask no more, and we'll take no less! Amen."

B. B. I. 5–8.
EDWARD C. RYAN.

There was one man, a local Confederate preacher, well advanced in years, whose eloquence and pathos were calculated to win all hearts as he dwelt on the justice of their cause and talked with quivering lips of his four sons in the western army fighting for the right. I was a frequent spectator at these meetings, and I always went away impressed with the sincerity of these men. On more than one occasion as I traveled from the Rebel prison to my own quarters, I could hear songs of praise arising to heaven from both the Rebel and Union soldiers.

I remember one Sunday evening in particular. The southern moon, assisted by the starry hosts of heaven, half lighted up the encampment, disclosing the white tents of the Union army with the cannon trained to deal instant death and destruction. Sentinels paced to and fro by the dark stockade of the Rebel prison, a guard walking across the top. The refreshing breeze of the balmy evening fanned the brow. I stopped to take in the scene. From the Confederate prison and from the Union encampment came songs of supplication and praise borne on the night air, their strains mingling as they ascended to heaven, both the Union and Rebel hosts sincerely worshipping the same God, both believing in the justice of their cause and devoutly asking high heaven to assist them in annihilating the other.

These incidents provoked serious thought on my part, and I could but ask myself the question, *Why is it that men so earnestly desirous to be in the right are left entirely in the dark as to their true position?* Instead of acquiring any light, both sides arose from their knees more firmly resolved to fight for the "right" as they saw it. They became better soldiers thereby, and when they again met in conflict, the slaughter was all the more terrible because of their faith and their prayers. Perhaps some theologian can explain all this, but I have never met one who could. Fifty years after the conflict some politicians tell us that both sides were right, and perhaps that should satisfy us for all the sacrifice made and the blood spilt in this fratricidal conflict.

Inspired in part by the Christian zeal of the Rebel prisoners, Chaplain Ambrose raised money through subscription to erect a chapel where religious services could be held in bad as well as good weather. Before this, services had been held in a small grove of pines near the camp of the Twelfth.

The new chapel was dedicated Sunday, December 27th.

Only one question caused a schism among the worshippers from the three New Hampshire regiments: Should the venerable Sergeant Osgood be excommunicated because he was a believer in universal salvation? This was deemed to be too dangerous a doctrine to be tolerated, much less to be openly communed with, and so without any other charge against him, he was voted out.

DH. B. D. 5–7½.
SERGT. THOMAS E. OSGOOD.

Soon after establishment of the camp, letters began to arrive for the prisoners from Baltimore and from the south via the blockade runners through Baltimore, and very many of these letters contained United States money. This provided a way by which many could obtain luxuries of the sutlers at the Point, but as they could not leave camp to make the purchases, the sergeants on duty were requested to make these purchases for them, and we did so willingly. This trade gradually increased, and the sutlers, quick to see the advantage of capturing as much as possible of this trade, gave us a commission on the trade we brought them, and this in time amounted to quite a little. Much of our spare time was devoted to this kind of work, while the prisoners still got their goods on the same terms as our own men. But this was not long to continue, for someone at headquarters had discovered the value of the trade with the Johnnies, and one day an order came for all the sergeants in charge to appear at brigade headquarters. We obeyed at once, and Adjutant General Lawrence addressed us, short but to the point: "I am directed by General Marston to say to you that if he catches one of you fellows purchasing any supplies for the Johnnies in the future, he will not leave as much as a grease spot of one of you." We were thunder struck. What earthly objection could there be to supplying these men with luxuries that they paid for? But it was unmilitary for us to reply or even to ask a question. We had simply to obey. The answer came next day. A sutler's stand was erected outside the stockade with an opening into the prison, where the Johnnies could spend all the money they had and be obliged to pay such a price as this sutler's conscience would allow him to impose without any fear of competition.

Another thing changed: All letters addressed to the prisoners were now examined by clerks at headquarters, and all money they contained was held back under the plea that they might use it to bribe the guard, and an equal amount in checks was substituted, which checks were only of use in purchasing goods of this particular sutler at his own price.

All letters that arrived for the prisoners and all letters written in camp were carefully read. Whenever these letters contained anything objectionable, either in the way of disloyal sentiment, giving improper information, or complaining of the situation, they were destroyed. It generally happened that those going in contained a stamp for a reply, sometimes quite a number, and those coming out had uncancelled stamps on the envelopes. All stamps on objectionable letters became the property of the clerk destroying the letters. The stamps taken from the envelopes were regummed and loose stamps substituted for sheets going in, and so the clerks had stamps in fit condition for sale. This supervision of the mail was necessary, but whether there was any abuse of the practice is left for those with a knowledge of human nature to judge.

Another source of income the Johnnies had was the making of trinkets for sale to the Union soldiers and visitors. They made a large number of rings from bones obtained at the cook houses and fancy fans made from one straight piece of wood, steamed, and then cut and bent to the shape desired and tied in position by ribbon purchased of the sutler. Some of these were decidedly artistic and brought good prices. The sergeants often bought these trinkets outright and sold them among the Union soldiers, or sold them on commission, and among all the trade of this kind I always noticed the same scrupulous honesty and square dealing between the men of the two armies as between men in our own army. Indeed the poor fellows shut up in that prison pen were objects of sympathy and respect to many a Union soldier. There was seldom ill will between the rank and file of the two armies.

The government allowed prisoners of war the same rations as men in its own army. This was true, but a full ration did not reach these men except during a short time after the camp was first opened. The government fixed the price of the ration at thirty cents a day or nine dollars per month, if I am not mistaken. Any company in the Union army could draw a part of the rations in money if it so chose and thus create a company fund with which to purchase delicacies not provided by the commissary. The same rule applied to prisoners of war, and at Point Lookout it was commonly reported, and generally believed, that the Johnnies themselves paid for all the luxuries that they enjoyed, such as a high stockade, cook houses and mess houses, hospitals, as extensive and costly as they were, though they could not be eaten. In other words, the savings from their rations, or from thirty cents per day, paid all these bills. Such a cut was enough to reduce the food to the lowest amount for each man, and even if the commissary was scrupulously honest and intended to issue the full amount to which the Johnnies were entitled after the cut, the details of the work must be executed by subordinates, and there were instances where the Johnnies did not get all they were entitled to, even at this early stage of the game.

However this may be, it was very evident that there was a further shrinkage after the food reached the prison camp before it reached the men. The prisoners of war in charge of the cook houses did not hesitate to live high and see that their friends lived well, for there was no one to call them to account or who had sufficient interest to call them to account, even if they had authority; and so at the final division, the amount was extremely small for each man. Meals were served twice a day at about 9 o'clock a.m. and 4 o'clock p.m. On tin plates, arranged on the tables, were placed small pieces of boiled pork or corn beef, beans and hard tack. When all was ready, the Rebel sergeants in charge marched their men in single file on each side of the table, gave the command, "Halt! Inward face!" and each man faced his plate and devoured his meal without further ceremony; but here again there was a frequent shrinkage. The strong, as they passed along, would sometimes grab from a plate the ration that belonged to another, and many a poor fellow as he inward faced found little or nothing on the plate before him. This state of affairs led to frequent fights, sometimes attended with fatal results.

One night a raid was made by dissatisfied and hungry men on one of the cook houses, and a hatchet thrown by one of the cooks buried itself in the breast of one of the attacking party, killing him instantly.

Treatment of Prisoners

Human nature was the same in the North as in the South, and those who suppose that prisoners of war from the Southern army were invariably treated well would probably revise their opinion could they know the full and truthful history of what the Southern soldiers suffered in Northern prisons. That many in this prison knew what the cravings of hunger were, there could be no doubt in the minds of those who could see the true condition of affairs.

As cold weather came on, there was much suffering on account of the cold. That could hardly be otherwise under the circumstances. When captured, these men were clothed for summer service in the field, and their clothing was of the scantiest. By the time cold weather came, there were ten thousand men in this prison and to have clothed, nursed and fed all these as humanity demanded would have cost a very large sum. Still the most destitute were relieved.

On the 24th of September, I succeeded in obtaining some clothing for the most needy of my five hundred men, and my diary says I issued that day twenty pairs of pants, forty pairs of shoes, five coats, and ten blankets. The shoes were supplied only to those who had none. Details of the prisoners were allowed to go out daily and cut wood in the neighboring forest, and the immense loads that these fellows would tote into camp on their backs was the marvel of all who saw them. But it took a large amount of wood to warm ten thousand men in the open air, and the number allowed to go into the woods each day was very small for prudential reasons.

That Northern men in Southern prisons were treated worse than Southern men in the prisons of the North, there can be no doubt. As a result, when exchanged, soldiers from the South were ready for active service in the field, while Northern men were so debilitated by their confinement that they were sent to their homes or the hospitals to recuperate. This condition grew worse as the war progressed, in part perhaps owing to the utter inability of the South to properly feed the thousands of men in their hands as prisoners of war. At one time there were fifty thousand Southern men held by the government in Northern prisons. To have exchanged these men for fifty thousand enfeebled Union soldiers would have meant a re-enforcement of fifty thousand men to the ranks of those fighting against the government—enough perhaps to have prolonged the war. Those who berate the government for declining an exchange and thus allowing so many of our soldiers to die of starvation in Rebel prisons should take these facts into account. The government was not seeking to save the lives of men, but the life of the nation, and for every thousand saved by an exchange, another thousand might have fallen in battle.

So there seemed to be some apology for some things that happened or existed; in other cases there was none, of which the following is a case in point.

A sentinel reported to the officer of the day that a prisoner had attempted to bribe him to allow him and others to escape. The sentinel was instructed to accept the bribe and to arrange to let the party out of the stockade at a certain hour that night. This was done, and the party, five in number, passed out of the stockade. They had proceeded but a few rods when their suspicions were aroused that the coast was not clear, and they started to return, when an armed party lying in wait fired upon them without even demanding their surrender. One was killed and others were wounded. The officer in command, a one-armed captain of the 2d Regiment, was said to have actually shot one man twice after he had surrendered, remarking, "This is in exchange for the loss of my arm." One of the wounded men, while in the hospital, stated to me that he was wounded after he surrendered. The Union soldiers doing guard duty at the Point universally condemned this, in writing, but no action or response was issued.

As was to be expected, there were frequent attempts to escape but only a very few were successful. Occasionally some of the wood party would secrete themselves in the woods, hoping at night to emerge from their hiding places and escape. Such generally found themselves surrounded by cavalry when they attempted to travel toward liberty. At one time a tent was erected on the parade ground in the prison, nearer the fence than the rest, ostensibly for the purpose of making brick. This finally excited suspicion, when it was found that this tent covered the entrance to a tunnel that had been constructed half way to the fence. On one occasion all the Johnnies were paraded, and while in line, their quarters were examined. Among the contraband articles found were two or three muskets, several oars, and boards shaped to be put together for a boat.

On another occasion while the men were bathing, I went to the beach which formed the eastern boundary of the prison. I noticed a barrel floating on the water out in the bay. I had given it only a casual look when close at hand a fight commenced among the prisoners. It assumed such proportions that I called on the guard to quell it. When all was over, I noticed there were no broken heads among the men, and no knives were used as was usual at such times and learned that night at roll call that the fight was a bogus affair. It was put up to attract my attention from the barrel because on the other side of the barrel was a Johnnie floating or swimming to liberty. He worked the barrel out into the bay and then to shore a long way from the stockade and escaped or was drowned, I never knew which.

To enforce discipline, tying up by the wrists was sometimes resorted to. This was a very painful operation and was used only in extreme cases. A rope was tied about the wrists and drawn so tight over a high support that a large part of the weight of the body was sustained by the rope. This soon produced excruciating pain and if long continued, was almost unbearable. It was said that a complaint by reason of this practice was lodged with the Confederate government, and that correspondence over the matter was carried on with the Washington government. It was reported that inquiries concerning the facts came to the Point from Washington, but they amounted to nothing.

In the spring of 1864, a colored regiment came to the Point for duty. To be guarded by their late slaves must have been the height of humiliation to the Rebels, especially to the officers. One of these officers was allowed to go to the commissary under guard of a colored soldier to buy some supplies. The officer did not seem to comprehend changed conditions and, the supplies being purchased, he ordered the black man as of yore to carry his bundle. The negro stood on his dignity and refused. High words ensued, and the difficulty was resolved by the negro shooting the officer dead in his tracks.

Fears of an uprising among the prisoners were at different times entertained. To meet such an emergency a section of artillery was planted opposite the main entrance, loaded with grape and canister ready for instant use. With ten desperate unarmed men against one armed guard, it is a wonder that the attempt was not made. The difficulty of reaching Virginia even if the guard were overpowered probably prevented the attempt. It is now known that when General Stuart made his descent on Washington in 1864, he included in his program the release of the prisoners of war at Point Lookout.

During the winter small-pox prevailed in the prisoners' camp. Dr. William Child of the 5th Regiment diagnosed all the cases in camp as fast as they appeared, and then the men were removed to the small-pox hospital nearby under charge of Dr. Samuel Carbee of the 12th Regiment, Notwithstanding the fact that the men were huddled so closely together, the disease was soon stamped out, and no great mortality prevailed at any time. My duties required me to come in contact with the disease daily. I could not avoid it, and therefore concluded not to fear it and I did not contract the disease.

My duties in the camp had hardly commenced ere some of the prisoners indicated a desire to take the oath of allegiance. I reported this fact to Brigade Headquarters and the matter was referred to Washington. The result was that printed blanks were sent us on which were a series of questions which we were to ask those desiring to take the oath. Their answers were written on the blanks and these were sent to Washington, and the application was approved or rejected as seemed wise to the clerk or officer inspecting them. This procedure amounted to but little as there was no way of determining whether the applicant was telling a truth or a falsehood. At first many who took the oath went North as they were allowed to do, but later most remained in quarters arranged for them with the expectation of their enlisting in the United States service. Enough of these men enlisted to form two regiments which were largely officered by men from the Second, Fifth and Twelfth New Hampshire regiments

The men who thus took the oath of allegiance were of various make-ups. Some took the oath as a stepping stone to return South to re-enter the Southern army; a goodly number claimed to be Union men who were forced into the Southern army, men from the hill country of North Carolina. These men made the best soldiers of any entering the Union from the prison pen. Then there were foreigners who cared nothing for either side and sought only to improve their condition, many deserting at a later date. There were some bright, keen men among those who took the oath and enlisted; yet about one-half could neither read nor write.

I have previously stated that there were only sixty-six muskets in the 12th Regiment when it reached the Point. A large number of men, sick or wounded, were in various hospitals or on furloughs, and these gradually returned, slowly increasing our numbers.

Among the first to arrive were George Currier and others of the drum corps who had been doing duty in the hospitals at Gettysburg since the battle there. The 6th of September brought a number of those who had been wounded at Chancellorsville, among them Port Hall, Albert Nelson and Louis Rowe, who brought with him the overcoat I placed over him after finding him wounded at Chancellorsville. Louis Rowe's wounds entitled him to a discharge but he declined it, preferring to return to the regiment. A few days later came Warren Tucker and others who were also wounded at Chancellorsville.

"The Little Corporal," Howard Taylor, whom we all missed and feared was dead, returned after being wounded and captured at Gettysburg. He had made a daring escape, and all rejoiced to see his young and shining face once more.

J P Fahey

SERGT. HOWARD TAYLOR.

Howard Taylor was wounded and captured with seven others at Gettysburg. He escaped from a Rebel prison hospital, the only one of those captured to ever return. Young, brave and daring, he was in every march and battle. At Bermuda Hundred he was struck in the head by a minie ball, but refused to leave the regiment for treatment. This wound was the cause of his insanity and death more than twenty-five years afterward.

As the fall wore away, preparations for winter were made. The boys raised the tents from the ground, in some cases several feet, with wood underneath and built fireplaces of wood and mud with a chimney of the same material outside, in true Virginia style. A board floor was placed in the large tent used for a chapel, and seats were procured. The Free Masons of the several regiments belonging to New Hampshire secured a traveling dispensation, organized and erected a hall of wood and did a flourishing business in raising Masons.

Arrival of the Subs

On the 13th of November the 5th Regiment, which had been to New Hampshire for recruiting, reached the Point. Its ranks were largely recruited with substitutes, and soon after, a goodly number of subs reached the Point for the 12th and 2d Regiments.

This was the beginning of trouble for the veterans. Previous to this all the soldiers had enjoyed the greatest liberty consistent with their duties. They could take a boat and fish in the waters of the river or the bay, or they could stroll into the country as far as inclination prompted and duty allowed. But when these fellows came, all these things were changed. Large numbers had deserted en route to their destination, and every precaution was necessary against the desertion of those that reached Point Lookout; a strong guard was placed across the Point, and no one was allowed to go into the country or use a boat without a written pass. Nearly all boats were destroyed.

Every few days a fresh supply of substitutes or Rebel prisoners would arrive in camp, but the latter were by far the more welcome.

The "subs" that arrived at Point Lookout during the fall and winter of 1863-4 were the result of a draft authorized by Congress to fill up the quotas of the different states by virtue of which every man whose name was drawn had to "play or pay" (the sum of $300). It was both unwise and unjust, for it discriminated in favor of the rich; many were convicts procured by consent of state authority, the criminal choosing to enlist for $16 per month rather than work for the State for nothing. From the moment of their arrival, the substitutes caused great hardship, concern and dissention among the honor-driven veterans who preferred the companionship, complement and care of Rebel prisoners to the "depraved vice-hardened subs" sent to fill the ranks of their fallen brave.

They represented the lowest class of human existence, though some of the worst were of good birth and education and were naturally the instigators of every effort to evade duty or to desert. Before their arrival common values, hardships and dangers over the months had made the veterans a band of brothers, and between the officers and men there existed the most perfect confidence and friendship. Punishment was uncalled for, as disobedience was unknown. When the all-subverting sub came, everything changed. Hard lines and severe military discipline were applied with a rigidness never before required.

The following incidents from the regimental history were recorded by foot soldiers of the Twelfth:

A boat had just brought another load of subs. Among the motley crew was one fellow, who was so badly hampered by lung trouble that he could walk but a few steps without sitting down. "What in the name of heaven are you out here for?" asked Captain Langley, who passed by where the poor fellow sat coughing and wheezing. "Fourteen hundred dollars," was the short but truthful reply.

In one train car loaded with subs enroute for the front, the following incidents took place. Although a free ride, it was in the wrong direction for the subs to be enjoyable and many of them had taken with them a thinner suit, of any color but blue, to put on. One of these fellows, with citizen pants under his others, noticed that the officer in charge of them had become annoyed by persistent efforts of the newsboys to get into the car at a certain city and was threatening to kick the next newsboy from the platform. Quickly pulling off his outside pants and turning his coat and cap inside out, he started for the door with a bundle of papers under his arms crying out,

"*Times! Herald! Tribune!*" He ran purposely against the officer who grabbed him by the shoulders and with a shove and a kick gave him a very acceptable send-off, while a roar of laughter arose from his comrades. As the cars were starting, another sub entered the saloon at the end of the train car where immediately a window was heard to crash, and while the guard jumped for the coattail going out of the window, two or three more coattails went out the door.

To keep them from running away was by no means the worst part that the subs furnished. To make them obey orders and perform duty, neither the patience of Job nor the wisdom of Solomon could avail. The officers were heavily taxed to find means of punishment commensurate with the multifold of daily offenses. In fact, more time and effort was spent overseeing and guarding the subs than the Rebel prisoners.

However much they were found wanting, with one thing they were well supplied and that was "greenbacks". With no relatives or friends they dared trust, they took their bounty money along with them; and, judging others by themselves, dared not carry it in their pockets but concealed it about their persons in every way conceivable. Despite all these precautions many had their money, as well as other goods, stolen by fellow subs.

Curley, who was one of the meanest and toughest specimens of his class was arrested for stealing $300. A drumhead court martial was instituted to try him, and in the course of the investigation, it was ascertained that he had gambled his comrades out of several thousand dollars which he had sent in separate packages to different banks all over the North. Once Curley made a cowardly attack upon Captain Barker. The Captain might have been killed but for the quick interference of one of the lieutenants. Another sub stabbed Lieutenant Gale, but his defending arm that received the knife thrust saved his body from a dangerous wound. The assaulting sub was subverted by a stunning blow from the fist of the strong Sergeant Piper.

Felonious assaults were common. The dangerous criminals among the subs would not hesitate to commit any crime that passion, avarice or revenge might incite. These men had plenty of money and spent it recklessly. They were known to pay as high as twenty dollars for a canteen of whiskey. One man paid twenty dollars for a canteen filled with water but wet with whiskey about the outside and stopper. He was told not to drink any till he reached a secluded spot. Then he discovered the trick.

They were a reckless and desperate class of men, and extreme measures were needed to bring them under proper discipline. One night one of these men stole a coffin from the carpenter's shop, used it for a boat, and escaped, but it was never known whether the coffin conveyed him to the bottom of the Potomac or to freedom.

Sometimes disputes arose between a haughty officer and one of his underlings in which the soldier, though knowing he would face punishment, would stand up to the officer. One night an incident occurred between a lieutenant and a corporal of the guard on the sentinel's walk:

The officer, wishing to prove by his vigilance that he was worthy of the rank he had just donned, crept stealthily up the stairs onto the walk, and before the guard could halt and challenge him, grabbed hold of the barrel of the sentinel's gun, thus making himself [the officer] master of the situation. He commenced to lecture his underling for being so easily outwitted, asking him what he would have done if it had been an enemy that had stolen up on him. "This is what *I* would have done," came the quick, sharp response of the corporal as, equally quick and sharp, the point of his bayonet backed up his tongue by a penetrating jab in the officer's rear. [History of the 12th Regiment]

On the 28th of October, I was detailed as sergeant of the provost guard at brigade headquarters under Captain Patterson, provost marshal. Although this was in the nature of a promotion, I obeyed the order with some misgivings. I had become very interested in my men in the Rebel prison, and I left them with many regrets. I spent many social hours in the company of prisoners and learned the unwritten work of Masonry from them.

The duties of my new position were various. I had charge of all those soldiers in confinement or under arrest for various offences. Refugees were constantly arriving from the Virginia shore and blockade runners arrested were turned over to me. I visited the dock on the arrival of every boat and examined all freight or express matter for the enlisted men to see that no liquors or other contraband articles were included. Many a box of goodies for the men contained tin cans labeled maple syrup or preserves went into the dock, much as I disliked to deprive the boys of a smile.

The refugees were men and families escaping from the South to the North and others who had visited the South carrying contraband goods and who then desired to reach the North to repeat the same operations. Others were arrested as spies. All these had to be cared for and detained under guard till their cases were disposed.

When I first assumed the duties of this position I found thirty-seven Union soldiers in the guard house. Some had been arrested for trivial offenses, and they had been allowed to remain week after week with no charges preferred against them, instead of being released the next day as regulations of the army required. I sent to headquarters a list of such as I thought ought to be released and was authorized to discharge eleven men at once. Others were released soon after. One of these men had been in confinement eight weeks without charges.

At headquarters I had a room in one of the summer cottages near the hotel where General Marston had his headquarters, and I messed with a company of others connected with headquarters and a Rebel prisoner to whom Captain Patterson had taken a fancy and allowed his liberty on his parole. This man was from New Orleans, a soldier in the organization known as the Louisiana Tigers. He shed his Rebel rags and dressed like a gentleman, as he really was; and at one time, to show his appreciation of the favors extended to him, he had shipped from New Orleans a large quantity of oranges which were enjoyed by all at Headquarters.

On Christmas day I took a horseback ride with the Louisiana Tiger into the country to visit some of the plantations a few miles from the Point. On this trip we rapped at the door of a planter's house. When a voice answered, "Come in," we entered. The woman of the house was holding in her lap a boy of perhaps seven years of age, and she apologized for not opening the door because she was obliged to hold her son, and the reason for this was that he was so drunk he could not stand. Then she added laughing, "Johnnie does not get drunk but once a year and that is at Christmas." I was told that this incident was the habit of many rural Marylanders at that time. Every planter kept whisky on hand as common as our farmers have ever kept cider.

In November I went to Washington with a blockade runner by the name of Hayden. Dr. Fowler took the same boat for home on a furlough and Benjamin Saunders on his discharge so I had their company as far as Washington. I turned my man over to the Provost Marshal at Washington, and by the *New York Herald* I noticed a few days later that my man Hayden had been committed to the Old Capital prison.

November 22^d a detail of forty men and two officers was sent to St. George's Island to capture a band of Rebels and blockade runners said to be located there. They were accompanied by a gun boat of the Potomac flotilla. They returned the next day with thirty blockade runners, refugees and deserters from the Rebel army. Among the number were three who had been prisoners at the Point two weeks before, refugees from Virginia who were given passes to go to the very place where they were arrested. I provided the group with rations and blankets and put over them an extra guard of ten cavalrymen and left them for the night.

On the 25th, twelve men, a woman and a child arrived from the Virginia shore. Eight were escaped prisoners of war from Richmond, the remainder refugees, so I then had a motley crowd of fifty-six under my charge.

That evening I attended a Masonic meeting and banquet at the Masonic temple. The topic of conversation was news from the front, the fighting at Chattanooga, of

Meade's advance, and Hooker fighting above the clouds at Lookout Mountain.

November 30th I arrested a man by the name of Weiner from Baltimore. He had come here from that city on a pass, and then had given his pass to a Rebel prisoner, who was outside the stockade, to enable him to escape.

December 5th the steamer *Key Port* arrived bringing a lot of boxes for the men from home. I got a box containing clothes, books, and eatables. It was my duty to open the boxes for the enlisted men. All the intoxicating liquor found in them was thrown into the dock.

December 11th a clerk in the dispensary — not an enlisted man — was drummed out of camp for selling liquor to an enlisted man. This was General Marston's way of punishing the man.

On the 14th of December Captain Patterson received information that a soldier was intending to steal a boat lying near headquarters and desert that night. Not wishing to take his chances with an ordinary detail, he requested two of the clerks at headquarters and myself to stand guard. We were to secrete ourselves behind bales of hay nearby and our orders were to fire without a challenge on whoever got into the boat. About two o'clock, the soldier arrived and placed a sail in the boat and prepared to embark. At that point the guard, one of the clerks, arrested him instead of firing as ordered. He was turned over to Captain Patterson, who handcuffed him.

In the morning Captain Patterson ordered me to tie the captured man up by the wrists which I did. I did not draw the rope tight enough to suit Captain Patterson, so he took a shovel and removed some of the earth from under the fellow's feet, mounted his horse and drove off, leaving orders that the fellow be left there till he returned. Hour after hour passed and the agony of the victim became terrible. He begged me to shoot him or kill him in any way rather than let him suffer longer. Only human compassion came to the fore, and thus, I took the shovel and crowded some earth under his feet to relieve him in part, despite the remarks of onlookers that I would catch Hell for doing it. After six hours of suffering, the captain returned and cut him down. It was hoped that such treatment would tend to lessen desertions, which were frequent among the new recruits, nearly all of whom were bounty jumpers and substitutes. A few weeks later a man of the 5th Regiment was executed for desertion.

On Monday morning, May 9th, at eight o'clock, in accordance with General Orders No. 15, the troops were marched to the open field opposite the grove, and formed three sides of a hollow square to witness the execution of Henry A. Burnham, 5th New Hampshire Volunteers. At twenty minutes of eight o'clock the prisoner, escorted by a detachment of twelve men of the provost guard, arrived upon the ground. After taking a position he was asked by Lieutenant Hilliard if he had anything to say, when he expressed himself as follows:

A Deserter's Confession

My friends: The time has come when I must die. I am willing to die and leave this world of sorrow. There is but one step between me and eternity, and I feel as if it were my duty to acknowledge that it is for a beloved country's good that I should die at the time appointed. I have forgiven all my friends in the Fifth New Hampshire Regiment. I have forgiven all who have ever done me wrong or injured me, and I hope to be forgiven by all to whom I have ever done an injury.

Beloved friends, I can address you as friends, for you have acted as such to me. It is necessary that we should all be prepared for death since we must all die. I admit that I am a sinner. I have not acted manly to the government that I have defrauded, not only once, or twice, but many times, and I now feel that I have done a serious wrong.

I suppose I am the first man who has been sentenced to pay the penalty of death on Point Lookout, Maryland, and I am satisfied to bear with it as an example. I have enjoyed in my life all the earthly comforts which money could give on this earth; but, after all, I was not happy, I was not contented, and no matter how badly he may have spent his life while on earth, when the time comes that he must die, he turns his heart to Christ for true happiness, and although I have lived a sinner, I want to die a Christian.

Alas! my dear father and mother! How many hours have they wasted away in instructing me. I forgot all their teachings; their hearts would be sad, indeed, to know the result of my waywardness. I never knew the worth of their teachings until within the last forty-eight hours. I must say farewell to all. May you never meet so sad a fate.

At the conclusion of his address he requested permission of the provost marshal to shake hands with the men who were detailed as the firing party, which was at once granted. He went through the ranks, accompanied by Lieutenant Hilliard, and clasped each man warmly by the hand. His step was firm to the last, and his voice clear and distinct. His memory seemed to catch inspiration from his position, as he did not forget even the most trivial matter which he wanted to settle. It encompassed in that brief space the work which might under ordinary circumstances have taken years to accomplish.

Having bade farewell to his friends, the spot was pointed out to him where he was to stand, and he walked to it with great coolness, though exhibiting symptoms of confusion. He stood for a few seconds with his hands clasped in prayer, and when he had concluded he was requested to bend on one knee, which having done, the word was given to "fire". This word, alone, told that his troubles in this world were at an end. Two or three throes of the body, and all was still.

A Trip to Washington

On the 23d of December it was decided that I should go to Washington with two or three smugglers. At my request Louis Rowe was detailed to go with me. The trip proved a memorable one. Our passes extended till the 28th. We arrived at Washington about 5:00 p.m. and at once turned our prisoners over to the provost marshal. We then proceeded to the rooms of the New Hampshire Soldiers' Aid Society where I met that distinguished nurse, Miss Harriet Dame, and her associate, Miss Swain. Miss Dame had recently been in Beaufort, South Carolina, where my brother Abbott was on duty as hospital steward, and had met him, which fact added much to the pleasure of my visit. That evening we attended a concert at the 13th Street Baptist Church and then took lodging at the New York Hotel on 7th Street.

While there we visited the Smithsonian Institute and inspected the personal effects of General Washington on exhibition at the Patent office. On Christmas day we went to Mt. Pleasant hospital and visited some of our comrades who were there by reason of wounds received at Chancellorsville and other battles. As it was Christmas the boys there enjoyed a turkey dinner, of which we partook.

That evening we visited Ford's theatre. The play of the evening was *The Drunkard* and one of the leading characters was J. Wilkes Booth who later in this same theatre assassinated President Lincoln.

The next morning we took passage on a boat for our return to Point Lookout. The cold weather of the two or three days previous had formed ice on the Potomac to the thickness of two or three inches, but the captain thought he could go through this all right and started. About the middle of the forenoon Louis Rowe and I were with the captain on the upper deck amusing ourselves shooting ducks, of which there were very many on the ice, when the captain was informed that the hold was filling with water. The ice had cut through the sheathing and woodwork of the bow, and the water was flowing in so freely that the boat was at once headed for the shore, a mile or two distant. The pumps were kept at work, but just as her bow struck the shore she went down, with the water on the level with the upper deck. Here we remained for some hours, with the signal of distress flying, when the *John A. Warner* of Baltimore came along and took us off and carried us back to Washington. There we remained till Sunday morning when we again started for the Point on another boat. We had proceeded but a few miles when the fog became very dense. We ran very slowly but came near running into a gun boat anchored in the stream, and the *John Brooks,* having President Lincoln and some of his cabinet on board, came near running into us. The President was on his way back to Washington from Fortress Monroe. As it was considered unsafe to run longer, the boat anchored and there remained till four o'clock in the afternoon. Then the fog lifted, and we proceeded on our way till seven o'clock when darkness prevented our going further. Later the moon afforded sufficient light to enable the boat to start again, and we arrived at the Point about nine o'clock Tuesday morning.

On our passage up the river we met the Russian fleet on its way from Washington. The presence of this fleet in American waters at this time attracted world wide attention, for it occurred when intervention by England was greatly feared, and this action was considered as a notice to England to keep her hands off.

During our absence from the Point, the President and some of his cabinet, on their return from a visit to Fortress Monroe, and General Butler and his staff had visited the Point. The troops stationed here made a part of the Eighteenth Army Corps commanded by Butler.

A day or two before the new year dawned about two hundred recruits arrived for the 12th Regiment. This raised the number to eight hundred and entitled the regiment to second lieutenants. During the last year all of the old second lieutenants had been promoted or mustered out by death or discharge.

On the 3d of January 1864, I was sent to Baltimore to arrest a German by the name of Seigel. This man had been a refugee or supposed blockade runner under arrest at the Point, and Captain Patterson had allowed him to go to Baltimore on his parole, and he had not returned. I went on the steamer *Wheldon* and found my man at his home but too sick to travel. I reported the facts to the office of the provost marshal in that city and was given papers to take back with me. I then took quarters at the Fountain house, spent a day looking about the city, and returned to the Point.

On the 12th of January, General Marston made a raid into Virginia. He took with him two hundred infantry and three hundred cavalry. Two or three gun boats accompanied them and furnished transportation for a part of the party. He returned on the 15th, bringing back a Rebel major, a captain, a lieutenant, and four privates, whom they captured at their homes on furloughs. They also brought back about fifty horses and mules for the government, while the boys brought over for their own use a lot of poultry and one or two live pigs. The only casualty was one man accidentally killed by one of the party.

The same day a squad of cavalry, which had been scouring the country north of us, brought in five deserters, four alive and one dead. The latter had been shot by one of the guard on some pretext which may have been thought sufficient by the authorities, but the surviving four pronounced it a cold blooded murder. Such incidents as these only go to show the little value placed on human life by men hardened by the scenes of war.

About this time a corporal and four men on guard at the wharf took a boat they were guarding and deserted. The night was bitterly cold, but they touched at some point after leaving Point Lookout and engaged a citizen to pilot them across the bay to the east. There they also secured another boat and proceeded, three in each. The next day a tug boat, from the lightship stationed at Smith's Point brought back to Point Lookout one of the deserters and the citizen. He stated that the boat was seen adrift during the night and a boat was sent to their rescue. One of the three lay dead in the boat, and the others were too chilled to ply the oars. The other boat was seen bottom up and all its occupants were supposed to have been drowned.

It was one of the duties of Lieutenant Bean, my immediate superior, each evening to go out into Chesapeake bay on a small steam-boat to intercept the mail boats that plied between Baltimore and Fortress Monroe and take on board the mail and passengers for the Point and examine the passes of the passengers, for no one could travel in that country at that time without a pass. Owing to the absence of Lieutenant Bean, this duty now fell on my shoulders most of the time, in addition to my other duties, and, as it was sometimes two o'clock in the morning before we returned, my duties were quite arduous.

About this time William A. Berry visited the Point on his way to Warrenton, Virginia to secure the remains of his brother-in-law, comrade Pratt. Dr. Fowler accompanied him from Point Lookout. We had as a guest, at this time, Reverend George Bryant, pastor of the Methodist church at Bristol, who spent a few days with us.

January 27, I received an order to report to the adjutant general at brigade headquarters. I was then told that General Butler was considering the organization of a regiment from among the Rebel prisoners who had taken the oath of allegiance and enlisted into the United States service and offered me a commission in that regiment. I thanked him and continued my usual duties till February 6th when Alonzo Jewett and Sergeant Hall got their commissions, and I was relieved from duty at brigade headquarters. Upon reporting to my company, I was made orderly sergeant.

Before the arrival of the new subs a case of punishment of one of the men was very rare. Now it was a common occurrence and various ways were devised. The culprit was required to do extra work, to parade the grounds with a placard on his back stating his offense, and to carry a load a long time. February 13, William Wilson of my company got drunk while on guard, and he was made to sit on the ridgepole of a tent all the afternoon, bearing a placard, which read, "I got drunk on guard."

Sunday morning, February 21, a salute for a major general announced the arrival of General Butler and staff, and then came an order to prepare for review. For a few minutes all was bustle and activity, when the several regiments fell into line and General Butler reviewed the brigade.

At another time an alarm called all the troops into line. "Load at will," was a command given. In response to this command, one of the recruits, said to be a Catholic priest, being unable to get a minie ball into his musket without removing the paper, put it into his pocket. I detected the movement and caused the ball to be placed in its proper place.

Furloughs for Home

As the time for the annual election in New Hampshire drew near, the boys became intensely interested in rumors to the effect that furloughs would be granted to some of the men to go home to vote. A little later this was announced as a fact, and I was one of the fortunate ones. Those from Companies C and D were sergeants Charles Brown and Uriah Kidder, corporals Louis Rowe, Albert Nelson, Hiram Ferrin, Charles Drown, and John Bickford, and privates George Currier, A.V.

Perry, and Robert Martin. None but Republicans were selected, and this fact was the cause, naturally, of deep-seated dissatisfaction, especially as some selected had but recently returned from New Hampshire, and some Democrats, as good soldiers as there were in the company, had not had a furlough since entering the service. But these men had been in the service long enough to know that open complaint would do no good so they suppressed their indignation.

On the morning of February 23, the steamer *Admiral Dupont*, which was to convey us to Boston, cast anchor in the stream, and we received orders to be ready to embark at five o'clock that afternoon with five days' rations. At five o'clock the time was changed to ten o'clock.

At the stated time we went to the boat, waited an hour and then were ordered back to camp and told to be ready at 6:30 a.m. the next morning. At that hour we again marched to the boat, when we were told to return to camp and be ready to embark at any time. As our furloughs expired March 15, every hour's delay meant just so much less time in New Hampshire, and we were impatient to be off.

That night, while the furloughed men were waiting for orders to take the boat, they naturally paid no attention to the Retreat or Taps as they sounded, and though the poor fellows doomed to remain in camp sought their bunks, the thought of their wrongs and the noise of the waiting men prevented sleep and put them in ill humor. There were in my company two brothers, one a Republican and the other a Democrat, consequently one was among the furloughed men and the other was not. That night politics was discussed, and the latter, failing to hold his own with his Republican brother, expressed himself thus: "'Well! my father was a Democrat and so I am a Democrat," to which his brother promptly retorted, "Well! I wouldn't be a damn fool just because my father was." This closed the discussion for the night.

Finally, at one o'clock p.m. on the 24th, we boarded the vessel, and she moved into Chesapeake Bay. There were about four hundred soldiers aboard from the 12th, 5th, and 2d New Hampshire regiments. In her normal condition the boat was not intended to carry one-fourth this number, but tiers of bunks had been put up in the hold so that each had a place to lie down, if he did not wish to stand on deck.

The afternoon was fine, and we enjoyed the ride down the bay. We arrived at Fortress Monroe at 8:00 p.m. where we passed the night. As we neared the fortress a sad accident happened. Our vessel ran so close to a schooner at anchor that the bowsprit of the schooner carried away a part of the wheel house, the railing on deck, and a boat hanging by its davits over the side of our boat. In the boat were four soldiers who were plunged into the water and one was drowned. Louis Rowe and I had selected this boat as a place to spend the night, but these men had taken possession while we had gone for our knapsacks.

At ten o'clock the next day, we resumed our voyage for Boston, and the day passed without any noteworthy incident. Saturday was stormy and very windy and the sea was very rough. All the hatchways were closed, and the large number of men in the holds soon rendered the air very impure and nearly all the men were sick. Some seemed not to care whether they lived or died. If they had any preference, it was to die. Never before or since have I seen men so totally indifferent to all decency as these. Though the waves swept the upper deck,

MUSTERED!

I made frequent visits to that side of the deck protected by the pilot house and obtained enough fresh air to keep myself in my normal condition, and I was not seasick at all.

On the evening of Saturday, the 27th, we arrived in Boston and at midnight disembarked and were quartered at the Soldiers' Retreat on Beach Street. At ten o'clock Sunday morning we took a special train for Concord, where we arrived at one o'clock.

We were met at the station at Concord by the militia of the city, a band of music, and a large concourse of people and were escorted to the city hall. At that place our party was divided and sent to the various hotels where we were entertained till we could take the train for home the next day.

Sunday evening an entertainment was given in our honor in Phoenix Hall. Music was furnished by the band, and the combined choirs of the city were led by Professor Benjamin B. Davis. Patriotic speeches were made by local talent and some of the officers of our detachments.

Not till three o'clock on the afternoon of Monday did a train leave Concord for Bristol, and we arrived home at five p.m. Our arrival was quite a surprise.

Our stay at home was one round of pleasure. We were lionized to some extent, and every evening was passed at parties, attending meetings and other gatherings, in receiving guests or making calls. One evening my father's home was filled with visitors, about thirty being present; another evening an oyster supper was given us at the town hall at which 350 were present.

Election Day

The second Tuesday of the month was Election Day. There were a few rightly called copperheads there, who did not disguise their displeasure at our presence. Such were watched for a sufficient cause for a demonstration, but the meeting passed without an open rupture.

Meeting adjourned early in the afternoon and the voters repaired to Central Square, where many of them lingered for gossip. It seemed that Dan Hight, of the copperhead class, who lived on Pleasant Street, had secreted in his home a Republican voter by the name of Pike, whose home was in New Hampton. Evidently thinking it was then so late that he could release his captive in safety, Hight drove through the village with Pike, going down Central Street to New Hampton. Some one suggested that Pike might yet be got to New Hampton town house in season to vote if he could be got away from Hight. Joseph P. Fellows and I at once volunteered to undertake this job.

A team was hastily hitched up for us at the stable and we overtook Hight and Pike on the New Hampton side of the river. Driving along side of Hight's sleigh we told Pike to get into our sleigh. It did not seem to make any difference to Pike where he went, but Hight at once showed fight and said, "No, he don't," to which Joe replied, "Yes, he does." We made the transfer, paying no attention to the hard words Hight rained on us, and we returned to the village with our capture and from there started for New Hampton, followed by half a dozen teams, filled with interested spectators. Half way there our sleigh was wrecked on a sand bar, but we transferred our prize to the next team in our rear and proceeded. We arrived at the town house a half hour before the adjournment of the town meeting, but only to find that Pike's name was not on the checklist. Hight followed us back to Bristol village, after losing his man, and there was greeted with rounds of ridicule as he passed through Central Square, to which he replied with a volley of high sounding words and pantomime that were evidently intended to deter the bravest from approaching him.

Monday morning following town meeting I left Bristol on my return to the army. On the way I passed a day or two at Cohoes, New York where my brother William resided, and reached Baltimore the next Saturday. At Baltimore I met a lot of the boys on their way back to Point Lookout, and about forty of us took passage on the steamer *Adelaide*, which was running between Baltimore and Fortress Monroe.

On Monday and Tuesday, March 21 and 22, there was a heavy fall of snow for Maryland, a cold wind blew and it was pitiful weather for those on guard, especially for those in the prison pen. Wednesday the sun came out and softened the snow, making it in just such condition as tempted the men of New Hampshire to throw snowballs. Many of the soldiers were boys still, and some of them commenced to throw snowballs into the camp of the 2^d Regiment. These were returned, and a pitched battle was soon on between the two regiments, in which nearly every man in both organizations joined. Charges and countercharges were made, and at one time the boys of the Twelfth held possession of the grounds of the Second including headquarters. Finally some of the thoughtless commenced to throw brickbats, and feelings were ruffled on both sides, when Major Langley, fearing more serious results, had the recall sounded and the boys retired to their quarters.

On the 6th of April 1864, General Marston was relieved by General Hinks, and ordered to report at Norfolk, or in that vicinity, and the next day the 2d Regiment followed him.

On the 10th, the Twelfth got orders to be ready to move at short notice, and that day, the Sabbath, was spent in packing up. Services were held for the last time in the evening. Our stay at Point Lookout on the whole had been so pleasant and comfortable that we left with many of the feelings with which we left Concord for the seat of war, only we realized more clearly what was probably before us, for we knew better what an active campaign meant.

The little trinkets and conveniences which we had accumulated during our stay there were thrown to one side as of no further value to us, and some thoughtless ones made a bonfire of them. Many of us gave them to the soldiers of the colored regiment who had come to relieve the 2d Regiment.

Little did I know then that my time with the boys of the Twelfth was quickly drawing to a close, and that time itself was drawing to a close for so many of them that remained.

MUSTERED!

CHAPTER X

Bermuda Hundred and Swift Creek

April 1864. Early on the 11th orders came for us to be ready to march at nine o'clock. While waiting for the order to fall in, I was surprised to receive an order to report immediately to Colonel Dimond at regimental headquarters. Colonel Dimond was to command a regiment that was to be organized of the "Galvanized Yankees," the prisoners of war who had taken the oath of allegiance and enlisted into our service. He wanted to meet the men who had been selected for commissions in that regiment and informed me that he should forward my papers for approval.

At noon of that day we boarded the steamer, *Thomas A. Morgan*, in waiting, and moved down the bay, soon passing the unidentified colored regiment going to the Point to take our places. The day was fine; on the water were a marvelous number of ducks, which excited our wonder and admiration, and drew from the boys a few stray shots, though against orders. At eight o'clock in the evening we reached Yorktown, and at two o'clock the next morning disembarked, and found the 2d New Hampshire Regiment there.

After making coffee and partaking of breakfast in the early morning, we marched to Williamsburg. Here the 12th and 2d New Hampshire, the 148th New York and 11th Connecticut were formed into the Second Brigade, of the Second Division, Eighteenth Army Corps. General Wistar was to command the brigade, General Weitzel, the division, and General Smith, the corps. This corps constituted a part of General Butler's forces, now termed the Army of the James.

The march of twelve miles from Yorktown was rather enjoyed by me though I carried a load of about fifty pounds. The road was good and we were traveling over historic ground where great deeds were enacted during the Revolutionary war and the early days of the present war. These thoughts occupied my mind and saved me from natural fatigue. We went into camp on a part of the battlefield of Williamsburg, where a year before Hooker and Kearny fought a much larger number of Confederate troops. To the old members of the Second, with whom we marched, everything was familiar and they told their sad memories of many brave comrades who fell on that field.

Our camp was laid out as with a view to permanency and tents were issued, which did not look like the opening of a field campaign. Perhaps this was to deceive the enemy. Daily drills were instituted for the benefit of the new subs in the ranks, which did not tend to increase the love of the veterans for the newcomers. They enlisted for money and sought the first opportunity to desert. Since leaving Point Lookout desertions had largely increased. It was reported that a hundred of these men had deserted in three days from our brigade.

It was evident that something must be done to check this exodus. Accordingly, James Scott, a twenty-two year-old native of Scotland, and Owen McDonald, a twenty-nine year-old Englishman, both members of the 2ᵈ Regiment were tried by general court martial, sentenced to be shot for desertion and were executed April 29 at Williamsburg.

The scenes of that day are still vivid in my recollection. The troops of the brigade were drawn up in line on three sides of a hollow square. On the fourth side, where the execution was to take place, two graves had been dug. Soon after the line had been formed, the funeral procession entered the square on the open side, marching to the music of the muffled drums. In the rear of the drum corps was driven an army wagon in which were two coffins; next walked, with apparent indifference, the two condemned men, followed by a guard, the chaplain and other officials. This procession marched close in front of the soldiers in line that all might see. The duty of one officer was to select the firing party as the procession moved along. When opposite us, the officer approached our company for a man. All shrank back at the thought of such a duty, but he laid his hand on the shoulder of Frank Marshall, who stood next to me, and Frank became one of the executioners. In this way twelve men were selected.

Arriving at the open graves, the coffins were placed on the ground and the condemned men were seated each on his own coffin; the muskets of the firing party were taken from them and eleven were loaded with ball cartridges by other than those who fired them, one being left blank so that no one would know whether he used a ball cartridge or not. They were then passed back to the men, the death warrant was read; the chaplain offered prayer; the eyes of the condemned men were bandaged; at a given sign, the firing party took aim; at another, it fired, and the lifeless bodies of both men fell backward on the coffins, pierced by a half dozen balls. The execution over, the troops composing the three sides of the square faced to the right and marched past the lifeless forms of the two men who had suffered the extreme penalty of the law.

Williamsburg was a place of much interest. On every hand were the marks of the battle a year previous, which interested the majority. It was one of the earliest settlements of the country and was for seventy-five years the capital of Virginia. Here, too, was William and Mary College, the oldest next to Harvard in the country. Yet little of its former self remained.

April 27, I received notice of an appointment as First Lieutenant in the 1st Regiment, U.S. Infantry. The next day, I received a letter from my brother Abbott of the 115 New York. He was acting hospital steward at Beaufort, South Carolina. At this time he was with his regiment at Gloucester Point, opposite Yorktown. Ordinarily a pass to leave one's regiment on the eve of an important movement was well nigh impossible to obtain, but, as I was awaiting orders, I resolved to try to secure a pass to visit my brother. General Wistar, in command of the brigade, granted my request without hesitation. I started for Gloucester Point at two o'clock in the afternoon and reached there at five o'clock, and readily found the camp of the 115th New York. A half hour later my brother came in from inspection. At first he did not know me and supposed I was still at Point Lookout. The next day in the afternoon, after a pleasant visit, I returned to my regiment.

On my way back I listened to a sermon by the chaplain of a colored regiment. Later I learned that I had listened to Rev. R.M. Manly, who was principal of Tilton School when I left there.

The scenes about Yorktown betokened a movement of large proportions in some direction. Butler was then preparing for his advance up the James River to Petersburg, from which point he was to enter Richmond by the back door, while Grant was fighting Lee north of Richmond. Butler's plans were well laid, but he had neither the celerity of execution nor the co-operation of his corps commander and therefore failed.

At this time at Yorktown there was great activity on every hand. A large number of troops were in camp making preparation for the move or being inspected as to their readiness for action. The waters at the mouth of the James were covered with crafts of many kinds — transports landing troops from distant points, or landing vast quantities of supplies for the coming campaign, and then dropping anchor in the stream waiting to transport troops in the movement up the river. The transports were all headed up the bay as though Butler thought to deceive the enemy as to his real intentions.

At Williamsburg an old offender, Jeb Hubbard returned under arrest. He had deserted six months ago at Fredericksburg after having borrowed the boots of a comrade to go in search of wood. He had just got back with the boots. Through the loss of records and other causes he escaped punishment and continued to build up a reputation as the most worthless man in the regiment.

On Wednesday morning, May 4, orders were received to march at noon with four days' rations. While camp-fires blazed with every combustible thing left in camp, the 12th Regiment right-faced into column, leaving behind its A-tents and taking shelter tents instead.

"Your command will march so as to arrive at Grove Landing when it is fairly dark to-morrow evening, at which time you will commence to embark," began the special instructions from General Smith to General Wistar, dated May 3. *"You will make your men comfortable. Show no lights, and permit no noise. About 2:30 a.m. you will move out into the stream so as to fall in rear of Heckman's brigade when it comes. Some signal will be designated to you by telegraph, by which you will know his rear boat."*

This order, together with the break-camp bonfire, indicated that Butler and his generals cared less that the enemy knew that some of the troops were leaving, but feared more that they might find out where most of them were going. However, how the general expected his brigade commander "to make the men comfortable" without fire to warm or feed the men was difficult to understand.

We marched a couple of miles towards Yorktown, past Fort Magruder to General Wistar's headquarters, and there we halted till dark. We then resumed our march through the woods to Grove Landing on the James. Arriving there, we were commanded not to make a noise or build a fire, just as though the enemy did not know we were there. Such an order was ridiculed by all the men, but had to be obeyed all the same, so instead of making coffee and warming ourselves by a fire, we shivered in the cold for an hour or two and then the brigade, late at night, embarked on four transports in waiting, and on these we passed the remainder of the night in great discomfort as the weather was cold and we were so crowded that few could lie down.

About eight o'clock the next morning other transports loaded with troops and boats of all kinds, from a freight barge to an ironclad ram or double-turreted monitor, were seen coming up the river convoyed by gunboats. They steamed past us and soon the river up stream and down for miles was covered with transports crowded with a mass of humanity. It was one of the most imposing sights I witnessed during the war. The river was filled with General Butler's fleet, the iron-clads and other war vessels, including the captured Rebel ram *Atlanta* under the command of Admiral Lee, taking the lead. Hour after hour they continued to pass until finally our own transport, the *Ocean Wave*, swung into line and we, too, moved up the river. We passed Harrison's Landing and the house where McClellan made his headquarters at one time, passed City Point, where many of the troops were landing, and just before dark we landed at a place we later ascertained to be Bermuda Hundred.

Butler had evidently surprised the enemy in landing in force at Bermuda Hundred and had he followed up his advantage by a rapid movement on Petersburg, he might have entered Richmond as originally intended by "the back door," but before he was ready to enter Petersburg, the enemy was there in force and he was shut out.

The next morning after reaching Bermuda Hundred, the reveille sounded at three o'clock and we fell in. At six o'clock the regiment moved toward Chester Station on the Petersburg and Richmond railroad, and after marching about four miles, a portion of the 12th Regiment was thrown out as skirmishers and the remainder of the regiment formed in line of battle with the balance of Wistar's brigade and were held as a reserve. There was no general engagement, the firing being confined to the picket line. The enemy fell back and the first day toward Richmond ended with but little results. That it had been a complete surprise to the Rebel authorities, there was ample evidence. Houses were found vacated with dishes and breakfast victuals on the table, half-eaten.

A large mansion, owned by a planter named Cobb, stood on a high plateau near the Appomattox. The engineers decided this was the best place for a redoubt and ordered the house demolished and the well filled up with bricks. This was done by a detail from the 2ᵈ New Hampshire Regiment encamped nearby. A negro hut left standing was used for a while as a signal station. Later a small fort was thrown up where the house had stood and close by a signal tower 130 feet high was erected, from the top of which Petersburg was in plain view and the steeples of Richmond could be distinctly seen on a clear day. This was known as "Cobb Hill Station" or "Butler's Tower". It was used both as an observing and transmitting station commanded by Captain Asa Bartlett of the Twelfth, who became the army's signal officer at Cobb Hill Station.

Some of the negroes, having more love for the Yankees than their masters, managed to hide away or linger behind in the hurry of the whites to escape. They then came into our lines. One, named Tom, who had been a slave on the Cobb plantation, was noticed sitting beneath a tree by his vacating owner. When admonished to leave, Tom replied: "No use to run, marsa, for 'pears 'they g'n' all o'er creation." He afterward acted as cook and groom for Captain Bartlett, our army's signal officer, at the Cobb Hill Station, and so remained on the plantation that his "marsa" had vacated.

MUSTERED!

The next day occurred a slight engagement known as the battle of Bermuda Hundred at which Brooks' division drove back the thin lines of the enemy and tore up two or three miles of the Richmond & Petersburg Railroad. Another day passed, and Butler moved forward by slow stages, but all this time the enemy was rushing troops to Butler's front, and by the time Butler was ready to enter the back door, it had been closed.

Soon after landing at Bermuda Hundred, I met Lieutenant John Fullerton, a clerk at General Marston's headquarters, who had lately been commissioned a lieutenant in the First U.S. Volunteers. and Captain Lawrence, A. G., on General Marston's staff. They ordered me to Fortress Monroe on appointment to organize and command the Galvanized Yankees of Companies D and I, First Regiment, U.S. Volunteer Infantry, organized by General Butler.

The Twelfth was falling in at dawn for an advance movement towards Richmond to re-enforce the Army of the Potomac. The sharing of privations and dangers in common during these years had cemented the bonds of friendship and made us all as brothers and I did not want to leave my comrades. Nevertheless, here my time with the boys of the 12th Regiment ceased, but not my connection.

Before leaving, Musgrove gave his journal to his tent-mates Louis Rowe and George Currier with orders that they must "keep recording, survive, and return the journal at the close of war". Louis and George did survive; and at the end of May, 1866, when Musgrove was mustered out, Currier and Rowe returned the journal to him along with others donated by comrades of the Twelfth.

DH. DR. L. 5-7.
CORP. LOUIS ROWE.

Louis Rowe was a Canadian. Although he never recovered from his wounds at Chancellorsville, he served in every battle. He mustered out with the regiment, but by that time was paralyzed from his wounds, the ball working downward into his vital organs, from which he eventually died. He was remembered by comrades as the kindest and most conscientious of men and the bravest of soldiers.

DR. B. L. 6-0.
GEORGE C. CURRIER.

George Currier served as both a drummer and ambulance assistant, carrying the wounded from the field. After the war, he took up a different type of drum stick, opening a small factory manufacturing crutches for the thousands of limbless war veterans. Thus, whereas he once assisted those who had lost their limbs in battle, he later helped supply them with new ones.

And it is not Musgrove alone who now narrates the continuing story of the Twelfth Regiment, for from this point forward, MUSTERED! *is supplemented with journal recordings and accounts written by his comrades along with those written and collected by Captain Asa Bartlett, historian of the regiment. Thus, the boys reunite for a final bivouac and raise their collective voices in telling the continuing odyssey of New Hampshire's Twelfth Regiment.*

The Twelfth moved with the rest of the division at daylight, marching down the turnpike toward Petersburg. Several were seriously affected by the heat, among whom was Major Langley, and once again Captain Barker took command.

Battle of Swift Creek

After marching a few miles, General Brooks found himself confronted by the enemy, who opened fire with artillery and a large supporting force of infantry. General Weitzel moved forward and deployed Heckman's brigade with its centre on the turnpike where one section of Follet's battery was posted. The division moved forward until it came up with Marston's brigade, Brooks' division. While this command was getting into position, General Heckman advanced his skirmishers and opened artillery fire. Enemy fire increased and Wistar's brigade moved forward and deployed on the right of Heckman's.

Here the veterans of the Twelfth found themselves exposed to lead as well as iron once again. For the substitutes it was a new experience, and it blanched the faces of those who had not yet managed to escape.

The regiment advanced into a narrow strip of woods where the battle roar came with frightful intensity. In the immediate front there was heavy musketry, and spiteful minies hissed all around. The Twelfth was near the extreme right of the actual battle-line, preceded by the 11th Connecticut, which received the first fire and suffered considerable loss. It soon fell back in some confusion, and the Twelfth advanced and took its place.

About this time some South Carolina troops charged against our centre, but they were repulsed by Heckman's and Wistar's brigade, and the enemy was driven back to beyond the church, leaving the ground covered with their dead and severely wounded.

The Rebels in the immediate front of the Twelfth had taken a position behind a rail fence, less than fifty yards from the woods. After the regiment opened fire upon them, they fell back, being outflanked by the advance of Heckman.

This engagement, which is recorded in history as the battle of Swift Creek or Harrowfield Church, was short and sharp. The church, riddled by bullet holes on both sides, stood for a while between the contending lines. According to rebel authorities, their retreat, if followed up, might have resulted in the capture of Petersburg. Later we were informed that Petersburg city was only two miles away. Butler had twenty thousand men with which to force his way there, more than enough to have overcome all the troops that the enemy had gathered to oppose him at that time.

At the battle of Swift Creek a remarkable coincidence occurred involving the Massachusetts and South Carolina troops between whom the severest fighting of that day took place. George E. Potter of the Twenty-fifth Massachusetts recorded the following:

> . . . Three regiments from each of these old rival states met face to face to decide on the field of battle what,

since Sumner, had long been disputed between them. The regiments concerned consisted of the *Twenty-third, Twenty-fifth,* and *Twenty-seventh* Massachusetts in one brigade, against the *Twenty-third, Twenty fifth,* and *Twenty-seventh* South Carolina troops in the opposing brigade. The commander of the Palmetto chivalry, seeing himself stubbornly resisted by the Bay State colors, ordered his *Twenty-fifth* to charge; and, as if by design, it was the *Twenty-fifth* Massachusetts that welcomed them. Colonel Pickett, observing that the Rebels in his front were getting ready to charge, ordered his men to cease firing; and when within thirty yards range, he gave the command, "*Fire!*" and Sumner was avenged.

The men slept on their arms that night but were called up three or four times to repel an expected attack.

The next morning a detail from the regiment helped bury the Rebel dead covering the ground in front of Heckman's brigade.

"That man is still alive," said a soldier from Company D to an officer of the Twelfth, pointing to a body that the officer had just stepped over. "You get down and see if he isn't," insisted the soldier. Looking to be as dead as his comrades around him, the officer's examination showed that he still breathed fourteen hours after having the back part of his head torn off by a shell.

An even more pitiable sight confronted them in the old church nearby filled with Confederate wounded.

"How quick the hatred of man turns into compassion at such a sight as this," remarked the officer.

To which the soldier tearfully replied: "This is all wrong. An hour ago at bayonet points we sought each other's lives, but now the brute becomes a man again."

About noon, amid the almost liquifying rays of the midday's sun, the brigade, started on a four-mile forced march up the turnpike to reinforce General Terry who was heavily engaged at Lempster Hill. When the men came up to the scene of action, the underbrush that had been set on fire was still burning in the blistering heat. A portion of the Twelfth was sent into these scorching woods from which Terry's men had been driven to form a skirmish and picket line. "Stand it for half an hour if you can, and you shall be relieved," said Captain Barker to his exhausted men as they advanced under the scalding sun into the smoke and fire. The lieutenant commanding Company B, hurrying back and forward to have his command connect before the enemy attacked again, fell exhausted upon the ground. Over one hundred of the regiment lay prostrated by the heat. On the 9th and 10th the brigade marched back to its last camping ground.

On the 12th of May the army started again at 3:00 a.m. in search of the enemy, and this time towards Richmond. Now it was rain and mud instead of sun, heat and dust. The enemy was soon found, but in small force and retreated as our army advanced. This continued for about four miles till Proctor's Creek was reached. Here night stopped the advance and the pickets of the two armies were almost within speaking distance from each other. So close were they that a detail from the regiment went on picket with orders to shoot at anything that approached without calling a halt. The men rested on their arms that night, but there was little sleep. Intense heat had given way to cold and then, to add to the discomfort, rain fell all night, chilling the men through. No fire was allowed for that would draw the fire of the enemy.

It is hard enough for men in the front line to lie all night on their arms in the cold rain, but it is even harder for the picket, who has to stand all night, where the snap of a twig or fall of limb or bark suggests the stealthy advance of a Rebel, or the blaze of a match to light his pipe is at the peril of his life. Sometimes imagination will give human shape to the darkness in the direction of the sound, and then, without a word, he takes deliberate aim at nothing. His musket discharge is followed by shots from the enemy's pickets, and answered by his own; and soon the reserves are roused up and stand to arms an hour or more. But this night the heavy rain and howling wind drowned out all other sounds, and no false alarm disturbed the tired soldiers' rest.

The next day the enemy continued to fall back as they were pressed by our troops fighting all the way till the Relay House was reached. This house was on the turnpike about half way between Richmond and Petersburg and about the same distance from Bermuda Hundred. Here the boys were revived by the cheering news that Grant had captured six thousand prisoners with forty guns.

While driving the Johnnies back across and beyond Kingland's Creek, and when the Twelfth was following up the skirmishers, a solid twenty-pound cannon-ball came slowly bounding and trundling along toward the centre of our line. Colonel Barker, seeing it coming some distance ahead, gave the command, "Open right and left, and let that ball through, so I can catch it!"

On the 14th occurred the attack upon Fort Stevens known as the Battle of the Relay House, which ended in the capture of the fort by the Union Army.

On the afternoon of this day, an incident took place that might have been of far-reaching result had our boys known the facts at the time. Jefferson Davis, the president of the Southern Confederacy, had left Richmond that day for a conference with Beauregard. Not knowing that the southern troops had fallen back so far, he came near riding into our Union lines. Had his presence been known, our troops could easily have swung round and captured him before he had time to retire.

The battle commenced early in the morning. The outer line of the enemy's defenses, on a commanding ridge of land, was abandoned by General Beauregard after a slight resistance. Beauregard thought it better to concentrate his troops before risking a general engagement. And the Army of the James, now extending from that river or near it, across and for some distance beyond the turnpike, advanced slowly and cautiously over the next rise of ground running back from the river nearly parallel with the first, and known as Drury's Bluff.

As the scene of the battle was reached, there came in sight an earth-work fort of the enemy. The Twelfth, still in the front line, advanced through a piece of woods, where the spiked tops of the felled trees made further progress both difficult and dangerous and suddenly debouched close upon the glacis of the small fort. Fortunately, the guns within the works were busy in checking the advance of the Union troops from another direction and did not notice the advance of the "Mountaineers"; otherwise the fighting record of the regiment would have ended then and there.

We made a rapid approach till a clearing was reached. Then our presence was discovered, and two howitzers opened fire with shell and shrapnel. It seemed now as if annihilation would be our fate, but the gunners of the enemy, in the excitement of the moment, miscalculated the distance of the assaulting party and shot over our heads. Shot after shot was fired with the same result, our boys pressing on and the gunners lowering their pieces, each time coming nearer and nearer the heads of our advancing party.

Before the Union sharpshooters who had crept up under the fort could silence the guns, a shell exploded in Company G, and nine men of that ill-fated company suddenly ceased their advance and lay upon the ground severely wounded.

The regiment advanced, but before the works were reached the enemy evacuated their position and took refuge in another earthwork, called Fort Stevens, and continued the fight. Our artillery concentrated its fire upon this fort, and in the engagement that followed, the colors of the enemy were twice shot away.

During the artillery fight one of the Union officers, who seemed to be stunned, rode daringly and defiantly into the very face of the enemy, mounted on a large white horse and wearing a broad-rimmed white hat. He galloped off in easy "cowboy" style towards the fort. Rebel minies warned him back, but unheedingly he rode on, not even quickening the pace of his steed, straight toward the smoke of the enemy's guns. It was first thought that he was the bearer of a message from General Butler to the commander of the fort, but he displayed no flag of truce. After approaching to within a few yards of the fort, he veered off to the left, his horse being urged onward by both spurs and bullets. He rode around the fort and back into the Union lines none the worse, but all the better for the entertainment he had given the on-lookers of both armies.

It had been a severe day for the regiment. From light till night it had faced the enemy without chance to drink or rest and twelve had been wounded, one mortally.

Sergeant Osgood, wounded in the battle, woke to consciousness in an ambulance lying beside a captured Confederate soldier who was suffering from a wound in his thigh. Noticing the perspiration falling in great drops upon the Rebel's face, the Sergeant raised himself upon his elbow and with his own handkerchief wiped the face and brow of his fellow passenger. After repeating this two or three times in silence, the Confederate soldier spoke:

"This is unexpectedly kind of you. . . How strange We are two deadly enemies, side by side, and one is wiping the sweat from the other's brow."

"Enemies? We are not enemies now," said Osgood. "Why should we have any ill will toward each other? I am not fighting you, nor you me. We are each fighting a cause the other believes in with all his heart."

"I reckon you are right," replied the Rebel.

And they continued to talk and soothe the wounds of battle until they had arrived at the Halfway House.

Sergeant Osgood concludes the story:

"What may I call your name?" I inquired.

"My name is Madison A. Brown. I belong to the Twenty-fifth South Carolina regiment." And my friend was carried into a tent. I have not seen or heard from him since, but I have often thought of him, as doubtless he, if living, has of me.

DH. B. D. 5–7½.
SERGT. THOMAS E. OSGOOD.

Sergeant Thomas Osgood, excommunicated from Christian services at Point Lookout for his belief in universal salvation, believed in a common brotherhood for all, declining to believe in a Creator less kind and forgiving than many of his creatures. He brought his dog, Boney, with him to the front. Boney, the regiment's mascot, followed them into Fredericksburg, Chancellorsville, Gettysburg, Point Lookout and Cold Harbor where, mortally wounded by a Rebel shell, he never 'turned tail' as he lay snapping and growling at the shells bursting around him. Sergeant Osgood was a carpenter, and the line by which he worked was as straight and true as that by which he lived. [History of the 12th Regiment]

There was no attack or advance attempted on either side. It was the lull before the storm. Smith and Gillmore, fearing it, suggested entrenchment to General Butler, who suggested to them that "HEARTS not SPADES were trump in the Army of the James." A few hours later, when he saw so many left to be covered up by the Rebel spades, he doubtless thought differently.

J.P. Fahey

CHAPTER XI

Drury's Bluff

May 1864. *Butler's army was now resting upon dangerous ground. Beauregard, one of the ablest of the Confederate generals, had arrived on the morning of the 14th of May 1864 followed by Jeff Davis. Confederate forces were gathering from all directions, concentrating upon Butler's front, determined to turn one or both of his flanks, cutting him from his base and destroying his army. How dangerously near they came to doing this is now history.*

In letters written in the field on the 15th, Captain Barker wrote the following account of the engagements at Drury's Bluff:

Close under cover of a Rebel earthwork which we captured yesterday does the 12th New Hampshire hold position this morning. Early yesterday our lines were ordered to advance and take the Rebel works, just through a belt of woods on our front. As I advanced my regiment through to near the edge of the woods there loomed before us about three or four hundred yards from the opening a small fort or redan, on which floated a Rebel flag, and from the embrasures of which belched forth intended death and destruction for us; but we were so near, and the shooting so high that without halt or hesitation we moved on over the glacis, which was so obstructed by fallen trees that our movement was necessarily very slow. Through fear of capture, the Rebels beat a hasty retreat, leaving this work to us; but about 700 yards beyond, from another fort with embrasures for six guns, they opened fire upon us. We came to a halt in position, where lying, we were slightly protected from their fire. Let me give you an idea of the position:

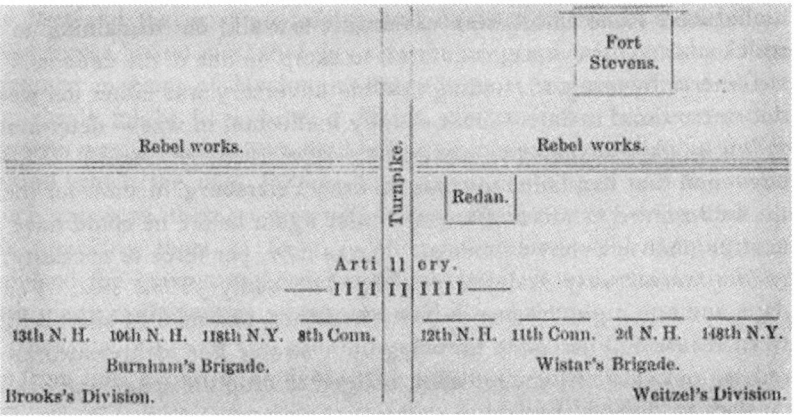

You will observe that Wistar's brigade (ours) is at the right of the Richmond and Petersburg turnpike, left resting on it. On the left is Burnham's brigade of Brooks's division, right resting on the pike. In front of the 12th you will observe the fort we captured, from which our sharpshooters pick off the gunners from the fort beyond. Brooks occupies the Rebel rifle pits, which, I can assure you, are very formidable. The short marks indicate our battery, four twenty-pound Parrott, four ten-pound brass pieces, and two small guns all trained on the Rebel fort.

During a portion of yesterday [the 14th] the Rebs poured a terrific fire upon us, but very soon our sharpshooters got in their work and silenced most of the guns in the fort by picking off the gunners. During the day we shot away their colors several times and blew up what some thought was their magazine, but this could not have been. One of the sharpshooters told me that he fired 120 rounds of ammunition and took aim every time.

[The following refers to the 16th:]

As promised in my last letter, I will give you the particulars of yesterday's fight. Little else than picket firing was carried on during the night; but at a very early hour in the morning, before light, the Rebels opened several pieces of artillery upon us, and the fact that nearly every shell burst among our guns and artillery horses was good evidence that their gunners were experts, and knew how to get range, even in the dark. The fourth or fifth shot blew up one of our caissons, killing several men and horses. For a long time we were idle, not knowing where to direct our fire. The Rebs were approaching under cover of darkness, and we were quite ignorant of their position. As soon as the day began to dawn and the fog, which was very dense, began to lift, we discovered the Rebel sharpshooters, less than a hundred yards away, picking off our gunners and battery horses. I directed Captain Bedee of Company G and Lieutenant Saunders of Company C to engage those gentlemen and drop every man that showed his head above the earthworks (a little to our left) to which they had advanced and taken shelter behind. I cautioned the men to waste no ammunition, but take deliberate aim at every shot. After one of the brass pieces at our left had been abandoned by its officers and men, Captain Bedee with a few of his men worked it on their own hook, delivering to the Johnnies charge after charge. While this was going on I observed to our right, just in front of the 11th Connecticut, a Rebel regiment advancing. Between the two was a thick growth of high bushes, so that within fifty yards neither regiment could see the other. I ordered the right wing of my regiment to open an oblique fire upon them, and at the same time a regiment appeared at our left upon which I opened fire with my left wing. Both regiments were so near that I could easily count the stars upon their battle-flags. The 11th Connecticut on learning of the presence of a regiment of the enemy on their front, opened so hot a fire upon them that they broke and ran, and while retreating the slaughter we made among them was terrible.

After all the battery horses had been killed, I sent word to General Wistar suggesting that some means be provided to take the guns to the rear. While awaiting his orders, I took a part of one company and dragged one of the Parrott guns to the turnpike, ready to be taken away.

The men were greatly disappointed and surprised at hearing the order for retreat announced, for everyone felt confident of our ability to hold the position. I called the regiment to attention, faced them about, but, reluctant to give up the position, faced them again to the front, and for a moment hesitated, hoping that the order might be countermanded. Finding the lines to our left retreating, I concluded there was no alternative for me but to obey orders. I again faced the men about and retreated, as if on parade; and from the fact that very little damage was done to us while retreating, I was more than ever convinced that we had most essentially crippled the enemy. Our loss was only one killed, nineteen wounded, and three missing. After the first retreat we manoeuvred about until nearly night when we returned to camp.

J.P. Fahey

We have been in sight of and within eight miles of Richmond, and fought a battle in which it seems to me the enemy suffered the greater loss — three to one.

A little past midnight on the morning of the 16th orders came from brigade headquarters to Captain Barker, commanding the Twelfth, to tear down the telegraph wire along the turnpike and stretch it a little less than knee high about eighty paces in front of the regiment.

Captain Barker gave this order to Lieutenant Bartlett. He selected three agile men from Company F, headed by Lieutenant Saunders, to assist him, and together they climbed the telegraph poles and detached enough wire to stretch two lines. The ground in front had been cleared a year or two before and thus not only did their stumps make good posts to fasten the wire, the thick growth of sprouts completely hid it from sight. With this double line of wire within close musket range in their front, the Twelfth, with flanks secure, could have withstood a good portion of the Rebel force. It was the only time that the regiment ever fought the enemy at an advantage of either works or position. And never before did the regiment inflict so great a punishment at so little cost.

Three or four hours later in the light of a dense fog there was a screech and a roll of musketry on our right and centre; soon our pickets came running in closely followed by the flash-marked lines of the enemy in rapid pursuit hoping to attack our main line before we were fully prepared to receive them. At the same time their artillery opened upon our lines with deadly effect, proving that they had been ready for action with the exact range of our position the day before.

The pickets from the Twelfth, not knowing that the wire had been put up between them and the regiment, had a rough but amusing experience in running against and tumbling over two lines of it in their hasty retreat. So quickly did they go down upon striking the first wire that some thought they had been shot.

The men jumped to arms, half awake, having no time to fully realize the situation before the Rebel infantry burst out of the fog upon them.

Along the whole line, the chief weight fell upon the Eighteenth Corps, forming the right wing and holding the ground between the turnpike and the river. General Heckman's brigade on the extreme right was soon driven back and he, with many of his men, was captured. The enemy then concentrated upon our centre with Wistar's and Burnham's brigades on the right and left of the turnpike.

Charge after charge was made, first on one brigade and then on the other. Four New Hampshire regiments, with as many more from New York and Connecticut, were there; and near the turnpike four twenty-pound Parrot guns and two or more ten-pound Napoleon pieces of Ashby's and Belger's batteries were aligned, presenting a dangerous front.

General Ransom, the Confederate commander on the field, seeing his troops as often repulsed as they charged, attributed the cause to our artillery, knowing nothing of the more potent but silent line of wires in the bushes. He ordered that the Union guns upon the turnpike be silenced by sharpshooters, and, if possible, captured. This made the position of Companies C and G on the left of the regiment dangerously "hot," for there was a sharp contest for the guns. The battery was getting the worst of it, the gunners being nearly all killed or wounded. The only officer remaining ordered his gunners to fall back, leaving the guns within a few yards of the enemy.

Seeing this, Captain Edwin Bedee and Lieutenant James Saunders grabbed ten men and rushed forward to the guns, which they manned and served so efficiently and effectively that the Rebel force which had so nearly captured them was driven back and the battery, for the time being, saved.

Before this, the Twelfth had repelled two charges; but their best, most unyielding and destructive line of battle was the telegraph wire. Had it been stretched in front of Heckman's brigade as it was in front of Wistar's, the result might have been a Union victory.

The strong array of infantry and artillery protected by the hidden line of telegraph wire within easy range of the ranks of musketry was too formidable even for a triple number of foe; and their efforts to break or drive back the Yankees at this point were all in vain.

The men were protected against attack in front by the double line of wire and a few logs behind which the men, by kneeling, could load and fire without exposure. Thus, when the order came to retreat, the Twelfth was reluctant to obey.

The regiment was unwilling to be relieved from the front line. This was so greatly in contrast with any battle experience they had ever had before—having protection in their front by the wires. They were enjoying watching the Rebels smack and stumble into the wires, and it seemed useless to abandon the field to the foe when, so far as could be observed, everything on this part of the field warranted an advance rather than a retreat.

That there was scarcely an attempt made to follow up our retreat is noted in the report of General Ransom who had the immediate command of the Rebel forces engaged. It is also evident from his report that a vigorous advance by our army, instead of a disgraceful retreat, would probably have changed the result of the conflict.

After falling back through a narrow strip of woods across an open field, the artillery was aligned on a ridge running parallel with the belt of woods, and the men were ordered to lie down just in front of the guns. Soon Rebel skirmishers were seen slowly and cautiously advancing. Waiting until a portion of their line had reached the edge of the woods, the officer in command of the batteries gave the order: "Half-second fuse, fire," and a swish of shells just above our heads burst upon the Johnnies jumping, dodging and running among the trees. This was the last we saw of the gray uniforms that day.

The men were so worn from want of rest and sleep that some were unable to march after the excitement of the battle was over. One of our officers who was unable to walk, but disdaining to take a sick man's conveyance in the ambulance, rode back to camp on one of the cannons.

General Beauregard, finding that his adversary was either too weak or too timid, determined to follow up his advantage with re-enforcements from General Whiting's command. He resolved to attack General Butler again before he could have time to strengthen his entrenchments. It was now that *spades* were *trump* and *hearts* obliged to sadly *follow suit*.

For two days and one night the men—first altogether, and then by short reliefs—were at work throwing up a strong line of breastworks with redans and bastions except when obliged to drop the spade and grab the musket against enemy attacks. We worked with our equipment on and our guns close at hand, ready to fall into line at a moment's warning. The Twelfth was called out to resist attacks three or four times and once during the night of the 19th, we were double-quicked about half a mile toward the right to help repulse a determined attempt of the enemy to break through that part of the line. The next day the regiment moved camp to its proper place in the line of works, which were soon completed.

On the morning of the 22nd Lieutenant Saunders recorded the following diary entry: "Last night was the first we have been allowed to sleep all night for three weeks or more. The boys are resting and we need it badly."

Quietness prevailed for the next few days. The Army of the James was safe but powerless, for it couldn't get out of the pen into which it had been driven. News came from the Army of the Potomac: Lee was retreating across the North Anna, and the boys gave a hurrah for Grant, and a groan for Butler, having to obey all orders and to do everything and know nothing. "Ours not to question why, ours but to do and die," wrote Lieutenant Saunders on the 25th.

It was known to the soldiers then, as well as afterward, that Butler's campaign was a sad failure; but the reasons why were not well understood. Those in the army and out attributed the cause of the defeat of the Army of the James, from which so much had been expected, to the inability of its commander. But the history of that campaign, when carefully read and considered, greatly modifies, if not reverses, what so long stood as the public verdict. It appears from the official records that Butler had enemies inside, as well as outside his entrenchments, and that his two corps commanders, Smith and Gillmore, were more interested in defeating HIM than the enemy. This, upon the authority of General Grant, seems to be especially true of General Smith. Concerning the inefficiency of the Army of the James, General Grant wrote to General Halleck that he [General Smith] "is obstinate, and likely to condemn whatever is not suggested by himself." He was afterward sent home in disgrace by Grant upon unmistakable evidence of treachery and falsehood.

If Butler's own account of his campaign is true, there was hardly an important order that he gave to either of his corps commanders that was executed properly. There were few who fought in the battle of Drury's Bluff who did not agree with the following extract from General Heckman's account of that battle:

> The press and the histories of the war blame Butler...but the opinions of intelligent officers who fought in the campaign...will rather lay the fault at the door of his corps commanders, Generals Gillmore and Smith. They did not seem to comprehend what was to be done, and then failed to cooperate in what attempts they did make....Grant himself shoulders some of the blame for having put Butler there with such a man as General Smith.

In 1883 General Butler claimed that his order was to extend the telephone wire across Heckman's front, but that, once again, his order was not carried out by his corps commanders. He expressed his surprise and regret that Heckman's front "where there was almost a necessity for a double line of wire, was left entirely exposed."

But whatever the reason for Heckman not having the benefit and protection of the wire, one thing is certain: that there was no lack of wire.

General Weitzel, after referring in his report of May 22 to the crushing of Heckman's brigade, reported: "The other seven regiments of my line did not move until after they had twice repulsed the enemy with terrible slaughter, they being piled in heaps over the telegraph wire, when we were ordered back."

Captain Ashby, commanding Battery E, Third New York Artillery, whose four 20-pound Parrott guns were planted on the turnpike reported:

> As they [the Confederates] advanced, the first charge was repulsed, but ....they poured continuous volleys of musketry. The fog and smoke were so dense that they could not be seen, and their exact position was doubtful. Very soon they charged again. At this time I was struck in the head and carried to the rear. Only one gun was saved." [*This was the gun that was hauled to the rear by Captain Bedee and Lieutenant Saunders.*]

General Weitzel, by copy from General Wistar's report, took notice of the action of Captain Bedee and Lieutenant Saunders and the men of Companies C and G in manning the deserted gun on the turnpike that belonged to Belger's battery:

> ... Captain Edwin E. Bedee and Lieutenant James W. Saunders, both of the 12th New Hampshire, with men from the same regiment, for some time loaded and fired one of the guns abandoned by Battery F, First Rhode Island Artillery. . . .These same officers limbered up a twenty-pound Parrott gun of Ashby's battery, deserted by its gunners, and moved it by hand some distance to the rear on the turnpike, where they turned it over to men of the battery with instructions to take it to the rear, which was neglected, and the piece abandoned without spiking. Captain Barker, commanding the 12th New Hampshire, had previously thrown forward sharpshooters, who dispersed and drove away the enemy's sharpshooters who attacked these guns.

MUSTERED!

The reports from Generals Wistar and Weitzel were of particular importance to Captain Bedee because while Lieutenant Saunders was complimented in general orders for his part in this affair, Captain Bedee was ordered before General Butler where he met two of the officers of Battery F, First Rhode Island Artillery, who had abandoned their artillery. They had entered a complaint to the General because of the vigorous language Captain Bedee had used at them because of their skulking. Captain Bedee admitted the charge, but explained the reason, upon which the General informed the officers of the battery that they could prefer charges against Captain Bedee for not addressing them as their rank demanded. No charges were preferred.

In a letter published in the *Boston Record*, Captain Barker relates the following amusing incident which occurred in conjunction with Captain Bedee's manning of the artillery:

> While directing the management of one of the abandoned field-pieces, Captain Bedee, unfamiliar with the artillery service and anxious to have it work as rapidly as possible, was greatly surprised and annoyed at its recoiling so far every time it was fired; and with an emphatic expression, ordered it placed against a stump to prevent it from backing out of the fight. One of his men, who knew more about the science of gunnery than he did, reminded him that if he wanted to disable the gun, that would be about the quickest way to do it.

The following incident involving the brave, yet brazen, ill-fated Captain Bedee was recorded by Captain Barker at this same time—though, thankfully, not submitted for publication:

While the regiment was reluctantly falling back from the front line that it had so easily held, General Butler, with his full staff and several orderlies, came riding along, and either for the joke of it or to make a show of his own self-composure, spoke to the men and said:

"Oh, don't be frightened. Don't be frightened, boys!"

Without waiting to hear any more which the general intended to say, the unrelenting Captain Bedee, who had already heard enough of that kind of talk, and in an ill-tempered mood for being ordered to retreat without cause, quickly replied:

"Who in Hell, sir, IS frightened?! I don't know of anybody, unless it's some of our commanding generals!"

"What are you falling back for, then?" snapped the General.

"Under orders, sir, of course! And if YOU did not give them, you had better find out WHO DID!"

For five days the 12th Regiment had been in the front line of battle and every day under fire and had lost two killed, twenty-nine wounded and three missing. The enemy had evidently suffered heavily and did not attempt to follow up its advantages and the Union army rested for a few days. The fact, however, that the Union army had failed in its advance movement had a very depressing effect upon the men, especially as news came that Grant's advance north of Richmond had caused Lee to retreat across the North Anna river. The boys were willing to fight if they could only see their efforts well directed and successful as they should have been.

General Butler, having failed to capture Richmond and feeling sore from Drury's Bluff, decided to make another attempt against Petersburg. But while he was diligently watching for his opportunity, his hopes of effecting his purpose were all nipped in the bud by Grant's unexpected call for 16,000 of his best troops to reinforce the Army of the Potomac at Cold Harbor. It certainly seemed as if fate was against him.

At the conclusion of the war Colonel Barker had a conversation with a Confederate officer who participated in the charge on the Twelfth's front at the battle of Drury's Bluff. The Confederate officer attested to the damage inflicted on their charging column by the telephone wire which Captain Barker and his men had strewn between the lines of battle.

"But," added the Confederate officer, "we got even with you at Cold Harbor."

CHAPTER XII

Cold Harbor

May 1864. The "wasp-nest affair" occurred at Port Walthall on the 26th of May. Around three o'clock in the morning, General Wistar's brigade was called up to reconnaissance in force toward Petersburg. General Butler had decided to make one more effort to capture that place and the brigade was sent to ascertain the position and strength of the enemy.

Crossing a branch of the Appomattox, a skirmish line was ordered to be sent out, and the Twelfth advanced in line of battle.

A Comrade's Cry

While moving forward there came with startling suddenness a shower of hissing minie-balls, followed by the roar of musketry. Company B, the right company of the regiment, had just reached the crest of a little hill, within plain view and close range of the enemy when the volley struck them. Every man of the company went down, killed or wounded. Seeing that some of the men were beginning to get up, Lieutenant Bartlett, close by, ordered them back down and was just getting down himself when a kind, old German recruit by the name of Lintner, who was mortally wounded, cried out:

"Oh! For God's sake, help me, Lieutenant! "

His dying cry pierced the air—and the heart of Lieutenant Bartlett who suddenly cared no more for Rebel bullets or danger to himself—only for his dying comrade. Jumping to his feet, with a hundred Rebels watching for the show of another head as a target, he stood erect and walked toward the dying man. No sooner had the Rebels seen what the officer was doing than their firing stopped as suddenly as it commenced. After comforting and easing the position of his dying comrade, he strode back over the hill, called for a stretcher, and then returned to the dying man. During all this time, even when Lieutenant Bartlett was walking or standing within speaking distance of the enemy, not a shot was fired.

After Private Lintner was removed from the field, Lieutenant Bartlett lay down with his men and awaited the order to fall back. Knowing that any movement now would bring upon his men another shower of lead, he ordered them to imitate the crawfish and crawl backward until over the crest of the hill and below the line of the enemy's fire.

When orders came to pack up and move at once in heavy marching order the following day, there was much wishing among the men that war was something more than narrow chances and sudden changes. But on the 28th of May, the Eighteenth Corps and two divisions of the Tenth Corps were detached from the Army of the James and sent to re-enforce the Army of the Potomac. The troops marched to City Point on the James river and then embarked on the transport steamer *G.A. Deveny* bound for some place unknown to the rank and file. Some thought it meant a change of base for the whole army and that Bermuda Hundred and City Point were to be evacuated. Others thought that Washington was again threatened by another Rebel raid, and that the Eighteenth Corps was on its way to the rescue; while others still guessed, rightly, and exclaimed, "Once more for the Army of the Potomac, boys! We're going up to help Grant finish the job with Lee!"

They little thought how worse than useless their efforts to help would prove, and that they, instead of Lee's forces, would be the ones to be finished up.

Surgeon Fowler got one of the hospital boats that he was in charge of pulled out of the mud in which it had stuck by assuming dictatorial authority and scaring the commander of another boat loaded with troops to do what the commander had just refused, which was to heave to, throw a tow line, and pull him out. The embarrassed commander later reported that Dr. Fowler acted as if he were "the self-ordained medical director of both the armies of the James and the Potomac".

The point of embarking was perhaps twenty miles southeast of Richmond on the James; their destination was about the same distance northeast of Richmond, on the Pamunky, and a march of perhaps thirty miles from one point to the other would have covered the distance. But the territory between the two points was held by the enemy and so could not be crossed; so the transports made their way down the James river into Chesapeake Bay, thence up the bay into the York river, thence into the Pamunky river to White House, a distance in all of about 150 miles.

The troops arrived at White House about noon the next day. Here General Griffin A. Steadman, Jr. took command of the brigade. The troops remained till the afternoon of the second day awaiting the arrival of ammunition. The Twelfth then took up the line of march and proceeded in haste till about ten o'clock and went into bivouac three miles from New Castle on the south side of the Pamunky river. The march was a hot and dusty one of about fifteen miles. The next morning orders came directing General Smith to proceed at once to New Castle Ferry, and there place his command between the Fifth and Sixth Corps. After reaching New Castle Ferry, instead of finding the Fifth and Sixth Corps, no troops were to be seen.

Someone had made a blunder in using the words "New Castle" instead of "Cold Harbor" in the last order of march, and the whole command had to "right about" and march back to where it started from, and then set out again on another road for Cold Harbor. The mistake was a big one for the Eighteenth Corps, for it not only lost time and distance, but obliged the troops to march in the hottest part of the day in the rear of the Sixth Corps, which they otherwise would have preceded. Marching behind a large body of troops in intense heat and dust made the march almost unbearable, thinning the ranks as many fell out, some dying of exhaustion or sunstroke.

At four o'clock in the afternoon, the Eighteenth Corps reached Cold Harbor, and there joined the Army of the Potomac, Second Brigade, Martindale's Division. While the men of the Twelfth stood awaiting orders to advance, twenty solid shots passed between their ranks and that of the 148th New York without doing any execution. The brigade advanced and lay on their arms in the woods all night, ready to resist an expected attack.

This continued during the following day, the air full of rumors of expected or intended charges from one side or the other, and not all unfounded, for during the day there had been as many as three orders received by General Smith and other corps commanders to prepare to attack at a certain hour, and each was countermanded except the last, which was to attack at 4:30 a.m. the following morning. How unfortunate for General Grant and his army that this order was not also countermanded.

Visions and Presentiments

Lieutenant Gorham P. Dunn had long carried with him the impression that he would not live to the end of his term of enlistment and carried in his pocket a piece of paper by which his body might be identified. This night, in a solemn talk with Lieutenant Hall, he stated that all his hopes and expectations for this life would end tomorrow.

B. L. L. 5-3.
LIEUT. GORHAM P. DUNN.

Lieutenant Dunn was cut down during the charge by bullets through both legs, but his fatal wound came hours later from a sharpshooter. He was talking with a wounded comrade who lay near him on the battlefield when suddenly he said, "Oh, dear!" and died. Captain Fernal brought his body from the field and removed his sword and sash to which was pinned his wife's picture.

MUSTERED!

Sergeant Henry C. Buzzell, who was mortally wounded the next day, had a clear presentiment of his death which he related to Andrew Small saying "I can tell you one thing sure, we are going to have another big battle in the morning, and it will be my last battle. I shall not be killed on the field, but shall be wounded and die." He lived nearly a month after receiving his mortal wound.

John S. Doloff, killed the next morning, had a mysterious warning that same night as testified to by both his tent-mates: "The evening before the charge," said Nate Plummer, "he could not sleep all night. I pitied him with all my heart, for I had learned before then that when a poor fellow got it, the sad event was always sure to come."

Charles H. Marden gave his watch that night to Sergeant Piper, telling him that he was going to be killed on the morrow. And Frederick Dietz gave Sergeant Tilton an address and $1,500 that he had worn in his waist belt requesting that Tilton send it home for him because he expected to be killed the next day. He fell as he had predicted, and the money was sent as requested.

And there are the following accounts from the widow of David Sanborn and his tent mate:

> **From his widow:** The night before the battle in which David was killed, I had a strange dream, though it seemed then and ever since to me that I was as fully awake as I am at this moment, but I suppose I could not have been. I saw my husband in the midst of the fight, and pushing bravely forward with his comrades toward the Rebel lines. And while watching, with a commingled feeling of pride for his valor and fear for his life, I saw him and others by his side go down, and I could hear the roar of the guns and was for a moment in the midst of the conflict and carnage.

I saw, oh, so painfully plain, my dear husband lie bleeding and dying upon the ground, with the dead and wounded all around him; and so distinctly vivid was the scene that I could see the outline of the field as it appeared to me and the particular configuration of the ground where David fell, and I have since been told by his company comrades who were in the battle that my description of the field and battle was as accurate as they could have given themselves. I arose in the morning feeling sure then and every day until the news came by mail, that my life companion would greet me no more, for I knew, as I told my relatives and friends, that I had received my last letter from him.

From his tent mate: On the night before the battle, David was detailed for picket. Early the next morning before the pickets came in, I drew his rations with my own. When he was relieved and came to his quarters, I told him that rations had been distributed and that I had looked out for him. He did not respond, and as I looked up at him, I saw his face, pale and troubled. But before I could ask him if he was sick, he solemnly replied: 'You will never have to draw any more rations for me because I have eaten my last ration. My last hour has come.' And so it proved, for before another hour had commenced he lay among the dead on the field."

B. I.B. I.. 5–8.
DAVID S. SANBORN.

MUSTERED!

David Sanborn *was killed in the first ten minutes of the charge. Captain Fernal and Sergeant Place were shot at several times while getting his body from the field. It was eleven or twelve o'clock at night before they had finished burying him and exhausted, they slept, using Sanborn's newly made grave for a pillow.*

What Private Sanborn and his comrades saw or felt as they stood silently watchful amid the surrounding gloom on that eventful evening remains unknown. Yet a foreshadowing entered their minds and hearts beyond the power of mortals to decide or explain.

And so night fell over the Army of the Potomac – the last night on earth for many a brave man.

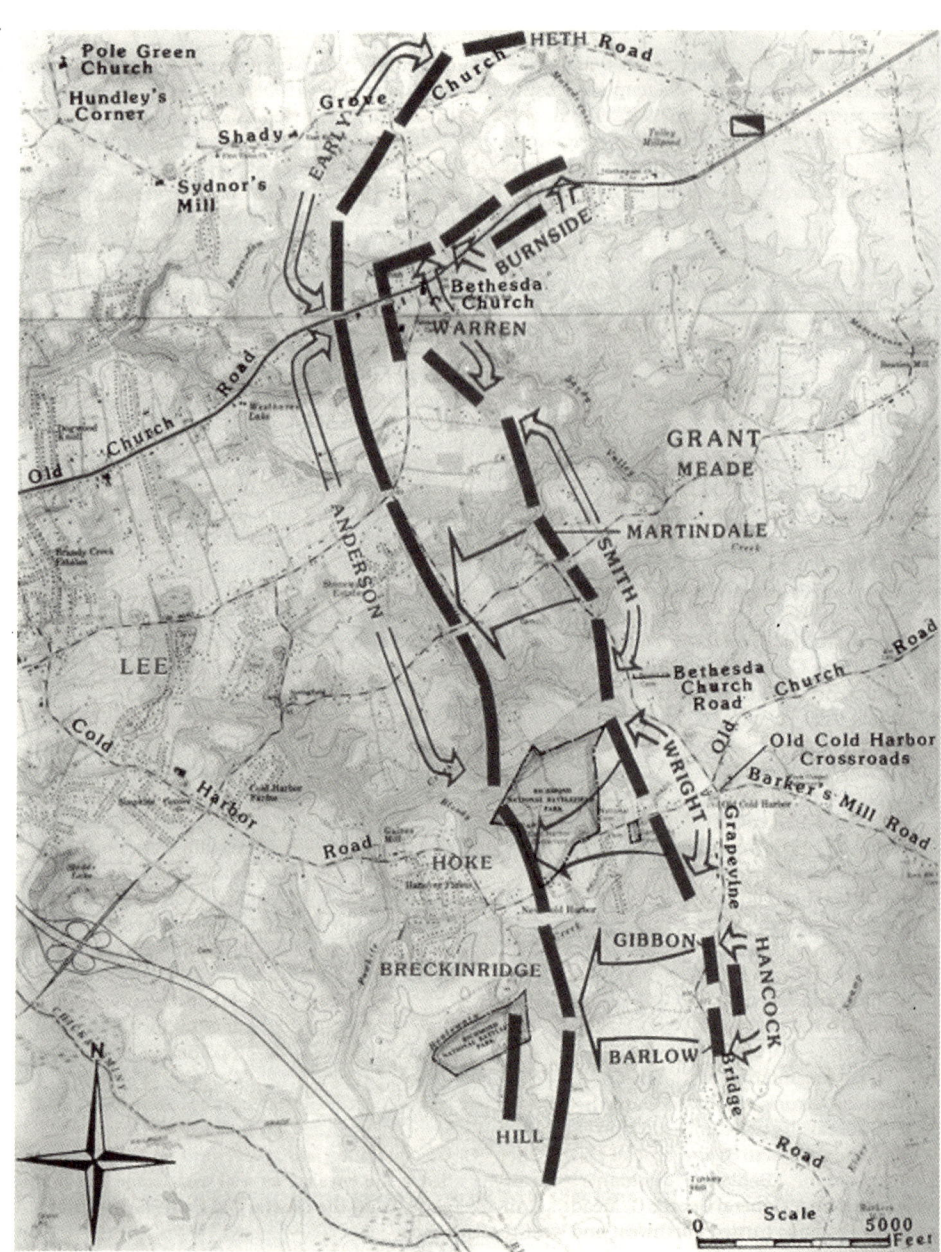

Cold Harbor
June 3, 1864

COMBAT STRENGTH
Union   114,000
Confederacy   59,000

CASUALTIES
Union   10,000
Confederacy   4,000

Slaughter at Cold Harbor

In the pre-dawn of June 3, 1864 began the most inexcusable slaughter of the entire war. No wonder General Grant said in his Memoirs, "I have always regretted that the last assault at Cold Harbor was ever made. No advantage whatever was gained to compensate for the heavy loss we sustained. Indeed the advantages were all on the Confederate side."

The hopelessness of the situation and the terrible loss sustained with its attendant suffering was another Fredericksburg, though on a smaller scale. The enemy was strongly entrenched in a semicircle, one of the hardest positions possible to assail.

If a mistake was made by the commander-in-chief in ordering the assault, another was made in the way in which the assault was made.

June 3, 1864

At 4:15 a.m., Colonel Steadman, using a ramrod for a sword, lead four regiments of his brigade, massed in column by division and headed by the 12th New Hampshire. They led in five lines of two companies each, though this formation was emphatically protested against by Captain Barker, the regimental commander. When too late, the mistake in the formation was admitted.

The men went down in rows, just as they marched in the ranks. They bent down as they pushed forward as if trying—as they were—to breast a tempest. The files of men went down nearly half a platoon at a time, like rows of blocks or bricks pushed over by striking against each other. Those unhurt heard no voice and saw so many comrades fall that it was thought an order had been given to lie down.

Sergeant Tuttle, thinking the order was to lie down, dropped himself among the dead and did not discover his mistake until his living comrades had advanced some distance beyond him. A.J. Farrar thought the same thing, and later wrote: "I saw them all go down! I thought the order was to lie down!"

Captain Barker, knowing that no such order had been given, but supposing the men were lying down of their own accord, yelled out with angry vehemence to Captain Bedee leading one of the divisions to bring his men up and forward into line, pointing at the same time with his sword to several files who had just fallen. The next moment Captain Bedee was among the prostrate men vainly trying by use of his sword and feet to do as he had been ordered. "I soon found," said Bedee, "that nothing but the judgment of the trump of the Almighty would ever bring those men upon their feet again."

Still the regiment went forward until cut to pieces or torn into fragments with no semblance of form left. The other regiments of the charging column quickly sought shelter behind the entrenchments in the woods from which they had emerged but a few moments before.

In less than ten minutes from the word *"Forward!"* there was no brigade to be seen, and of the leading 12th New Hampshire over one-half lay dead or disabled on the field; of the remaining scattered ones, at least two of every ten were severely wounded.

The day after the battle Sergeant Benjamin Clarke of Company G sketched the following diagram. It outlines the relative positions of the regiments of the charging column and the line of works and artillery of the enemy at the time the charge was made.

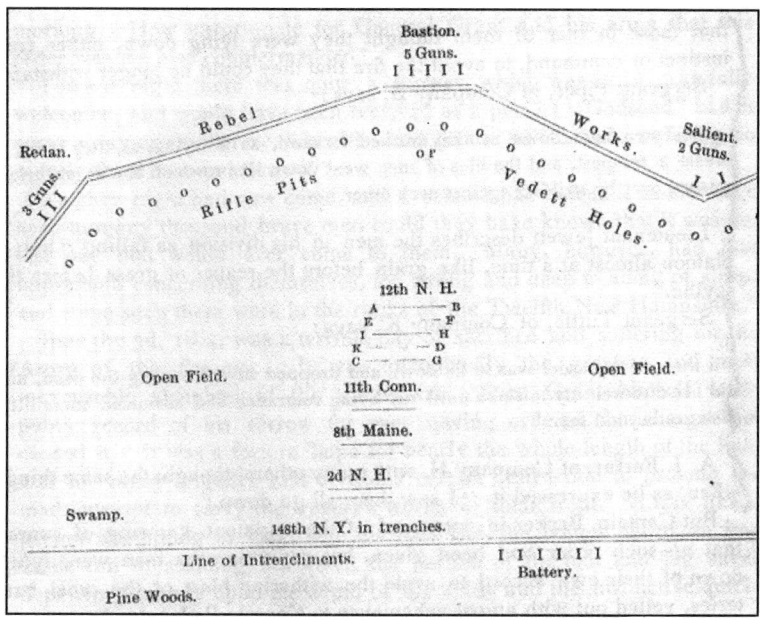

The letters on the right and left of the straight lines, representing the divisions of the regiment, show of what companies those divisions were formed and their flank positions.

The 148th New York Regiment was sent forward as skirmishers but never went farther than the outer line of entrenchments, the other regiments going over them when they made the charge.

To advance a massed column of troops into such a semi-circle of destruction as here portrayed, with front and back flanks entirely exposed to the converging fire of eight or ten pieces of artillery and more than half a mile sweep of battle-lined musketry, is fearful to contemplate but much more fearful to experience.

Some of the living lay within a few yards of the enemy's works, not daring to show any signs of life, fearing that a Rebel bullet would number them with the dead. Here those who continued to survive were obliged to lie all day upon the burning sands under the scorching sun until night or death brought relief. One, hopelessly shattered by a shell, was seen to end his sufferings by cutting his own throat with his jack-knife.

Captain Barker, with a heart to feel as well as courage to act, stood up before his superiors in rank while the enemy's shot was still flying around him and denounced in righteous wrath the General, high or low, who was guilty of ordering such a murderous charge.

Adjutant-General Reynolds referred to Napoleon as making all his charges in solid column and thought it the most effectual way. "The most effectual way of murdering men, and there is the evidence of it!" shouted the Captain, as he pointed to the field in front. The next moment General Reynolds himself was wounded in the shoulder, the effects of which he afterwards died.

Battle Observations

A letter written by Captain Barker, headed and dated "In a trench one hundred yards from the Rebels, June 4, 1864," describes the details of the charge:

At four o'clock yesterday morning our brigade left our breastworks, marched a few rods to the left and started on a charge with pieces uncapped and bayonets fixed. The 148th New York Regiment had been deployed as skirmishers. The 12th New Hampshire led in column by division. We passed through a distance of some four hundred yards with but very little loss. As the 148th appeared at the edge of the open field, volley after volley belched forth from the Rebel works about 500 yards ahead, and the 148th New York gave way. I tried my best to get Colonel Steadman, commanding the column, to deploy; for I deemed it rashness to charge the enemy's works so strong and threatening in column. He would not allow it but said, *"Go as you are,"* and we did go — into the most deadly fire that ever met an opposing force on the field of battle; and when within about fifty yards of the enemy's works which we were all rushing for, a battery opened upon us with grape and canister on our left and musketry from the right. Seeing that to advance further in this formation was annihilation to the regiment, I endeavored to deploy the column, but it was too late, it could not be done. The color bearer, Sergeant Hoyt, was shot and got separated from the regiment and for a time we thought we had lost our colors, and not until we had formed in support of Standard's brigade did we know where they were. Then Corporal Wallace came bringing them in and presented them to me. You ought to have heard the cheers with which the old flag was greeted. I made the corporal color sergeant on the spot. Up to the present time, we know of twenty killed, eighty wounded and about one hundred missing, all the last are probably killed or severely wounded.

George Place survived the charge but couldn't stop the flow of scenes and faces that replayed themselves in his head. Sometime after midnight he recorded the following poignant account of the apparitions that haunted him:

We are in line of battle, close column by division. We are ordered to take the caps from our guns and fix bayonet. We are now in the woods and can see nothing of the Rebels. Everything is quiet. Ah! It is such occasions as this which try men's nerves. I study the faces around me. Every face is paled. Thus we stood, all ready for the charge; I know not how long, but it seemed a long time to me, for at such a time, with men's nerves strained to their utmost tension, a minute seems an hour.

Finally, the Colonel drew his sword – *"Forward march,"* and the regiment started. We had not gone ten feet, when a Rebel battery on our left flank opened fire. I wondered how the Rebels knew so soon that we had started, for being in the woods, they could not see us. The guns were so arranged that the iron storm swept past us about two rods in front. How it crashed and howled through those pine trees! For a moment, the regiment halted, shocked. As it did so, I turned and looked at Colonel Barker. I shall never forget the expression that came into his face as he beheld that halting. His eyes dilated, and it seemed as if I could almost see the fire flash from them. He flung his sword above his head and shouted with a voice that seemed as if the Rebels must have heard, *"Forward!"* Instantly we started again, yelling as we went.

There was no more halting after that until, swept down in killed and wounded, we lost all semblance of order. That artillery discharge was immediately followed by the opening of musketry. I passed close by one of the 148th New York vedettes in a rifle-pit, hugging the ground as close as he could and trembling like an aspen leaf. Past the vedettes we immediately entered an open field, bare of vegetation. All over that field little puffs of dust were thickly rising, occasioned by the Rebel bullets striking the ground. A line of breastworks ran zig-zag, one in front, the other on our left. We could not see a man in these works, for a dense cloud of battle-smoke rested all along the line.

From the works in front and the other works on our left, arose a musketry fire so heavy it seemed almost like one continual crash of thunder, while artillery on our left poured in the shells. Just as we entered the field, a shell plunged into the ground at the left of our column and immediately burst, throwing dirt and pebbles over us. Some small missile struck me just under the left eye causing a sharp sting, and I felt the blood trickling down my face. James Rollins was at my left, Charles Marden next to him and the next beyond was Charles Bunker. Rollins threw up both hands, uttered a yell and fell over on his face. A bullet had gone through the calves of both legs.

I looked for Marden and Bunker to dress by, but they were missing; indeed, there was such a wide gap on my left —I was almost on the right of the column—that I thought I had fallen behind my column and hastened to catch up only to find myself in Company A, who were in the front column. We were now so near the breastworks that I could see the flash of their musketry quivering through the bank of smoke that lay about them like lightning through a cloud; and I was just thinking of the hand-to-hand struggle that would come when we reached the breastworks, when a bullet went through my right arm. My hand instantly flew open and my gun dropped to the ground. All the fingers on that hand turned back to nearly a right angle with the back of my hand and quivered. I caught hold of my fingers and straightened them out. About this time the regiment began to fall back. Just before I re-entered the woods, a flank bullet grazed the small of my back and left quite a scar, which is there today. As I received the third blow, that familiar expression, "Hit 'im agin, blue jacket, he's got no friends," passed across my mind.

I reached the field hospital and sat down among a group of wounded men. As I raised my eyes, I saw that I was seated near an amputating table. The spectacle was too harrowing and I arose to go away, but immediately grew faint and had to sit down again. I was compelled to sit there nearly an hour. Twice during that time a load of arms, legs, hands, and feet was carried off on a shelter tent and dumped into a ravine.

G. B. D. 5-7¼.
GEORGE E. PLACE.

George Place, the Regiment's poet, wrote verses, at a rate of five cents each, for his comrades to send to mothers, wives and female admirers. He was captured by Jackson's forces before the battle of Chancellorsville and, as a captive, witnessed the evening before the main battle when Jackson's forces scattered the Eleventh Corps and stuck a staggering blow to Hooker's whole army. During the raid, he made a harrowing escape. After the war, he used his talent by making contributions to literary magazines and the press.

After the charging column of the brigade had been hurled back, and while the enemy's fire was sweeping every foot of the front occupied by our troops, the heedless wit and daring of John Emerson made him an object of attention to friend and foe. Standing up entirely exposed, he made mocking gestures at the Johnnies until a Rebel battery directly opposite sent a terrific discharge of grape and canister targeted at the tantalizer. Untouched and undisturbed, he stepped up and stood out even higher and bolder; then he beckoned toward the Rebel battery and shouted: *"Good enough, Johnny! Send us over another can of strawberries!"* A general, standing behind a tree nearby, inquired about his name, regiment, etc., asking, "Is he always that fearless? Or has he just gone mad?" (His comrades answered with a resounding 'yes' to both.) [This incident has been summarized from the regimental history]

Bk. B. D. 5-10½.
CORP. JOHN A. EMERSON.

Although the Second, Sixth and Eighteenth corps had been relied upon for the grand charge, General Grant, with characteristic stubbornness, allowed General Meade to order the attacks renewed. Repeated efforts were made to get the corps commanders to push forward other heavy assaulting columns, either in concert as first attempted or independent of each other as last directed, but all to no effect.

The men "unanimously refused to obey any such an order, for they knew success was hopeless and refused to be sacrificed to no purpose." [Greeley's American Conflict, Vol. II, page 582] *Grant, convinced at last that he was attempting the impossible, ordered a cessation of all further offensive operations.*

The battle was brief but terrible and when it ceased, the suffering and agony of the wounded did not so quickly end, for worse even than the charge itself was the sight of beloved comrades and tent-mates lying helpless in their suffering, in plain sight, with no means to aid them. They were within two hundred yards of the enemy's lines, and though the battle was over, there was no cessation of hostilities for five days. Rumor gave as a reason that there was fear of a Rebel refusal as there were no enemy dead or wounded to be cared for between the lines.

Many regiments had suffered severely but none lost so many in proportion to its number engaged as the Twelfth New Hampshire. Such was the hopelessness of their undertaking and the peril of their position as they debouched from the woods at the head of the charging column that one of the Confederate officers said to some of the regiment on the day of the truce, "'It seemed almost like murder to fire upon you." Lieutenant Colonel Murray of the 148th New York, in talking to other officers about the perilous position of the 12th when leading the charge, made the following remark to officers of the Twelfth: "My God, I never expected to see a regiment march into the jaws of death without flinching as your regiment did."

Alvin Mitchell was the first man hit after the charge was ordered (just as the line left the woods). At about the same time, several other men had their muskets shattered in their hands, and one had his gun barrel cut entirely off.

Most of the companies had less than a dozen men left in their ranks after the charge, some less than half that number. "Company A," said Sergeant Lawler, "came out of the charge with only five whole men." It had advanced a few moments before with one officer and twenty-one men. Lieutenant Dunn and ten men were killed and six were severely wounded.

Company B went in with the same number of men and came out with but four left; and those, like the five saved from Company A, had their clothes and equipment perforated by bullets or pieces of shells. Three were killed and fourteen wounded, but not all of the latter were reported. Company H was so reduced in officers that Corporal Daniel Huntoon was the only man of any rank left to command the company.

After the brigade had fallen back to the first line of entrenchments, the officer in command of the provost line came up from the rear and reported that most of one of the regiments were back in the ravine, referring to those who had escaped unharmed from the charge. In reply to an inquiry if there were any of the 12th New Hampshire back there, he replied: "Yes, lots of them, but all severely wounded."

General Smith's account describes the closing battle scene:

> At the close of the battle, the front of General Martindale was less than two hundred yards from the enemy's line, and in the open space between were many dead and wounded. For three days no cessation of hostilities was asked for . . . Some of our wounded were brought in by men who risked their lives in the act, and some were rescued by digging trenches to them.

Such a picture of war does not often present itself even to the veteran of a hundred battles: Two armies so closely confronting each other that their main lines in some places are scarcely a rifle shot apart, while on the narrow space between, in plain sight of both sides, are lying thousands of dead, wounded and dying – all unprotected and uncared for.

Rescuing the Dead and Wounded

Seeing that nothing had been done for their comrades through that long, sad day, the remaining men of the Twelfth welcomed night as they never had before — that they might go themselves to the rescue.

Forty men — nearly half the remaining regiment — went out with Captain Fernal and Lieutenant Saunders on a mission of mercy. In little squads of double files, they silently approached the centre of the field where most of the dead and wounded lay. The work of searching for the living was their first objective. Nearing the enemy's line, they crawled on hands and knees ever watchful of the strong line of Rebel pickets outlined against the sky a short distance away. In silent darkness they crept among the still more silent dead, listening for some deep sigh or low moan that would tell them where among the dead they might find one of their comrades alive. With whispered caution the rescuers warned each wounded comrade to make no cry of pain or groan of agony as he was gently lifted up, a blanket put under him to drag him away.

Captain Fernel describes the rescue mission:

Each night we crawled upon the field and brought off such of our comrades as we could; but a form moving in the darkness or a noise made in the work of humanity was sure to draw the fire of the enemy. Many of the wounded were again wounded and some killed as they lay exposed on the ground, and Rebel soldiers fired at the still living, wounded, and even at the dead.

To those who were nearly under the dark shadow of death, it was no small consolation to once more grasp hands and listen to the tender words of their companions in arms . . . and to send by them a last, loving message to the dearly cherished in their far distant homes. . . . Some lived only a few moments after being found or brought into our lines, and only a few of the wounded recovered so as to reach their homes. . . . The groans of those who could not be reached grew fainter and fainter until they ceased.

Sergeants Gordon and Gray found and brought in Lieutenant Emery; Captain Fernal and Sergeant Place secured the body of Lieutenant Dunn; and Sergeant Clarke and others succeeded in getting the sword and watch of Lieutenant Whittier but were fired upon while trying to remove his body and had to leave it. Sergeant Cheney, though seen alive between the lines during the day, could not be found and his body was never recovered. His brother, Daniel, long sought in vain for him or his body, inspecting the faces of the dead by the carefully secured light of a match.

The night after the terrible charge, Sergeants Gordon and Thompson, while rescuing the dead and wounded from the field, ran their poles under the body of a fellow to carry him to the rear and bury him. He proved to be a live picket stretched at full length upon the ground, fast asleep. Exhausted, he could not keep awake even when right in the face of the enemy; and although he could sleep well enough among the dead, he protested at being buried with them. (He was not reported by the sympathetic sergeants.)

Sergeant Clarke attested that "Twenty-eight of our dead were brought in and buried in one trench on the night of the fourth, making fifty already brought into our lines and buried." How many of the living were rescued there is no means of knowing; nor is it known how many of the dead were brought in on the night of the 5th. The boys were too busy to keep count.

The rescues went on for three nights until all of the living and most of the dead were removed. However, the wounded were allowed to remain in suffering helplessness upon that field day after day. Not until just before dark on the 7th of June, five days after the battle, was a flag of truce raised.

It was supposed at the time that no efforts were made for a cessation of hostilities for the purpose of caring for the dead and wounded; yet it is now known that General Grant entered into negotiations with General Lee two days after the battle, but that two days were consumed in the negotiations so that until that hour, none were brought from the field or cared for except those rescued at night by their own comrades.

For ordering the charge under such adverse circumstances perhaps an excuse can be found, but for permitting wounded heroes of that charge to suffer as they did, no justification can be made.

In the afternoon of June 3d some twenty-five or thirty men from the left of the regiment under the command of Captain Bedee were deployed as skirmishers and advanced a few yards just to the left and rear of where the charge was made. Suddenly the Rebels spotted them and barraged them with open fire. In a few moments every man was underground. They had sunk themselves into the earth, gopher style, assisted by a vigorous use of jackknives and bayonets for axes and picks, tin dippers and plates for spades and shovels. After dark, the men were relieved from their cramped positions in their gopher holes and found that only three had been wounded. Later that evening, the men released the horrors, fears, and frustrations of the day's battle with humor, recalling what their gophering must have looked like to the Rebels who witnessed how quickly Yankees could cover themselves from southern sharpshooters when every second was likely to be their last.

The night of the charge, the brigade was advanced several yards nearer the Rebel line and threw up a new line of entrenchments which they occupied the next day. It was within easy musket range of Rebel pickets, who quickly fell back after discovering it by the first light of day. But the enemy was returning bullet for bullet. Their artillery gave the new redoubt a severe shelling several times during the day. Nathaniel Briggs was mortally wounded by a Rebel sharpshooter while carrying water to the boys in the trenches.

On the morning of the 4th Captain Bedee was wounded in the head by a musket ball that rendered him temporarily insane, and was sent to the hospital. Captain Bedee was always very particular about having all his military papers made out and forwarded in proper shape and time, especially his ordnance returns. As soon as he recovered enough to know where he was, he looked up to one of the officers standing over him and said: "If anything should happen to me see that my ordnance return is all right." When shown the ball that struck him, he remarked: "Didn't the fools know better than waste their powder on my pate when they had tried it in vain with twenty-pound shells at Chancellorsville?" Sergeant Tebbetts looked straight-faced at Bedee and said for the benefit of on-looking officers, "Yep, struck him right square in the head and *stove the shell all to pieces!"*

The regiment remained in the same line of trenches until dark the next day when part of it was advanced as skirmishers in front of the position held by the Twelfth and Second. The men quickly threw up another line of works a short distance in front of the line thrown up a night or two before. This was done so close upon the Rebel pickets that serious trouble was expected, but the work was done so quickly and quietly that only two men of the Second Regiment and one of the Twelfth were wounded

It was thought that Grant, having failed to *drive* the enemy out of his lines, was now trying to *crowd* him out. Later that night after firing caused by the picket advance had died away, a last effort was made to recover the bodies of the men still left upon the field. The search party was fired upon but succeeded in getting several more of the dead, among which was found one young recruit still living.

Between the hours of 6:00 and 8:00 p.m. on the evening of the 7th, there was finally a two-hour truce for burying the dead still left between the lines. On the day of the truce Captain Sanborn paced off the distance between the lines in front of the regiment and found it to be only seventy paces.

MUSTERED!

The morning following the truce, a staff officer came up to the line of entrenchments where the regiment was lying and was about to look through his field glass at the Rebel works when Sergeant Tilton dryly advised the staff officer that he had better look out for Johnny Sharp while he was looking through his spy glass. The staff officer sneered a reproachful glance at Tilton, who thought to himself, "As he resents my advice, I will say no more, but I will have that eye glass in a minute." And he did, as the officer had no further use for it, having taken his last look.

Exposure of the men to disease and danger was now becoming serious. The lines were so close together in some places that pickets could not be sent out by either side without running into each other, making a continuous skirmish between the pickets by night and constant rifle and artillery practice by the opposing lines through the day. The great strain upon the nervous system due to lack of food, water, and sleep as well as exposure to the extreme heat and noxious vapors would soon become more dangerous to the army than Rebel bullets.

On the 11th of June, after being for ten days and nights in the front line of battle or in the trenches, the 12th Regiment was relieved and marched a short distance to the rear, and the next day took up the line of march for White House landing.

What this move back from the enemy's fire meant, no one of the regiment knew, but when it was continued the next day in the direction of the White House, hope was strengthened that they were on the return route to the Army of the James, and this proved to be fact.

The long line of ambulances had passed over the road several days before carrying many of the Twelfth, two of the bravest and most seriously wounded being Captain Shackford and William Welch:

Captain Nathanial Shackford

Captain "Shack" was second to none when it came to pluck and luck. Riddled with minies during the Cold Harbor charge, he walked twelve miles to White House Landing hospital, arriving with his grit and wit as good as ever, for as he entered, Doctor Fowler heard the Captain's voice calling out as gleeful as ever, "Doc Fowler here? I'm goin' a fishin'. Got my bait all cut with me."

B. B. L. 5-4½.
BVT. LIEUT. COL. NAT. SHACKFORD.

William Welch

None were more conspicuous for cool, determined bravery than William Welch. On June 3, when charging the enemy's works, he fell with a terrible head wound within a few yards of the breastworks. While lying on the field unable to crawl away, he was riddled with balls, no less than six piercing his body. Here he lay for thirty-six hours exposed to the hot rays of the sun. When at last he was carried from the field, he lay for another two days without having his wounds dressed, the surgeons supposing he would live but a short time. At last he said, "If you won't dress my wounds, in God's name carry me to my surgeon," and he was carried sixteen miles over rough roads to Dr. Fowler at White House Landing. Dr. Fowler and his comrades recalled that "not a groan was ever heard to escape his lips."

MUSTERED!

B. B. L. 5-7.
WILLIAM B. WELCH.

Contrary to all expectations, William Welch returned to duty, partially paralyzed, and mustered out with the regiment. Though he remained an invalid, he lived for another nineteen years before dying of his wounds.

Thus ended the battle of Cold Harbor. Nearly fourteen thousand men (10,000 during the first day's charge) had been cut down, and this appalling sacrifice was made without the slightest advantage gained or a single purpose effected.

As at Chancellorsville, the 12th New Hampshire was destined once again to become a forgotten regiment. Its contribution and sacrifice in leading the brigade's charge in the pre-dawn of June 3, 1864 was never reported in official records. War Department records listed the Twelfth as having "63 mortally wounded," but no report was ever made of the more than 114 men who were severely wounded, many of whom died from their wounds. Many regiments had suffered severely, but none had lost so many in proportion to its number engaged.

At White House landing, the regiment embarked on two transports and returned to the Army of the James. They landed at Bermuda Hundred and Point of Rocks on the James on the 15th of June and soon after rejoined the Eighteenth Corps which was already in motion for Petersburg which had been nearly deserted by the Confederate troops to meet demands for help in more exposed positions nearby. The Eighteenth Corps was moving for the capture of the city. But again it was too late, for before its arrival, the city was occupied once more by Rebel troops, and instead of capturing the city by an assault, the Siege of Petersburg began.

CHAPTER XIII

Siege of Petersburg

June 1864. *The Siege of Petersburg extended from the middle of June 1864 until the evacuation of Richmond on the first of April 1865. During this time the experiences of the 12th Regiment were in common with the rest of the investing army — a tale of privations and constant fighting in the trenches.*

Immediately after returning to the Army of the James, the 12th Regiment became part of the investing forces and was under fire nearly all the time they remained at the front. The lines of the two armies were but a short distance apart, and the approaches were slowly made, for every foot of ground was stubbornly contested. From the rifle pits dug at the commencement of the siege, a few Union soldiers would advance a short distance on a dark night, the rain falling in torrents; and while lying on the ground, they would dig a hole with tin plates or other implements sufficiently deep to conceal their bodies from the sharpshooters when daylight appeared. There the regiment remained during the day. Its numbers would be increased the following night by others with pick and spade, and thus the night work would be carried on till a continuous rifle pit was constructed.

Here the men lived day and night without protection from the burning sun or drenching rain until by constant work, the trench was made deep enough and broad enough to permit a shelter of boughs to be constructed or a hole excavated, called "boom proofs," sufficiently large to shelter the men. In spite of constant vigilance, men were killed or wounded every day by sharpshooters who were constantly on the watch for a head or hand that might appear above the earth. In time, these new trenches were connected with the old by cross trenches, sometimes covered; but reliefs to those in the outer works were always made at night. No man in the outer works or in the works further to the rear was safe for even a moment if within sight of the sharpshooters.

During the entire time of the siege, the batteries and siege guns were constantly pounding away at the works of the enemy. This was sometimes continued all night, and it was rare when the men were not lulled to sleep, or disturbed during the night, by the roar of big guns from some part of the investing lines.

And yet the great loss from shot and shells was less than that by disease. The constant exposure to all kinds of weather and the impossibility of observing even ordinary sanitary precautions told fearfully on the health of the men. Large numbers were constantly being sent to hospitals at the rear and elsewhere. By the middle of July the regiment was reduced to 115 guns.

Life during the siege was one continuing routine day and night, whether lying in reserve beneath a shower of shells or lying in the trenches overheated by the scorching sun or half-

filled by drenching rains. Most of the troops were more exposed when out of the trenches than in. To the soldiers of both the Blue and the Gray, the siege was a continuous wearing of muscles and nerves that broke down even the strongest constitution. Men in the outer lines or in the rear of the works were being shot down almost every hour by long-range riflemen perched behind trees, stumps or rocks.

The following excerpts from diaries and letters written by foot soldiers of the Twelfth highlight daily routine, memorable incidents and notable events:

JUNE 15, 1864. Here we are in front of the enemy again, and from the way they hurried us here it looks as if a fight for the possession of Petersburg is close at hand. Line of battle formed by our brigade about six o'clock near the outer works exposed to enemy's shells. Two men wounded in Company B. It is reported this evening that our advance of colored troops has taken the outer works of the enemy and has captured sixteen guns.

JUNE 16. Sergeant Clarke and six men were ordered to scout the front; they found our gunboats shelling the fort. Why was not our success of last night followed up before now? Hancock's Corps has arrived. Fighting all night on our left. Oppressively hot.

JUNE 19. On the skirmish line all day. The Twelfth advanced thirty yards nearer the Rebel works than any other regiment up to this time. Relieved from the fort after dark; marched about three miles toward Bermuda Hundred and bivouacked for the night. Sergeant Lane and John Clay wounded and sent to hospital. Sweltering hot.

JUNE 23. Johnnies made an attempt to drive us out last night about twelve o'clock midnight. Regiment in trenches until evening, then relieved and bivouacked in ravine. Enemy attacked Hinks' colored troops in the night but was repulsed. Shells flying about us "right smart" today. Very hot day. Colonel Barker has drawn this pen picture of the quarters: *A carpet of cedar sprigs and a roof covering of locust, cedar, and oak boughs, and green corn stocks, supported by poles laid across the top of the parapet and through which the bullets are constantly rattling, some with a low hum and some with a spiteful hiss.* No less than twenty shells have been thrown by and over my quarters since writing this letter.

JUNE 24. The regiment has been under fire twenty-six days and nights and in five pitched battles since leaving Williamsburg about six weeks ago. John Clay, wounded on the 19th, died today in hospital.

JUNE 30. Charge made on Rebel works at 4:00 p.m. After, they shelled us unmercifully. Heavy musketry and artillery fire for two hours. Thomas Dalton, drummer of Company D, killed; Frank Glancey, Company G, severely wounded. Dalton lived but a few minutes and when asked if he wanted to send any word to his mother in Manchester, he said: "Tell her I am dead."

JULY 2. "Petersburg Express" running all night. One of the shells set fire to a house in the city; could plainly hear the bells ringing. To-night go back into trenches; Captain Barker's horse killed by a shell.

DEATH OF POOR CLIPPER

One day when the regiment was in the ravine in front of Petersburg, Colonel Barker and Adjutant Heath thought they would take a short tour of observation on the left to see how General Grant was progressing in that direction. Their horses had been brought to their tents and Colonel Barker stood by his horse talking with the Adjutant about the superior merits of his charger, and jokingly asked him if he didn't wish he had as good a horse. Scarcely were the words spoken, when there was a *whuzz* and a *thud* and the horse lay dead at the Colonel's feet with a twelve-pounder hole through its body.

The equine war veteran was bought in New Hampshire by an adjutant as his war steed before the regiment went to the front. When the adjutant's military career ended after the battle of Chancellorsville, he sold him to Captain Langley; and when he also left the service, he was bought by Captain Barker [recently appointed Colonel].

He was named "Clipper," because it turned out that he had been stolen from a man in the State of Maine—much to the sorrow of his purchaser who had to pay for him twice!—and his hair, mane and tail, clipped off so that he could not be identified. When he fell, so far away from the green pastures of his early home, the thief, who indirectly brought him to his sad end, was serving a five-year sentence in the State prison.

JULY 5. Regiment in second line of works all day. From trenches to ravine to-night. Brave Dennis Kelly, Company F, shot by a Rebel sharpshooter, died this morning. Company F draws rations for only seven men to-day.

JULY 9. Several wounded. Another welcome supply of much needed food and medicines from the Sanitary and Christian Commissions. God bless them. Isaac Stevens, Company K, wounded; Caleb Holt, Company C, severely wounded and feared mortally.

JULY 10. Very hot and dry; roads like an ash heap. Regiment in reserve, many sick and discouraged; dark days. During the thirty-eight months I have been in service, Richmond never looked so far away as now.

JULY 12. Heavy thunder–not from Rebels but from heaven, a welcome change. Colonel Davis, 39th Massachusetts, killed by a shell while sitting in his tent. Sixth Army Corps gone to Washington. If the Rebs get our capital before we do theirs, goodbye to Uncle Sam. Lying in trenches is wearing the life out of the men. Give us anything but a summer siege in Dixie.

JULY 13. Chaplain Ambrose is constructing a temporary hospital of boughs and vines. Can only move here with any safety under cover of night and silently, as every sound brings a bullet.

JULY 19. General Ord assigned to the command of Eighteenth Army Corps in place of General "Baldy" Smith who was sent home in disgrace to New York. That's the way the generals go; but the boys are left to fight on. "Petersburg Express" making its regular trips every fifteen minutes today again. Thomas Edwards, Company K, wounded in neck.

JULY 24. Sad Sabbath day. Chaplain Ambrose wounded and carried away. Shot by a sharpshooter while up to the front attending the sick. Pray that he is not fatal. Heaven can wait better than earth can spare him.

Chaplain Ambrose was carried to the rear and died Aug. 19 at Fortress Monroe. He was clearly beloved by the men of the regiment because of his spotless Christian character and his devotion to the welfare of the men. He spared not himself in his efforts to serve others. When he received his death wound, he was seeking to alleviate the sufferings of the sick at the front, and to do this he did not hesitate to expose himself to the fatal fire of the sharp shooters.

JULY 27. Rainy. There are whispers of an assault which are heard with ears and mouth open, for the boys are ready for anything for a change even if we go from the fry pan into the fire.

JULY 28. An oldish man and a staff officer came into the trenches to-day and took several looks through the port holes. While looking through one not far from me, a Rebel bullet struck close by at which he dodged back and smiled. I asked the staff officer who he was and he told me it was General Meade. He had no stars on.

JULY 30. This has been a terrible day. Rebel fort blown up at 4:40 a.m. followed by terrific cannonade from our side. Then the assaulting column (part of the Ninth Corps) charged into the breach but was driven back and the whole thing was a sad failure. Big blunder somewhere. . . . thousands slaughtered for nothing; oh, the dreadful suffering of the wounded men lying nearly all day under scorching sun in that crater of death! Colonel Barker got up on tip-toe in his stirrups when forming the brigade line.

Cemetery Hill (Battle of the Mine)

The 30th of July was a memorable day. A Rebel fort that had been mined for the Union forces was blown up. Lieutenant Colonel Pleasants of the 48th Pennsylvania, who had had experience in the mines of Pennsylvania, conceived the idea of mining one of the Rebel forts, Elliotts Salient, blowing it up, and in the confusion resulting therefrom, to break and hold a portion of the enemy's line.

The fort was located about three hundred feet from the front line.

A tunnel was dug to the fort, where a chamber was made, and in this were placed eight tons of powder. This was exploded while the enemy was evidently in blissful ignorance of any danger from the source. The explosion was a fearful one. The entire fort was hurled two or three hundred feet into the air, and there was left in its place a hole in the ground thirty feet deep, sixty feet wide and nearly one hundred feet long. The explosion was a success. Of those occupying the fort few were left alive, and all the Confederate troops in that vicinity were so paralyzed that for three hundred yards on either side their lines were deserted, and a half hour elapsed before they were rallied to make any resistance. And yet in spite of all this, the grand opportunity of advancing and breaking the enemy's line was lost through the inefficiency of the Union general in charge of the assault. Delay in grasping an opportunity was fatal to success, and about the only result of this effort was the loss of thousands of men and the discouragement and depression of the whole army from its failure.

How could the mining of the fort so perfectly conceived and successfully executed by the 48th Pennsylvania go so terribly wrong in the easier follow-up part of clearing the breach and entrenching the troops? After the mine had been completed, Generals Meade and Burnside argued about how and by whom this last part of the undertaking should be accomplished. Burnside, the only general who believed in the success of the venture, had drilled and trained one of his divisions of colored troops to perform this important task. The colored troops looked upon their selection to lead the assault as an acknowledgment of the confidence their corps commander had in them and had trained long and hard for the heroic effort expected of them. Every night they could be heard chanting their war chorus:

We-e looks l-i-kes men a-marching' on,
We-e looks li-kes men-er-war!

General Meade objected to letting colored troops lead the assault, and the matter was referred to General Grant who unfortunately decided for Meade – not only as to the troops to lead the assault, but also to the plan of attack.

As the time approached for the grand assault that was to follow the blowing up of the enemy's works, hopes increased and spirits improved with every hour, until when the fateful morning came, almost every one of the officers and men were quite confident of success. But the unexpected and disastrous result brought with it depression, and this despondency increased. The colored troops, when told that the order for them to lead had been countermanded, fell into sullen silence, and their songs were heard no more.

After all reasonable chances for success were gone and the crater breach was choked up with untrained and unwilling white troops, the black men, as a last resort, were ordered forward. Had they not been impeded by the white troops in advance—over some of whom they charged—they would have reached the crest of Cemetery Hill. As it was, they captured about two hundred prisoners, a stand of rebel colors and recaptured the colors lost by a white regiment. We witnessed the following courageous and amusing incident:

As the colored column was moving by the left flank around the edge of the crater to the right, the colored file-closers were compelled to pass through the mass of white men inside the crater. One of these file-closers was a massively built, powerful, and well formed sergeant stripped to the waist, his coal-black skin shining like polished ebony in the sunlight. As he was passing up the slope to emerge on the enemy's side of the crest, he came across one of his own who was lagging behind. He was accosted by the sergeant with "none of yo' damn skulkin' now," with which remark he seized the culprit with one hand, and lifting him up in his powerful grasp by the waistband of his trousers carried him to the crest of the crater, threw him over on the enemy's side and quickly followed.

The explosion of the mine was an awe-inspiring sight, and for an hour or more there was an air-quaking and earth-trembling artillery chorus. Just before the enemy's guns got dangerously close, Grant, Meade and Ord came along in front of the Twelfth. Grant was cool and impassive, but Burnside and Meade seemed nervous as they looked through their glasses in vain for some sign of success at the front. The visiting shells soon came closer and caught their attention. And as they turned to seek safer ground, one of the men shouted, "Oh, don't get disgusted so quick now; we all endure it every day." The trio moved on without comment or reprimand.

After the war, the owner of the land upon which the Rebel fort was blown up, fenced off a few acres around the crater, collected a lot of broken muskets and swords, shells and shot, and pieces of equipment of every description and charged twenty-five cents as an admission fee. This place soon became the chief point of attraction for visitors to Petersburg.

During the Battle of the Mine, the Twelfth received orders by the adjutant general of the brigade to move to the left and front to support a battery, and while executing this order General Steadman, seeing that his order had been misunderstood by his adjutant, gave the direct command to move the 12th Regiment to the rear and right. While changing its direction to comply with the last order, General Ord, commanding the corps, rode up and called out: *"What is that regiment falling back for?"* Colonel Barker, without waiting or caring to know who the question was directed to, stood up on his toes in his stirrups and half turning his head toward the questioner, loudly exclaimed: *"God Almighty! This regiment was never known to fall back yet without orders!"* And judging the few left of the regiment by the spirit of its commander, Ord tipped his hat in deference and moved on.

The battle of the mine deeply affected the armies of both sides, for each side thought the ground under them was being honeycombed by mining operations of the enemy. On August 5th a loud explosion was heard which was caused by the explosion of a Rebel magazine. Each side thought one of their forts had gone up, rushed to arms, and lively cannonading ensued. The brigade at once was ordered to the front amid a shower of shells, and many men were lost. One shell exploded between Colonel Barker and Captain Bedee who stood within twenty feet of each other, though both escaped without being wounded. A similar excitement occurred on the 9th of August, caused by the explosion of two barges at City Point loaded with ammunition. Many were killed or wounded. Every day brought excitement of some kind, and all nerves were constantly keyed to a high pitch.

AUGUST 5   A loud explosion this afternoon, thought to have been another fort blown up but proved to be the explosion of a Rebel magazine. We thought it was one of ours, the Rebs thought it was one of theirs; so both sides sprang to their guns. Our brigade was ordered to the front under shells, losing many men. Go into front line of works this evening.

AUGUST 6.   Colonel Steadman breathed his last this morning from wound received last night from Rebel sharpshooter. The announcement that Steadman is dead carries sorrow to every heart in the brigade. Roasting all day in rifle pits.

AUGUST 10.   Explosion at City Point yesterday proved to be two barges loaded with ammunition. Many killed and wounded.

AUGUST 15.   Terrible deluge. Great damage done to commissary and sutler stores and several men reported downed — as many as seventeen. News to-day of the fight between the *Alabama* and *Kearsage*! Daniel Webber wounded this morning, fear it will be fatal. Few better boys ever in the regiment than he.

AUGUST 18.   This morning at ten was a terrific shelling from the enemy's works in our front, a shower of shells that threatened general destruction of everything within its sweep. Witnessed it about two hours, dreaming of a Fourth of July celebration back home, when orders came to have the regiment under arms at once ready to repel an attack after the cannonade. This is the third or fourth time that our regiment has been in the very centre of the enemy's fire and escaped with little losses. Each of us left must be proof against shot and shells by now. Fifty men go out on picket to-night.

AUGUST 22. Another salute from the Johnnies this morning and our brigade catches it again hot and heavy. A long, loud reveille they give us every morning lately; evidently don't want us to become sluggards. At 2:00 p.m. got orders to pack up expecting to follow the other troops that left yesterday. Moved about dark thirty paces to the left, two hours more again, but this time one hundred paces toward the right. Spent half the night in doing it. "This is military" as the boys call such absurd movements, and there are many of them.

AUGUST 24. At dark, orders came to march to Bermuda Front, but were soon countermanded and ordered to be ready to move into the entrenchments. Packed up ready to move to the front or rear, but remained in camp all night. Deserters report that Rebel government is conscripting everyone old and young who can carry a gun.

AUGUST 25. Break camp at half past four this morning, march to and across the Appomattox and halt near our old place in the works at Bermuda front.

On the 25th of August, a day of relief came at last for those remaining in the ranks of the Twelfth. The regiment was withdrawn from the rifle pits before Petersburg and sent to Bermuda Front. Since the 15th of June they had been in the trenches, almost constantly under fire, and so removal to a less exposed position where some needed rest could be had was joyously welcomed.

The march to our old camping ground on the north side of the Appomattox was a short one, but the day was excessively hot, and we were completely worn out; so when a halt was called, we threw ourselves on the ground to rest before any attempt was made to prepare a camp for our short stay there. At this time the rank and file numbered only about one hundred, and only a few of the commissioned officers remained.

CHAPTER XIV

The Bermuda Front

August 1864. Rest and rest alone was the order of the day on the 26th of August, but the next day the regiment went on picket down by the "Old Mill," as it became known to the men. It became quite a trading post for the pickets on both sides. The first time the regiment went out on picket, the following incident occurred:

> Soon after taking his position, considerably in advance of the other pickets, one of the boys thought he heard something moving not far in front of him. He heard quite distinctly the breaking of a dry limb that convinced him that probably an armed Rebel was approaching. The next moment he was under cover and on his guard. Raising his head just enough to watch, he discovered a pair of butternut colored legs moving swiftly behind a tree. The young Confederate foot soldier, was not of the Louisiana Tiger type, thirsting for blood, for he responded with his tongue instead of his gun
>
> "Halloo there, Yank! What ye hunting for?"

Not wishing to be outdone in picket-line *socialistics*, the young watchful Twelfth soldier replied, "Oh, *I'm* not hunting; only watching to see what *you're* hunting for."

"Well, I was hunting for the Yankee pickets, and I've found one, I reckon."

"You're right, Johnny, but what do you want of them?"

"I wanted to find out if the damn niggers were still on your picket-line, but as they are not I reckon that you'uns and we'uns might as well be friendly as to shoot each other for nothin'. What do you say to that, Yank?"

"All right, Johnny, if you mean what you talk."

"Well, see if I don't," was the quick reply of the daring Rebel scout as leaving his gun, he stepped boldly out from the tree. "And I am ready to meet you half way and shake hands as a pledge of good faith."

But what if the Rebel carried a revolver or dirk knife, neither of which he possessed himself? he thought. Still he didn't want to show less courage than the Rebel had, so he advanced to meet him. And he had quite a long chat with the Rebel, who had volunteered to go out in advance of their line to ascertain whether the colored troops were still in their front.

"We'uns are plumb down on nigger soldiers," but he promised before leaving his new enemy-friend, "I shan't forget ya'll if we shall meet again."

And they parted, each to his post of duty, and both with stronger impulses of comraderie than they had felt before.

After resting for two days, a camp was regularly laid out, for here the boys expected to remain. The quarters of the men were made of uniform size, ten feet long by four wide, and the walls, made of logs with the crevices filled with mud, were four feet high, on the tops of which were placed the shelter tents for roofs. In the rear of each, on the outside, was constructed a chimney, made of the same material as the walls. In each of these huts were comfortably quartered four men. Not content with making for themselves comfortable quarters inside, the boys graded and improved the company streets and the parade ground, and thus again established their old reputation of having the best and most comfortable quarters of any regiment of their corps.

While the regiment was sent here primarily for rest, they relieved other troops, taking their places at the front and were regularly on picket and continually on duty as guards on the river, which was the line between the two contending armies.

The relations between the foot soldiers of the two armies were most cordial, and the river and both banks of the stream were neutral ground. But fraternizing was not allowed by either army, and the Confederates policy imposed was to kill all violators in their own ranks who fraternized with Union soldiers. Still, the men bathed together and fraternized on both banks with a watchful eye out at all times for Confederate officers.

One quiet starlit night, Almon Farrar and several others were on the Confederate side of the stream enjoying a game of cards with the Johnnies when a mounted Confederate officer suddenly appeared in the woods close by where Almon was playing with three Confederate foot soldiers. There was no time to escape. Quick as a wink, one of the Rebel foot soldiers grabbed his blanket from off his shoulders and threw it over Almon's shoulders, while another snatched the blue cap off the Yank's head, and put his own slouch hat in its place. The Confederate officer rode up, was saluted by all—including Almon—and passed on. The Johnnies sitting with other Yankees further along on the officer's path, all bravely imitated the actions of their comrades, and the games went on till the officer rode away.

On the 15th of September, Colonel Potter, who had been absent from the regiment since the battle of Chancellorsville, May 3, 1863, returned and at once assumed command of the brigade. But the hope of a long stay in our new quarters was soon dashed to the ground, for on the 20th of September came an order to move, and the regiment marched two miles towards Bermuda Landing. We left our comfortable quarters with keen regrets.

Arriving at the new encampment, Colonel Potter's command was detached from the Eighteenth Army Corps and made the nucleus of a provisional brigade for the instruction of recruits, mostly short-term men who were arriving in large numbers. Here he soon had a brigade of nine regiments, and selected a staff commensurate with his command. He selected several of his staff from the 12th Regiment. Captain Andrew Heath was appointed assistant inspector general; Captain John Johnston was made assistant provost marshal; Captain John Prescott, aide-de-camp; and Captain Edwin Bedee, special staff officer.

Again comfortable quarters were made, but on the 28th of September the brigade was ordered forward to take the place of the Eighteenth Corps, which had moved across the James river. Here we were again on the front line and entered quarters just vacated by the 13th New Hampshire Regiment.

Battle of Fort Harrison

The next day occurred the battle of Fort Harrison, when a portion of the Rebel line was captured and held against desperate efforts of the enemy to retake it. Fort Harrison was the most formidable work on the Rebel line north of the James from Chapin's Bluff on the river to Fort Gilmer. It was captured at quite a heavy loss, especially of officers who were picked off by Rebel sharpshooters in their advance over a wide space of unprotected ground leading up to the fort, located on a steep elevation.

The whole of the regiment was not engaged in this fight, but a portion of our men were used as skirmishers and sharp shooters, contributing largely to the successful attack upon the fort. This small band of men was called the "Dirty Dozen" and had been detailed as sharpshooters months before from many regiments. Without their aid and heroic efforts in being the first to scale its parapets, the fort might not then have been taken. The Dirty Dozen actually captured the fort and had they been at once properly supported, there would not have been so severe a contest to hold it, for the defenders had time to recover from their surprise and rally for the final hand-to-hand struggle before any Union troops got up to the works.

William Gray and Almon Farrar were two of the Dirty Dozen sharpshooters and were among the few who drove the Rebel gunners from their guns and entered the fort.

DR. DB. L. 5-10.
CORP. ALMON J. FARRAR.

B. D. D. 5-10½.
SERGT. WILLIAM S. GRAY.

Almon Farrar and **William Gray**, *both farm boys from the villages of Gilmanton and Stafford, were part of a battalion of sharpshooters commanded by Captain Cooley and were almost constantly in the front line. At the battle of Fort Harrison, eight of them were ordered to creep up under cover of darkness and get a position from which they could pick off the Rebel gunners in the fort. "We fell in with the Rebel relief when they appeared and captured four or five of their pickets as fast as they were posted," recalled Farrar. "We got across the ditch, climbed up over the parapet and took the fort by surprise before it was barely light and before our forces had fired a single shot." Farrar and Gray were detached as sharpshooters for nearly every engagement.*

Farrar was eighteen when he enlisted and was wounded at Cold Harbor and Bermuda Hundred, where he escaped capture by rolling and crawling between the corn rows. At Petersburg, Farrar exchanged shots for thirty days with a Rebel sharpshooter with whom he used to meet between the lines, shake hands and have a friendly chat. At High Bridge, where Union forces were confronting the remnant of Lee's army, a minie ball passed diagonally through his body from breast to back, yet did not disable him. **William Gray** *was wounded at Chancellorsville and at Chapin's Farm where minie balls took off the sight of his rifle and his left thumb while he was engaged in silencing a gun in one of the Rebel forts. He was severely injured at High Bridge a few days before Lee's surrender, yet escaped permanent injury and remained in active service throughout the war.*

Farrar *and* **Gray** *were mustered out with the Regiment and returned to farming. Their close encounters with Rebel sharpshooters brought them mutual respect and friendship among the enemy, and until their deaths, they both continued to correspond with two sharpshooters in the Carolinas.*

After the battle, the Twelfth worked with spades to strengthen the works so as to prevent recapture by the enemy. Then they worked with picks in constructing a new line of works between the fort and the river. Here they worked in the rain and in a constant shower of shells thrown from Rebel gunboats on the river. Again the regiment occupied the trenches, and this time to the right of Fort Harrison.

Almost immediately after occupying the trenches, they were ordered to report to the Third Brigade of the First Division, commanded by their much loved and admired Captain Barker, now a Lieutenant Colonel. His brigade consisted of the 2nd and 12th New Hampshire, 58th and 188th Pennsylvania, 21st Connecticut and 92nd New York. Although these six regiments could once have mustered a little army of five or six thousand men, they now were only an aggregate of remaining remnants amounting to less than six hundred. Yet every man was a battle-scarred veteran.

The brigade occupied the trenches at this time, between Forts Harrison and Gilmer, the latter being still held by the enemy. On October 9th the regiment extended its line so as to relieve the Third Division, and a few hours later moved still farther to the right to the rear of the Tenth Corps. During the night, in a cold rain storm, they relieved a portion of the corps in the trenches, but. a few hours later another order came. This time Colonel Barker was ordered to report to Colonel Potter on the Bermuda Front and once again the 12th Regiment was under the command of their old colonel, between the James and the Appomattox rivers.

For some time there had been a growing apprehension in the mind of Colonel Potter that the enemy would attack his line, and the return of the Twelfth to his command was in compliance with his request that his old regiment might be returned to him. General Weitzel, then commanding the Eighteenth Corps, in asking permission of General Butler, remarked:

"I think I had better send the 12TH New Hampshire over to Potter at once. That place is weak, and this regiment would give Potter much confidence. Shall I send it?"

To which Butler, at 10.05 p.m. of the 13th, replied:

"Send the 12TH New Hampshire to Potter at once."

While here, twice in one night, the long roll was sounded for the boys to fall in to repel an expected attack of the enemy, but the firing proved to be that of the Rebel picket line, firing at deserters who were leaving their ranks for the Union lines. Such was the discontent among the Confederates and their desire for the war to close that vast numbers were constantly deserting. General Grant in his memoirs estimated that the loss to the Confederate army from desertions at this time amounted to one regiment a day.

"The 10th was a very foggy day and the sallow-faced supporters of the crumbling Confederacy came into our lines by tens and scores," recalled Captain Bartlett. "A company of about fifty started to come in, but were mistaken in the fog for an attacking force, fired upon by our brigade, and driven back."

On the 20th, the victory of Sheridan over Early in the Shenandoah valley was celebrated in the Army of the Potomac and the Army of the James by a hundred guns each, loaded with shot and shell, and discharged against the enemy. This was the single most brilliant victory of the Union arms. It electrified the entire North and gladdened the hearts of the men in Blue, for they knew it to be in honor of Sheridan's second great victory in the valley.

The celebration of Sheridan's victory in the Shenandoah by a hundred gun salute had just ended. After the artillery guns had stopped their roaring upon both sides—for the salute was a "shotted" one to which the enemy replied—a musket fusilade was heard in Colonel Potter's brigade just to the left of the Twelfth. In a few moments a staff officer went dashing by, and as he rode up to the commander of the Pennsylvania regiment, which had joined the army for the first time just a few days before, he saw the whole regiment of about a thousand men blazing away at their very best over the earthworks.

"What in Hell are you doing here?!" yelled the staff officer to the colonel, who was encouraging his men to fire as rapidly as possible.

"Firing a salute, sir, and I have had no orders to stop yet."

When the colonel of the Pennsylvania regiment found out that his was the only regiment that was "firing a salute" along the line and that even the artillery was silent, he began to excuse himself by repeating that he had received no orders to stop and had not noticed that the other regiments had done so. At this the staff officer had another hearty laugh and then kindly explained to him that the order for a shotted salute was meant for the artillery alone, not for the infantry, and that no other regiment except his could claim historic honors for having taken such an active part. "Firing a salute," was the joking reply to many foolish inquiries among the boys after that.

October 27 another attempt was made by General Grant to get possession of the South Side Railroad on the extreme right of the enemy's line of defense. To assist in this General Butler's command was ordered to make a demonstration against Richmond on the north side of the James.

On the same day, either as a part of the general plan, or simply to get the new troops used to "war alarms," Colonel Potter received order to make a feint of attacking the enemy in front of him on the Bermuda line. The troops were ordered out in light marching order. Lines of attack formed with the Twelfth in front deployed as skirmishers at half distance and supported by the other regiments.

After dark the brigade was ordered forward over the works, and the Twelfth, with only sixty men (a few being out on picket) advanced to about half way between the lines, where it was halted, as supposed by the men, preparatory to a charge. But after waiting there in silence and darkness, the order came to fall back over the entrenchments again. Some of the "hundred-day men" were so badly frightened that they broke away from the ranks when they found they were to go outside of the front line of works and ran for the rear.

About this time some southern families who had remained inside the lines on pretense of being Union people were arrested upon suspicion of giving information to the enemy, and the ladies were brought in ambulances before Colonel Potter, who after questioning them awhile, ordered them reconveyed to their homes. Their own statements were neither contradictory nor inconsistent with their assured innocence. And yet these women were in daily communication, by signs, with the enemy. A few days later Captain Johnson, of Col. Potter's staff, conveyed orders to one of the families, named Barr, to be removed from Port Walthall, where they then resided, to some other location not seen from the enemy's lines.

Election of 1864

In the presidential election of November 1864, the soldiers in the field were allowed to vote. It was perhaps the most important presidential election ever held, for it was for the people to decide at the ballot box whether the war was a failure — with the demand for an "immediate cessation of hostilities" to be obeyed by Grant, Sherman and Sheridan in the field — or whether the blood shed and lives sacrificed should not be in vain. A large majority of the North believed that upon the ballot box, even more than the cartridge-box, depended the fate of the Nation. Confederate officials knew that their only hope would disappear forever upon the re-election of Abraham Lincoln.

"It is too good news to be true," said a Rebel officer to a Union officer upon hearing that McClellan had been nominated at Chicago as they met between the lines for their regular rendezvous to exchange newspapers.

A few weeks before the election, an intelligent Rebel sergeant who had come into our lines was asked what effect the re-election of Lincoln would have upon the rank and file of the southern army. "It would leave more rank than file," was the quick and witty response.

The leading anti-war Democrats of New Hampshire and other states bitterly opposed giving the soldiers a right to vote in the field, for they well knew that they would "vote as they shot" against the enemy, and they feared the result in the general count.

The count in the 12th Regiment was eight-six for Lincoln and thirty-nine for McClellan. This was a larger vote for McClellan than in any other New Hampshire regiment except the 10th Regiment, which was largely Irish, who gave a majority for McClellan.

In one officer's diary under date of the 9th is the following entry: "Great cheering all along the line for the news comes to-day that the Union is safe. The Rebels heard it, well understanding its meaning, and their bands commenced playing "Dixie". We responded with "Yankee Doodle," "Red, White and Blue," and "Rally Round the Flag."

From the 24th of October when the regiment returned to the south side of the James until the 17th of November little of historic interest, not already referred to, occurred. But this short run of good luck was about to receive a sudden and serious change.

Capture of the Twelfth

On the 17th of November something out of the ordinary happened. The Twelfth was on picket. At its right and left on the line were raw troops. The line was attacked by a small force of the enemy, and the raw troops at once fell back. Through this break, the enemy gained a position in the rear of the men, and fifty officers and enlisted men of the Twelfth were captured.

The regiment was so reduced in numbers that its detail for picket duty that day was too small to reach across the exposed space without leaving the line too weak; so enough men from the new regiments, stationed upon either flank, were deployed in right and left connecting with the Twelfth to cover the full distance.

The enemy, being aware that our troops were up early on the alert, concluded to test us at the other end of the day. They made their attack just after dark instead of just before light. Although the Rebels made quite a vigorous assault, the men thought it nothing more than a lively "corn-popping" entertainment for the evening until to their great surprise, they found the Rebels in their rear as well as their front, loudly demanding their surrender. The new troops, fresh from fields of peaceful husbandry, concluded that they must either run or die, and they struck out for the rear, some of them not stopping until they reached City Point.

Lieutenant Charles Towle, in command of the Twelfth detail that the Rebels were flanking, ordered his men to fall back, but hearing nothing to confirm his belief as he brought them to a halt, he ordered them to advance again. Both orders were heard by the attacking Rebels who were close upon the flanks of the Twelfth line when it fell back, and who were glad to hear the order for our men to advance, for its only effect was to give them more prisoners.

Before some of the men had regained their posts, they were entirely surrounded and most of them captured. A few managed to escape by dropping flat into the ploughed furrows of a field that had been cultivated until the Rebels passed over them from their rear, and then rolling from one furrow to another until far enough away to risk a run in the darkness.

In the meantime officers and men from the other regiments came running back to the reserve, then under the command of Captain Fernal, with all sorts of stories, but no news of the Twelfth. Thus what the exact situation at the front was, no one could tell. That there had been a serious break and a stampede of the raw recruits was only too evident.

"But what has become of my fifty or more officers and men in the Twelfth?" Colonel Potter was impatiently asking. Not only was he anxious for the fate of his old regimental boys themselves, but he knew that upon their safety depended the security of the line.

"Where are the Twelfth boys?" he would ask as he walked up and down in front of his quarters.

"If the line is broken as all these run-away cowards are telling, why don't we hear something from the Twelfth?"

"We shall before long, if it is true," replied Colonel Barker, who with Captain Bedee and two other staff officers, was waiting and listening.

In desperation, Captain Bedee was sent out to learn the truth of the matter. When he left headquarters for the picket line he said, "I'll soon let you know what's up and where the Twelfth is, if I have to go to Richmond or Hell to find out." Bedee did not return to report, for he was captured like the rest.

After Captain Bedee's exchange and return to the regiment, he was asked, "Well, Captain, did you go to Richmond or to Hell?" To which he quickly and emphatically replied, "Both," and it was full of meaning to all the men who had been captured and supplied with free board and lodging at "Libby's Hotel" in Libby Prison.

Potter was about to send another officer forward to investigate, when news came, written by the messenger himself, Sergeant Charles Place:

MUSTERED!

At Bermuda Hundred, on the night of the 17th of November 1864, the Rebels thought they would straighten their picket line to bring a portion of their line where ours then was, and that portion was then occupied by a detail from our regiment. The enemy charged both right and left, and their intention was to capture us all, which, through the unreliance of green troops upon our flanks, they nearly accomplished.

When I was ordered to surrender, the Johnnies being all around us, I turned and ran from them, and a volley of bullets came whizzing about me. I kept on and came in over the works and reported to Captain Fernal.

I think I was the only man who escaped capture that advanced to our former position after having retreated.

At Colonel Potter's headquarters, I told him that our pickets were all captured, and that the enemy occupied our line; but he did not credit my story, and told the captain to put me under arrest. The captain did not, however, but sent me into his tent, and told me all would be right, for he knew full well that I was telling what I believed to be true.

After this he sent out what was left of the regiment, but their reconnaissance only proved that the enemy held our line, as I had reported, and that to retake it would require a severe contest.

The loss of the regiment was three commissioned officers, one wounded and two captured; one enlisted man killed, six wounded, and thirty-five captured.

The Confederates continued to hold the new line they had so easily established against us until General Ferrero's division of colored troops relieved the provisional brigade on the Bermuda front. And they retook the old line we had lost.

The men left in the Twelfth remained on the old line until December 3, when they again moved to the north side of the James, where they were assigned to the Second Brigade, Third Division, Fourth Army Corps. The Eighteenth and Tenth were discontinued, and the Army of the James was re-organized into the Twenty-fourth Corps, consisting of white troops, commanded by General Ord, and the Twenty-fifth Corps, consisting of colored troops, and commanded by General Weitzel. This new organization still left the Twelfth under the brigade command of Colonel Potter.

After the colored troops took the place of the whites on the Bermuda front, all friendliness between the opposing pickets at once disappeared. The Rebel soldiers were ordered to fire upon the colored pickets at every opportunity, and there was a constant interchange of shots between them.

On December 12th Sergeant Albert Bacheler and Private Benjamin Thompson, who were among those captured, returned. It was an occasion for celebration by their comrades who feared they would never see them again. Here is the story of their perilous escape from Libby Prison, written by Albert Bacheler:

Escape from Libby Prison
LIBBY AND HOW WE GOT OUT OF IT

At the time of which I write, we and the Rebs were making the best of the "bottled up" situation, and daily, on the picket-lines between the hostile earthworks, you might have seen us making the usual exchange of coffee and salt for "terbac," or swapping *New York Tribunes* and *Baltimore Americans* of yesterday for *The Richmond* morning sheets damp from the press. Not a few of us struck up friendships in our stolen interludes with the Rebs.

MUSTERED!

All the veteran regiments except our own had been withdrawn from the Port Walthall front to reinforce Grant before Petersburg, and their places supplied by the greenest of all green troops, Pennsylvania Dutch regiments high up in the two hundreds. Johnny Reb knew of the change almost as soon as ourselves, and very soon thereafter arranged the tea party of which I write.

The night of November 17 came still and moonlit. Pickets had been relieved at dusk, and the fresh guard had just settled in for another of the quiet nights we had enjoyed so long, when at ten in the evening the Rebs charged on the new troops on either flank of the 12th. The "greens" were off like sheep, and the Johnnies closing in our rear coolly began to blaze away at us at point-blank range. The game was up, there was no dodging that, for they outnumbered us ten to one, and before we knew it forty-six of us were gobbled without waiting to hear any objections on our part. Over the Rebel breastworks we were hustled and there disarmed; all overcoats and good hats or boots being especially contraband. By a sheltered path we reached a wood near the Richmond & Petersburg Railroad. Morning came, and after a breakfast of pea soup we were crowded aboard a freight car, and in a short hour found ourselves in Richmond. The tramp through the city was enlivened with jeers and greetings of the crowd: "Say, Yank, gib yer yo choice, Libby House or Castle Thunder, both right smart hotels, I reckon, fare high, 'ropean plan, sah." These and other kindly touches compelled us, despite our forlorn circumstances to put on sickly grins that in their chilliness betokened no small lack of genuineness.

We soon reached our destination, a large two-story brick structure, with the ominous sign at one corner that said: *Libby & Son, Ship Chandlers and Grocers.* In the lower room, popularly known as the "reception room" by our boys, we were left for that day and the succeeding night without food, and with only such opportunities for sleep as were afforded by the damp brick floor. Next morning we were ordered to "fall in," strip ourselves, place our clothing on the floor before our feet, and wait our turn at being searched. Money, watches, and pocketknives were especially contraband, as being possible aids to an attempted escape through bribery of their own soldiers.

It would hardly be respectful to the gentle reader to relate the extremities to which we were put in concealing these obnoxious articles; it is enough to remind him that though Yankee ingenuity was taxed to its utmost, it was, in most cases, equal to the occasion, despite some temporary inconvenience at one or another part of the body caused by unwonted burdens. Our next move was to the second story of the building, to which we were conducted by a tall, gaunt Virginian named Pryor. This man in *ante-bellum* times had been a noted "whip" among the plantation slave-drivers..

Never shall I forget the sight that met our gaze as we entered. Several hundred haggard countenances, in every degree of emaciation, were upturned in answering stare. In the universal filth and squalor it was hard to recognize in the creatures before us comrades once as well fed and cleanly clad as ourselves. The tell-tale blue, that here and there appeared through the dirt, was a silent, though convincing, witness. Instantly we were surrounded by eager inquirers, — our regiment, how we were captured, what Grant was at over there by Petersburg, had we heard any talk about an exchange of prisoners, did we bring a spare hardtack; these and hundreds more were the questions we tried to answer. Meanwhile a drum had called us into line for breakfast. The meal was served at ten o'clock each morning and always consisted of a standard dish—the refuse of Richmond markets— bones, bits of beef, pork, and mutton, indiscriminately mixed, were first boiled in large kettles, cut into bits, and served with corn-meal bread and frequently was sour on being served. My first piece of meat was a choice morsel of pork-rind, apparently fresh from the sty, and as I

MUSTERED!

was not yet starved to such fodder, I threw it with some spite on the filth of the floor. "Never you dun mind," said Pryor, "you'll jes thank me fur its like fo yer out er thes yer." The scrap was kicked about and trampled for some time unobserved until a drummer boy of sixteen or so, captured by Moseby in the valley the summer before, caught sight of it, and before I could protest had devoured it with all its filth in evident relish. At four in the afternoon the drum called us to the same fare with this variation, that to the water in which the morning's meat had been cooked, were added a few black beans, and more black bugs, and after cooking, a pint of the mixture was doled out to each prisoner. The ratio of nutritious elements in this soup can best be estimated by the formula current among us Yanks for its manufacture: Two beans and seven gallons of water, if too rich add water seasoned with skippers. This without any variation constituted our supply of food.

  The day was cheerless enough in our crowded and filthy quarters, but the night was even worse, and would come upon us all too soon. There was small comfort in lying on the hard floor, crawling with vermin, while the searching December winds blew unchecked through the casements where once there had been windows. With scanty clothing and no blankets there was nothing for us but to spend half the night in promenading the floor, or lying close-packed, "spoon fashion," to utilize what heat we might through contact with our neighbors. Even at this late day, I recall the methods in use for relieving our stiffened muscles and aching joints. After a troubled sleep of two hours, someone, whose aches had passed the point of endurance, would sing out, "Yanks, attention! Company right turn! March!" Woe to the unlucky dreamer who was tardy in his motions! Worse woe if, in the bewilderment of his first waking, he mistook the direction of his turn! No apologies were accepted, and he was at once compelled to sleep by himself until voted into the ranks again by unanimous consent. So passed the weary days, and still more wearing nights.

We watched each other grow thinner, and paler, and more haggard. We saw the finer instincts of kindliness and goodwill die out into the universal selfishness that asserted itself under the guise of self-preservation. We saw, in not a few cases, reason dethroned. We saw some of these madmen, true to the one mastering instinct for food, gather the very vermin that had fattened on their emaciated bodies, and, with these eke out their scanty fare. We saw despair with its blackness taking possession of face after face. We saw the dead, day after day, carted off to unnamed graves.

The only ray of sunshine was when the boys, with husky voices, sang some of the old camp songs, and "Tenting To-night," or " John Brown's Body," or "Star Spangled Banner" rang out through the dingy halls. Once when we had reached the last verse of "John Brown," a council of war was held to settle the question of completing the song with "hanging Jeff Davis to the sour apple tree." It was decided to venture by a unanimous vote, and we were well on our way through the lines, when old Pryor burst into the room with an oath, and cried out, " Now jes be dun with tha' cher, and no mo' of it," and at the same instant the guards outside blazed away at the open windows with the evident design of reminding us where we were. No one was hit, however, and we were careful afterwards to omit all reference to the obnoxious verse.

It would be quite unlikely that men in circumstances like these should fail to discuss, in subdued tones but ever-deepening interest, the chances of escape and the means for accomplishing it. One of the men captured with me was Ben Thompson, a native of Wolfeborough. He was one of the best specimens of the traditional Yankee,—shrewd as a lawyer, keen at trade as a Jew, full of resources, and plucky. He lacked all reverence for dignity or rank, and would always succeed in worming his way into the confidence of officers without appearing intrusive.

The following story, told at Ben's expense, illustrates his character better than any words of mine: Ben had been detailed for picket duty one day, and scenting a chance to turn an honest shekel, he filled his haversack with commissary coffee, and watching his opportunity, traded it off during the day with the Johnnies for tobacco and papers. Next day Ben was sick, "unfit for service," so the surgeon said, and was missing from sight for some hours. Everybody supposed he was asleep in his tent. Nothing of the sort. With his surgeon's release from duty in his pocket, and his haversack on his shoulder, Ben struck for the James, hired a darky to row him across in his dugout, and turned up late in the forenoon at Dutch Gap canal, then two-thirds dug across the narrow tongue of land where Butler was cutting off a seven-mile reach of the river. For two hours Ben drove a thriving trade, and found the troops at work in the canal, hungry for both news and the weed. He was nearly done with his traffic, and had begun to congratulate himself on the generous pile of greenbacks in his possession, when General Butler, with an orderly or two at his heels, made his way on foot into the big ditch. Thompson failed to see the General until he was close upon him, and knowing that he had been driving a contraband trade, he naturally feared a confiscation of his gains. However, drawing a bunch of choice Havanas from the depths of his haversack, a reserve fund apparently provided for an emergency, he ran up to the General with, "Good morning, General, I've been trying to find you for a week, for I did want you to try some of my fresh cigars, and I hope you'll do me the honor to accept them with my compliments." Before the General could refuse or accept the proffer, a ten-inch bomb from one of their mortars was dropped by the Johnnies in somewhat anxious proximity to the group. Exploding as it buried itself in the ground, it did no further damage than to cover the General and his escort with mud. But Ben, taking advantage of the excitement of the moment, cried out, "Good God, General, if that's the manners you show a kindly disposed person like myself, the sooner I'm out of this the better! " And with the words he ran like mad out of the canal, and was soon lost to view around a bend of the river.

Seeing Ben in a brown study one day, a fortnight after we reached Libby, I inquired what he was thinking about. Instead of any direct reply, he asked if I knew anything about shoemaking, and on my replying in the affirmative, he told me of a chance turnkey Pryor had offered him to make shoes for the Confederacy. "And who knows," said he, "but there'll be a chance for us to skedaddle out of this, if once we get into the shop." Next morning thirty of us were detailed as shoemakers, and found ourselves in a building adjoining the main prison hard at work on shoes for the Rebel army. There was a partial division of labor among the gangs that brought the stitching to me and the fitting of the soles to Thompson. Early in our work I noticed Ben went through a curious process of cutting deeply across the outer sole of every shoe, on the reverse side at the front, where shank and heel meet. Of course it ruined the shoe, which would do well if it served the wearer while he was walking away from the quartermaster's. "That's my mark," said Ben, at my inquiry. "Escape valve, you know, for the guilty conscience of a fellow at work aiding and abetting the enemies of his country." Neither of us ever met a Johnnie afterwards, but we ached to ask him if he had ever worn any of the patent brand manufactured by the Yanks at Libby.

Across Water street from our shop was a large warehouse used for any overflow of prisoners, but empty at the time we were there, on the second floor of which, in a small room, old Pryor kept a variety store. It was a sort of perquisite to his office of prison keeper, and aided in eking out a scanty salary. Pryor was accustomed almost daily to conduct squads of half a dozen prisoners to this store, and sell them bread, pies, apples and other eatables. His prices were outrageous, fifty cents for an apple, one dollar a loaf for bread, two dollars for an apple-pie baked in an ordinary saucer. This process of sale was thought altogether safe, as the warehouse was within the prison enclosure and always surrounded by the line of sentries. When Ben and I had studied the situation and formed our plans for escape, we broached the matter to our fellow shoemakers and endeavored to induce some of them to join us. But the danger of recapture and the terrors of Castle Thunder proved stronger than our arguments. It was fortunate for us that they were so, for we learned by experience that the smaller the number in an escaping party the less likely were the rebs to pursue and retake them. However, nearly the entire shop wrote anonymous letters to their friends, and these we agreed to deliver to the mails within a reasonable time, Ben remarking that if anything happened to that particular penny-post he should bring suit in the court of claims against the Southern Confederacy.

December 12, the day we had chosen for our attempt, was dark and stormy. Holding off as late in the afternoon as we dared, we informed Pryor that we needed something to eat, and with four other comrades who were in on our secret, were taken over the street to the store. Thompson and I made our purchase first, and then stepping aside, our companions engaged the keeper's attention while we noiselessly crept up a second flight of stairs to the third story. There we were fortunate enough to find an immense pile of condemned tent-cloth, much of it with the stamp of the United States upon it. Working our way deep into the pile, we anxiously waited for any sounds that would indicate we had been missed. Comrades have since told me that Pryor at once inquired for us, but on being assured that we had returned to the shop, seemed satisfied and returned the remainder without further questions. Six hours of weary waiting followed, for we had agreed to wait for midnight, as the safest hour for our attempt. Nothing broke the dull monotony of the time save the sleepy "Post Number 1, all's well," of the drowsy sentinels, carried in turn around the prison by each succeeding sentry.

J.P. Fahey

Soon after twelve we were astir. Cutting the tent-cloth into long strips, we braided a triple strand into a passably strong rope of some thirty feet in length. Fastening one end to a table we had found near by, we dropped the other from a window. It was short by ten feet, but we had no difficulty in dropping that height. Thompson slid down first and I followed. Once at the bottom we found ourselves inside a board fence fifteen feet high, with the smooth side next the prison. Luckily, however, there were lying about the remains of the boards and timbers of which the fence had been built, and having piled these up cob-house fashion, I mounted the pile, and Ben mounted my shoulders. He could just reach the fence top, and being muscular, he was over in a twinkling, and had dropped me a piece of the tent-cloth and pulled me to the top. We found ourselves in the back yard of a private dwelling, and working our way toward the street were attacked by a ferocious bull-dog, whose howlings alarmed us even more than his bite. The cur quickly yielded to Ben's suavity and caresses and left us for his mat on the doorstep.

In glancing over the front fence we were startled to see a sentry standing with his piece at order arms only a few feet away on the brick sidewalk! There was nothing for it but to put a bold face on the matter and leap the fence. Hastily agreeing to meet at a neighboring street light, Thompson, was first over, and coolly walked away whistling. In ten minutes I followed without the whistle, and shortly rejoined Ben at the appointed place. Just why that Johnny failed to challenge us we never knew, but the probability is that overcome by drowsiness be was stealing a nap over his gun. As neither of us had more than a general knowledge of the streets, such as we could gain by our first march through them, or by our study from the prison windows, we tramped on with only the vague notion of reaching the suburbs and concealing ourselves until the succeeding night. Now and then we passed a watchman or some belated traveler, but the pieces of tent-cloth we had brought along so completely disguised us that no one asked any questions. An hour's hard tramping found us bewildered, and once more in the heart of the city. Then affairs took a serious turn.

We dared not inquire of those we met, nor at the houses, but hurrying on at our best pace found ourselves in another hour climbing the parapets of the third or inner line of works surrounding the city on the north. We saw no troops, as most of the Rebels were with Lee guarding the Petersburg front. The ditch in front of the works was deep and half filled with water, but creeping along in the darkness we soon reached a log laid over the chasm for the use of their troops. Over this we were threading our dizzy way, when Ben, who was ahead, slipped and tumbled in. He disappeared for a moment, but soon came up puffing to the surface. I ran along the bank and dropping him my canvas soon fished him out to terra firma. Every rag of clothing on him was saturated, and the bread in his pockets converted into mush.

Faint streaks of dawn now showing themselves admonished us to be pushing on, and despite Ben's condition we hurried away for something that looked like woods in the distance. We found the woods, a swamp, thick-grown with trees and underbrush. Exhausted and faint, we found a spot somewhat more solid than the rest, where we lay down in the shelter of a large cottonwood tree. After an hour's sleep we both woke shivering and chilled to the very marrow. Ben was the worse off, the result of his morning's ducking. To add to our discomfort a drizzling rain set in, and I was soon as badly off as my companion. We dared not light a fire even if we had had the means; the most we could venture on was to rise occasionally to our feet, stretch our benumbed and aching limbs, and return quietly to our drenched beds on the ground.

Soon after noon the sky cleared somewhat, and sounds of voices began to be heard; these indicated the presence of a camp on the opposite side of our swamp. Not long after, the men seemed to start a hunt, and some dogs had evidently treed an animal. Soon we heard the clip of axes, the tree was felled, and then dogs and men pushed on for the interior of the swamp. Nearer and nearer they drew to our hiding-place, and in a moment I saw the gray squirrel they were after dart into a hollow oak not three rods from us. Three dogs and fifteen or twenty men were close behind. We fugitives instinctively hugged the sod beneath us. Foiled in the chase, the men gathered sticks and dry grass or bark and started a fire in the hollow butt. The smoke soon forced the squirrel from his retreat, and with a leap he took to the nearest trees; the dogs rushed over in hot chase, but failed to molest us; the men taking a shorter cut avoided us altogether, and in a few moments we knew by their shouts that they had bagged their game and were on their way to camp. It was a narrow chance, and Ben remarked, as we began to recover breath, that if that was a specimen of what we were to encounter, the probabilities of our escape were slim.

Darkness, our best friend, came at last, and we crept out of our hiding-place as fast as our chilled and stiffened limbs allowed. With the pole star as guide we steered northward, in order if possible to cross the Chickahominy and put that stream between us and any pursuers that might be on our track. Carefully avoiding the roads, except when it was necessary to cross them, we tramped on through the weary hours of the night, startled now and then by the snapping of a twig or the movement of some animal more frightened than ourselves. At times we were up to the knees in mud and water, and again were climbing steep banks, or working our painful way through thickets and underbrush where we suffered severely from the thorns and briers. Near dawn we crossed a second and less pretentious line of parapets and were rejoiced to find these, like the last, unoccupied by troops. Soon after, we crept up to the negro quarters of a Virginia plantation and stealthily pushing in the door, we entered. At one end of the room was a large fireplace, and stretched on the floor of unbaked clay, in a half-circle, were the dusky forms of half a dozen slaves, with heads turned toward the fire that was now smoldering low on the hearth. After some vigorous shaking we succeeded in rousing the sleepers, and begged for a chance to dry and warm ourselves.

Trusting to the innate sense of justice in the slave, we did not hesitate to confide in them our secret. The story seemed to hasten their endeavors to make us comfortable. The family was soon astir, and the matron quickly mixed corn meal into a hoe-cake, raked the hot ashes aside, patted the cake into passable shape, and tossing it among the embers soon had it ready for us. "Good Lor', massa, af yer'd only tole dis when yer fuss come, mabbe yer'd done goo an had dis hoe-cache eat up to now," said the kind creature, half apologizing for her tardiness in preparing the meal. Never before was food so sweet; for though a little of Pryor's bread still remained, we had found small opportunity to eat, compared with the comfort of this humble home. The meal over, we talked of shelter near by, and the man of the family, a brawny negro, a plantation hand of the best type, offered to stow us away on a loft of loose boards over the fireplace.

We slept out the entire day in comparative comfort. On coming down the ladder at nightfall, the good fellow told us that his mistress had spoken of soldiers who had called at the house to inquire for prisoners that were said to have escaped two nights before from Libby. So we knew we were missed and that no stone would be left unturned to retake us.

"Endu'in de wah sah, we's cullered fo'ks s'hd mighty hard times, an we's han't dun awishin an aprayn yer Linkum fo'ks cum right soon," said our host as we bade him good-by. We now pushed for the Chickabominy and crossed it near midnight a few miles west of Mechanicsville, where we leaped the stream without difficulty, it being hardly more than a brook. Once over, we turned southward determined to use the stream as a guide, as we knew it would finally bring us to the James, where we were sure of finding

Union troops. As the night wore away we again sought the help of negroes at a plantation cabin. This time, after getting warmed and clothing dried, we were conducted to an open shed, fifty rods or more from the house, where the man of the family stowed us away deep under the cornstalks that filled the shed. Giving us a large hot stove for our feet and piling above us many an armful of the fodder, he bade us keep quiet, and promised to come for us after nightfall.

About four in the afternoon the sound of voices roused us and we heard a cart approaching the corn-rick, "Ise dun gwine ter gib dis yer mule no mo' co'n, case he's jus fass gettin good fer nuffin," said the voice of our friend to the boss man on the place. A gruff answer we could not make out was made to his remark, and then we heard the cart back up to the stalks, and the two men began to load. Their voices grew more and more distinct as the pile over our heads grew thinner. " Whit furs yer gwine ter kill dat ar mule?" complained the slave. "Cart's dun loaded nuff an mo'." But the master bade him keep on; he even took, the fork himself and eased the slave for a moment. Again and again the two men walked over us, and once the fork tines passed through Thompson's trowsers but luckily missed wounding him.

At last the expostulations of the slave in the mule's behalf had their effect, and the cart drove off. We breathed freer for the moment, but would cart and master return? Ben pulled his jack-knife from his pocket, and opening it scanned the only weapon of defense we possessed. Then, shaking his head, said, "It's no use, Bach, we're gone as sure as thunder if he comes back, and even if we get the best of him in a fight, he'll rouse the neighbors and we'll be gobbled." We saw there was nothing for it but to be out and off; so gathering our traps, and seeing a piece of woods near by, we ran for it, and seemed to have escaped observation. Though it still lacked two hours of dark, we concluded to continue our tramp.

MUSTERED!

A light snow had fallen during the day, and half melting snow not only quickly soaked our army brogans, but made it almost impossible for us to halt for rest with any degree of comfort. We had marched an hour perhaps, when, skirting a piece of woods, we suddenly came to a junction of three roads, and saw before us a mill on the bank of a small stream. The ruins of a much larger mill were near at hand, and we soon learned that this was Gaines's Mill that had figured so prominently in the seven days' fight before Richmond. Some men were at work on the mill, and a squad of Confederate cavalry was cooking at a fire near by. So sudden had been our approach that almost before we knew it we were in plain view of the group, and not ten rods away. I would have sold my chances cheap, and Ben afterward told me that he saw Castle Thunder for an instant as plainly as if he were in it.

"Come on," whispered he, "It's no use running, but remember to let me do the talking." I gladly noticed that the boldness of our manoeuvre had completely thrown them off their guard. We asked each other in turn the natural questions at such a meeting. Ben told them that we were officers of the Eleventh Virginia Infantry, and had volunteered to go as spies into the Yankee lines to find out the progress Dutch Gap canal was making.

Our dress of Union blue seemed to confirm our story, and in fact Thompson volunteered the information that we had secured the clothing the better to escape observation. "Do you know Captain Polk of the Eleventh?" said the officer in charge of the picket. "Well, I reckon," replied Thompson, " he belongs to my mess, I left him only a day or two ago. Fine fellow, Cap." A part of this was literally true, for in exchanging the courtesies of the picket-line at Port Walthall, we had met the officer referred to. Questions over, we were invited to share the supper of the party, and regaled ourselves with bacon roasted on a stick over the fire, and corn bread cooked at a neighboring farmhouse. With many wishes for the success of our venture, and a promise on our part to call on them on our way back and relate our adventures among the Yanks, we parted the best of friends. "Take care of yourselves, boys, them Yanks are mighty sharp," were the last words that followed us moving down the road casually so long as the light of their camp-fire was in sight. When out of sight, we struck for the woods, and after getting under cover took up the double-quick for a mile or more without a halt. By that time the excitement of our adventure had subsided enough to allow us to speak, and Ben turning to me said, "Bach, another one like that'll be too much for me."

Early that night, the third since our escape, and only a couple of miles from Gaines's Mills, we found ourselves tumbling about among the intrenchments and bomb-proofs of Cold Harbor battle-field. A field where, on the third of June preceding, our regiment at the head of Humphrey's division, had made the fatal charge that cost us more than half our men in the short space of five minutes. No Twelfth New Hampshire boy hears the name Cold Harbor without a shudder to this day.

Traces of the savage fight were lying about everywhere. Canteens, cartridge boxes, shattered muskets, and here and there the bleaching bones of comrades looked up into our faces, white and distinct in the darkness. Damp and chilly as it was we could have enjoyed a short nap, even in that place, had I not, in groping about for a smooth spot, struck something hard and round, and upon carrying it to the light, seen the grinning features of a skull looking at me with its sightless eyes. We could endure fatigue better than sleep with such companionship and resumed again our weary tramp. It was a hideous night; blackness all about, but light enough for us to distinguish the scattered bones of the dead which now and then caused us to stumble, and wonder what the poor owners of seven months before would have said to this rude intrusion on their long sleep.

MUSTERED!

At eight o'clock that night a light ahead gave warning of a dwelling. It proved to be a negro cabin. Within, a father, mother, and three adult daughters were at work at their task of shelling corn, a task which they assured us must be finished before they could receive their rations of food for the next day. Despite their own dire necessities, they begged us to remain the day out at their cabin and offered to share with us their scanty fare. With some hesitation we concluded to stay, worn out as we were with anxiety and travel. A few dirty rags spread on the floor of a loft in one corner of the cabin served as a bed, and so completely worn out were we that, though the family continued their usual occupations, neither Ben nor myself knew what was occurring. Early the succeeding night, after thanking our host, and promising to free them from their bondage when we had conquered the Rebs, we were on our journey. Getting bolder with our increasing distance from Richmond, we determined to take the roads instead of avoiding them as we had hitherto done.

By ten o'clock we had reached Barker's Mill, the scene of another fight of the Peninsular campaign, and an hour later were passing the ruins of Tyler's house. The two roads leading down to Sumner's grapevine bridge over the Chickahominy river were to our right. We had learned that these bridges were no longer passable, and hurrying on our way, we crossed the Richmond & York River Railroad and struck the highway leading to Bottom's bridge. There we had determined to recross the stream and strike for camps of our troops that we knew to be on the north bank of the James, and some twelve miles distant. About three in the morning we approached the bridge, and much to our surprise found a bright camp-fire at the centre of the road and about four rods from the farther end of the bridge. Horses were picketed near by, their saddles on, betokening readiness for prompt movement.

A sentry stood dreamily looking into the fire at his feet, his carbine at "secure". Thompson and I hastily retreated into a thicket by the roadside. We discussed the situation in whispers. There were two alternatives open to us: A tramp of seventy miles down the peninsula to Fortress Monroe with all the risks of capture such as we had already experienced, or an equally hazardous attempt at crossing the bridge in the face of an armed guard with almost the dead certainty of ending up back in Richmond. Pros and cons were carefully weighed. So evenly balanced seemed the chances that we could not make a choice. "Lie still, Ben," said I, "while I go out and look them over again." Leaving him in the woods, I crept along on my hands and knees to the end of the bridge nearest us.

The road was an embankment as it approached the bridge, and high above the level of the ground on either side it reached the crossing at a dead level. The river, a black, ugly stream, flowed sluggishly by. It was fifty feet or more in breadth. Anyone attempting to cross must move the entire distance in the face of that picket standing there by his fire, and nearing him at every step. There were six men, at least, under their blankets near the fire. If there were but one, we might dash upon him and overpower him. I returned to my companion and reported. "There is one chance in a thousand," I said, "and that is the best I can make of it." Ben suggested lots; agreed. He cut two twigs, "Long one means the long road; short one, the bridge." He fixed them; I draw. It is the long stick! Off we start down the long pike, trying to think we have done the best in choosing. We can hardly drag one foot after the other. Our feet are par-boiled with their constant soaking; every motion of the body is torture; the terrible strain of the last five days has begun to tell, not only on our physical endurance but on our will power as well.

"Ben," I say at last, "this is slow murder. I'd as soon starve in Libby as walk myself into the grave. What do you say to trying the bridge?" "I'm agreed," said he, and back we tramp over the half-mile we have just come. We agree that I shall lead, and Ben keep close behind; if the guard challenges us we are to rush for the woods, and run the chances of his missing us when he fires. Once on the bridge, we drop on hands and knees and creep cat-like across. Every inch brings us nearer the picket; he stands like a statue. He seems to nod once, but as I wait for another look he stoops down and tosses some brands into the fire. We move on; each thinks the other makes twice the noise he needs to. We are at the end of the bridge. My eyes are almost bursting from their sockets as I watch that man at the fire. A yard more, and we are safe! It is the longest yard I have ever traveled. It ends at last, and I creep down the embankment at the roadside farthest from the guard. Ben sticks close behind, and is the last to be out of danger.

We steal away through the bushes and take the first long breath, and as we do so the sentry for some reason—we never knew what—rouses his sleeping companions and they stand to arms. A mile away under the shelter of some pines, we stretch out on the pine needles and are fast asleep in a twinkling.

The sun was high before either of us awoke. We concluded it was best to lay off for the day and not run the chance of meeting scouting parties of the Rebs. As soon as darkness permitted, we were again on the road, and happy in the thought that it was our last night out. At the first farmhouse we reached we very incautiously walked up to the door and knocked. A white woman appeared, evidently the mistress of the house. I asked for food, she answered by asking who we were and why we were there in that plight. Ben interposed with the same story he had used at Gaines's Mills with such good effect.

It was all to no purpose. "You'uns ar jes Yanks, you don't talk like we'uns down here 'n Henraker," was all the answer we got in reply to our request for food. "We've caught a Tartar," I whispered to Thompson, and without pressing our claims on the woman's larder, we bade her good night and hurried off through the fields towards the James. Directly we reached some negro quarters belonging to the same plantation, and making our way in asked for hoe-cake. The woman began to prepare it and while we made ourselves comfortable at the fire a negro lad ran in, out of breath, and told his mother that his mistress, as soon as we were out of the house, had dispatched a son to some neighbors a mile away to rouse the lads to be after some Yanks that had been there. An older son was home on furlough from the Petersburg lines and had gone to a dance at a neighbor's. "It's time we were out of this," said Ben, and without waiting for the hoe-cake, now about half done, we made good time over fields and through woods for a couple of miles until the rough jungle forced us to take to the road again.

We tramped along for half an hour, perhaps, neither of us speaking meanwhile, when an overpowering desire came over me to rest. I declared to Ben that I would go no farther till I had rested. He urged our keeping on. "We are nearly through," said he; "only seven miles and we should reach Harrison's and then we could rest for good". But I was stubborn, and Ben was as determined as I. "Then I am going on alone," he said, and started ahead. I walked into the open field by the roadside, fifty feet or so and stretched out on my canvas. Thompson, after moving on a little, changed his mind, came back where I was and lay down by my side.

We were lying there quietly, with the moon looking us in the face, it being now between ten and eleven, when the rumble of a wagon fell on our ears. Nearer and nearer it drew to us, coming from the direction in which we were bound. We should have met it had we kept on. As the team reached us we saw it was a countryman, whether black or white we could not distinguish, with a load of wood. His mules stopped to breathe in front of us, and almost in the same instant a cavalryman coming from our rear drew rein in front of the team. He was mounted on a gray horse and heavily armed. "Have yer seen a couple of fellows on the road as yer come along?" he inquired addressing the teamster. The man answered that he had not. The soldier then went on to say that two chaps that looked like escaped prisoners had stopped at his mother's an hour before to ask for food, and not being granted it, had hurried off through the field. "One of them," said he, evidently describing Ben, "was a stout fellow with a Yank's cap and heavy moustache, and the other short and slim like, and with a slouched hat. They both had Yanks' uniforms," he added, "and carried some sort of blankets over their shoulders." To the two fugitives who were being thus accurately described, this conversation was becoming decidedly interesting. It is needless to say that I never hugged any five feet of ground closer in my life. Neither of us stirred. There we lay in the open field in bright moonlight, and took in every word. One glance of the rider towards us and he must have seen us. To our infinite relief he said at last, "I reckon as how the rascals must have turned off on Long Bridge road," and then turning his horse he kept the mule team company on the road to our rear. We listened to their voices as they died away in the distance, and congratulating ourselves on this last narrow escape, kept on our way—Thompson ahead and looking out for dangers in advance and I behind with an occasional backward glance to warn of trouble from the rear.

Faint streaks of dawn were appearing in the east when Ben caught sight of a mounted horseman standing statue-like in the road ahead. Fearful of making a mistake, we reconnoitered for some time before venturing to make ourselves known. Negroes had told us that a colored regiment with gray horses were doing picket duty at the Landing. Ben finally sang out, "Hello there, don't shoot, we're friends, we want to come in." "Corporal, the guard!" answered the picket without noticing us directly. In a moment the corporal and three men charged down on us at a gallop with carbines ready for instant service. However, we had no difficulty in proving who we were to their satisfaction, and in a few minutes we were made welcome by the Eighth United States Colored Cavalry. Once back with the picket reserve we were furnished hot coffee and extra blankets, and turned in for sleep—and such sleeping as we did that morning! On waking, someone passed us a mirror; neither Ben nor I could recognize ourselves, and no wonder. My own weight had fallen off, as I afterwards learned, from one hundred and forty-five pounds to ninety-six pounds, and Ben's in like proportion. Our complexions had sallowed, and the vile stench of the prison hung about us for weeks despite new uniforms and frequent baths.

To tell how we took the boat the next day to Chapin's Farm where our corps was then stationed; how the boys turned out as we drew near the camp and boosted us on their shoulders and rode us into quarters perched high in air; how the officers made us welcome to their mess; how General Weitzel ordered us a thirty days' furlough; how we received commissions as officers; and how when we took Richmond the following April, I paid old Pryor a visit and relieved him of some of the arms he used to flourish in our faces—all these are things not germane to my story, which amounts to this: that next to the wear and tear of life in Libby and all that implies, is the wear and tear of getting out of Libby and all that includes.

D. B. L. 5–6½. DB. DB. D. 5–8.
LIEUT. ALBERT W. BACHELER.   CAPT. BENJAMIN B. THOMPSON.

Albert Bacheler *of New Hampton was the son of missionairies. He was attending Tilton School when he, Musgrove and others* *answered the call. He was wounded at Chancellorsville and again at Gettysburg, where, carrying a wounded comrade and under fire, he took from the death grasp of Sergeant Howe a piece of the State flag left behind. With the exception of the time he spent in capture, he was never absent from the regiment during its service. After the war he became a teacher at which profession he was many times recognized for his contributions to students and his community.*

Benjamin Thompson, *on the other hand, "went out with the rest of the boys," as he once told his comrades, "but went where I pleased after I got there." And the Rebel picket line was never the boundary of his perambulations. He ventured to Richmond with about the same ease that he did to Washington and is said to have acted as a Union spy. He attributed his escape from Libby prison as little more than one of many amusing episodes. His relatives believed he had been murdered after the war, though none of the 12th ever believed it. His continuing adventures are not known, for after shaking hands with his comrades on Independence Day 1965, he again "went where he pleased" and was never seen or heard from again.*

CHAPTER XV

Chapin's Farm—Last Winter in Dixie

December 1864. The new encampment was upon Chapin's Farm within seven miles of Richmond. Here the boys once again built winter quarters.

The winter was one of unusual severity, making the picket duty in front of the entrenchments very severe. December brought many cold nights when the orders were that no fires be built upon the picket-line so that the enemy would not know the position of that part of our army.

On one of these cold nights, "Old Teb" while on picket duty, could stand his shivering no longer; and so he gathered together some dry sticks and leaves and applied the match. While warming his benumbed fingers by a good cheerful blaze, the Colonel came riding furiously up and angrily asked the Corporal if he did not know the order was to have no fires.

"O yes, sir," was the cool reply from the old vet.

"Then sir, what is this? Do you not intend to obey orders?"

"Well, I guess I'm "puty" well up to the average in that respect, Colonel; but, Hell, I might as well be shot to death as froze to death."

MUSTERED!

The Colonel left "Old Teb" in command of his post with his comfortable headquarters undisturbed.

B. G. L. 5-6.
SERGT. EDMUND TEBBETTS.

"Old Teb"

During the winter of '64-65 there was little fighting north of the James or on the Bermuda line, the majority of troops being sent to the extreme left where Grant was almost constantly pounding away upon Lee's right flank. Life was one of continual drill, and much attention was given to bayonet exercises so that the men might be effective at close quarters should the enemy attack.

The Union works were often thinly manned because of lack of troops, and great vigilance and double duty, especially for pickets, were required of the small force allowed to remain. The men were frequently obliged to turn out an hour or more before light and stand to arms until roll-call, but duties here were neither severe nor exhausting as in earlier days, and the boys bore it with submissive patience, for they fully believed that their time together was drawing to a close. They had heard of the successes of Sherman in the South, Thomas in the West, and Terry at Fort Fisher and Wilmington, and there were the increasing desertions from the Rebel ranks to add to their encouragement.

During the months of December and January, the boys heard first-hand the discouraged deserters' stories of scant food and insufficient commissary supplies. For the Rebel foot soldiers, it became a daily debatable question of whether they should "stay and starve" or "leave and live".

In his book, *Virginia Campaign of 1864-5*, General Humphreys explained the bleak situation that existed for the Southern Confederacy:

> The winter of '64-65 was especially severe to the Confederate troops, with their threadbare clothing and meager food . . . . In a secret session of the Confederate Congress the condition of the Confederacy was declared to be: that there was not enough in the Southern Confederacy for the armies in the field; that there was not in Virginia either meat or bread enough for the armies within her limits; that the supply of bread for those armies to be obtained from other places depended absolutely upon keeping open the railroad connections of the South; that the meat must be obtained from abroad by blockade runners; that the supply of fresh meat to General Lee's army was precarious, and, if the army fell back from Richmond and Petersburg, there was every probability that it would cease altogether.

The condition of the deserters who came into the lines of the 12th Regiment during the winter appeared to prove the above. On the picket line, more than one member of the regiment secretly exchanged food with Rebel pickets for whatever scant offerings would sustain the honor of the Rebel pickets, for their close encounters during the Siege—and particularly at Bermuda—had made them more intimate comrades than enemies. They called each other the "Fed-well" and the "Corn-fed".

One day, while making an exchange with a Rebel picket, one of the boys jokingly told the Rebel, "We're not allowed to use any long-range guns on our side any longer 'cause your Confederacy is getting so thin that we're afraid of shooting plumb through it and killing our own men." In truth, the Whitworth long-range gun used so effectively by the Confederate forces was still the envy and fear of any Union soldier.

The regiment at this time was in camp near Butler's famous Dutch Gap canal. Fort Darling, a strong Confederate fort, stood at the north end of a long detour in the James river and commanded the river so effectively that no Union gun boats dared attempt the passage. A few miles south of this fort, the river above Fort Darling came so near the river below that General Butler conceived the idea of cutting a canal from one point to the other, thus enabling our gun boats to visit Richmond without passing Fort Darling. The idea seemed reasonable enough, except to professional engineers who made it the butt of ridicule, and all the money and labor expended amounted to nothing. On Christmas day 1864, the last explosion was made on the canal and its bulkhead removed, uniting the stream above with the stream below. Water flowed through the gap, but not in sufficient volume to float a rowboat, and no further work was done on this famous canal.

At the time work was being scheduled on this undertaking, and a date frequently reset for when it would be completed, a general court martial was convened of Regular army officers by General Butler to try an enlisted man of the Regular army. Butler had some of the Regular army troops in his command, and an enlisted man of this branch of the service could only be tried by officers of the same branch. The court found the man guilty and sentenced him to three years' hard labor on the Dutch Gap canal. The findings of the court were sent up to Butler for approval, but he promptly dissolved the court and ordered the discharge of the man.

Corporal Julius Davis, a friend of the accused soldier, led Colonel Barker to the 5th Maryland Regiment, where the soldier was hiding out. By virtue of a reward offered by the War Department to any soldier who would give information that would lead to the apprehension and conviction of this soldier, Corporal Davis was entitled to a thirty days' furlough and thirty dollars in money. Some of the regiment blamed Davis for informing against his friend, with whom he had been intimate even after the soldier was found by him in the Maryland regiment. Davis' comrades in the Twelfth accused him of betraying a confidant solely for selfish gain. But Davis insisted that he only answered to the inquiry made of him by Colonel Barker.

On January 7th, Butler was removed from his command, and no further work was done on the canal. General Gibbon succeeded Butler. General Potter became Chief of Staff for General Gibbon, and Lieutenant Colonel Birney, of the 9th Vermont, succeeded Potter as brigade commander. The first day of his command, General Gibbon had a corps review. While this was in progress, he received word that Fort Fisher had fallen into our hands with over one thousand prisoners of war. Butler had been sent to North Carolina to take this fort a few weeks before but returned without making the attempt, although the fort was but weakly garrisoned. Now, after being heavily

MUSTERED!

re-enforced, it had been taken by General Terry. This news was received with much enthusiasm by the men.

Just above Dutch Gap, the Union forces had placed obstructions in the James to prevent the gun boats of the enemy from going below that point. On the night of the 23d, the men were aroused from slumber by heavy firing, proceeding from their gun boats at this point. They made a vigorous effort to pass the obstructions with three iron-clad rams, five armored steamers and three torpedo boats, and to proceed down the river and destroy the depot of supplies at City Point. This was a dismal failure, and the fleet later in the day withdrew, leaving one ram so firmly grounded that it could not be moved.

Late in February, Lyman Merrill, O.P.(Opey) Hall and George Dockham, who were captured with the regiment on November 17th, returned with the horrific account of their life in a Confederate prison den. Opey Hall recorded the following:

> We were captured on the 17th day of November, 1864 while on picket on the Bermuda line. We were first taken to Richmond where we stayed one night in the old Libby prison. We were then sent over across the street to the Pemberton building, where we remained about two weeks. About December 6th we were taken to Salisbury, North Carolina where we were thrown in a hole in the ground. We had a very small piece of corn bread and a little rice water. They gave us a small piece of meat once, which is all that we had while we were in the hole [over two months]. We were drowned out of our hole three times and had to get out and stand in the rain until it stopped. The hole would fill up full, and we would have to dip the water out as best we could, having nothing but

a tin cup to do it with. When it was all out, we would crawl back into our hole again to keep from suffering from heat or cold as the season might be. We stayed there until the 22nd day of February, 1865. What a glorious Washington's birthday it was.

As winter wore away, Union soldiers saw the Southern Cross fast fading away as they kept their night watch. The spirits of the boys rose as they daily saw fresh evidence that all their sufferings and privations were soon to result in the complete success of our arms—despite all the blunders and incapacity of some high in command.

One of those who had had enough of the "blunders and incapacity" of those in high command—and whose spirits had been raised, not entirely unaided by spirits of a liquid sort—was Private Nudd. He had just returned from a furlough granted him for superior deportment, and on this night he was outfitted in dress parade trim, marching with his musket at "right shoulder shift" toward General Weitzel's headquarters:

"Look! There goes Nudd for another furlough," exclaimed one of his comrades to another. "I'll bet you he gets it, too," replied the other. They did not know that he had got a little too much of the "spirit" which brings trouble instead of furloughs, for he had the firm and measured step, erect carriage, and proud bearing of one of the king's foot body guards. But it was no such trifling object as a furlough that he now vied for. His aim was much higher, and the spirit within him stirred his blood and fired his ambition to dare and do great and noble deeds. Soon he reached the General's tent, and with arms already at a "shoulder" he demanded immediate admission as a bearer of verbal orders from the highest authority and of the greatest importance. The General, who had overheard his brief parley with the guard, admitted Nudd himself. Marching in and saluting the commander of the right wing of the Army of the James, he assumed the stone-stern rigidity of a statue, and speaking in tones of unquestioned authority, he said: *"General Weitzel, I have come to relieve you of your command!"*

The attack upon Fort Steadman convinced the Union leaders that the hour of final action was at hand. General Ord, now in command of the Army of the James, was ordered to take with him the First and Second Divisions of the Twenty-fourth Corps, one division (colored) of the Twenty-fifth Corps, with quite a large force of cavalry, and march at once with all possible secrecy and celerity to join the Second Corps at the extreme left of the Union line, where they would be ready to fight or chase Lee, in the anticipated effort of the Rebel commander to save his army from capture.

This march of thirty-six miles was so quickly and quietly made that the enemy knew nothing of it until several days after, when they found their right flank imperiled by the presence of troops that were supposed to be nearly forty miles away. It was one of the most timely and successful movements ever made by the Army of the James.

But this movement of troops, though largely contributory to greater results than even hoped for, was a risky one because it was made in the face and eyes of the whole of Longstreet's corps that had been sent north of the James only a few days before to meet an attack or take advantage of the withdrawal of our troops.

Had Longstreet known what General Weitzel, left in command of Bermuda and Chapin's Farm, did—that little more than a picket line remained to hold the works protecting Grant's right wing—it would have been the Union instead of the Confederate right that would have suffered first, if not most. It was because of this danger that every precaution was taken, both by the troops leaving and those remaining, to deceive the enemy until his right flank was imperiled by Grant's strongly reinforced left. The Twelfth, along with others of the Twenty-fourth Corps, left to hold the line nearest Richmond, were constantly fearing an attack. Luckily, the enemy remained ignorant of their weakness, and the last "onward to Richmond" was over deserted works instead of the wounded and the dead.

One of the best soldiers in the regiment was Daniel Bohonon, who was gifted with superior intellectual endowments, but who was so careless and indifferent about his dress as to often excite the jests and ridicule of his comrades. He always wore his pants about six inches too low, leaving a huge gap between his pelvic area and the seat of his pants, turning up the pant legs that much at the bottom to keep them from dragging.

One night during a brief skirmish, a piece of shell passed between his legs just high enough to tear away the seat of his pants in front. He grabbed himself where the hole was, and holding the seat of his pants in front with both hands, he whirled around and looked to see if he had been *"unmanned"*. Finding no loss of parts when he halted to examine himself, he uttered an exclamation of disgust at his own fright and sight and returned to his skirmishing.

Bk. D. L. 5–11.
CAPT. DANIEL W. BOHONON.

Captain Daniel Bohonon *had a love for learning and books were his constant companions. He attended Tilton School with Musgrove, Bacheler, Currier, Farrar and other comrades who enlisted from there. Although he cared little for military honors, his intellectual merits could not remain hidden, and after the war he was appointed Government Revenue Officer at Richmond where he married a "southern belle" he had met while in Richmond with the 12th. His quest for learning took him to Europe, and upon his return, he extended his scholarly reputation as a visiting lecturer at universities and the military academy. His untimely death on his thirty-fifth birthday brought his comrades back to Virginia with evergreen branches which they spread over his grave in Oakwood cemetery in Richmond.*

Daily, nearly hourly, came the order: "Hold your men in readiness to move at any moment," and picket orders and duties were so rigidly exacting and constantly recurring due to the scarcity of troops, that the men hardly got time to eat or sleep.

"On the evening of April 2nd," wrote Colonel Barker, "the musicians were kept busy until after nine o'clock for the double purpose of holding Longstreet in our front as long as possible and preventing him from making an attack by inducing him to believe that there were three or four times as many troops in his front as there really were.

But Ord's, Wright's, and Parks' guns in their early morning attack upon the enemy's lines to the left and in front of Petersburg had sent Longstreet in that direction many hours before our musical entertainment, intended for his delusion, had commenced."

All night General Weitzel watched for signs. One of his staff, climbing to the top of a signal tower, discovered a bright light, like the burning of a building of some kind, in what he thought to be the city of Richmond.

Earlier in the evening a deep, heavy sound had been heard from the same direction, soon followed by two or three others resembling the first. These reports were heard by many of the soldiers in addition to those on picket. Among such were several officers and men of the Twelfth, who, while watching, had seen the light and sounds and agreed that they were not either cannon or mortars. They concluded that the Rebels were blowing up their gun-boats and arsenal preparatory to evacuation.

By three o'clock in the morning, from reports of deserters and the story of a trusted negro who came riding into the line in a buggy, it became certain that Richmond was being evacuated.

CHAPTER XVI

Richmond

April 1865. On Sunday, April 2nd, the advances of the army around Petersburg had made the position of the Rebel army untenable. Jefferson Davis was so informed while at church in Richmond, and the evacuation of the city at once commenced.

Around three o'clock in the morning on the 3d of April, the picket line of the 12th Regiment was ordered forward. The enemy's outer line of works was quickly reached and surmounted, but no Rebels, armed or unarmed, were found, and silence alone remained to challenge their approach.

Captain Sargent and Lieutenant Bohonon were the officers in charge of the picket detail, and Lieutenant Bohonon was the first man to mount the enemy's works. After the picket line passed the fortifications, all semblance of marching order was lost in a wild race that they might be the first to enter Richmond.

The *Richmond Whig* on the 4th of April, 1865 stated: Captain Warren M. Kelley, 10th New Hampshire Volunteers, in command of the [picket line] of the Second Brigade, commanded by General M.T. Donohoe, Third Division, Twenty-fourth Army Corps . . . [and] Captain H.Q. Sargent, 12th New Hampshire Volunteers, in command of the left wing [picket line] were the first organized body of troops to enter the city.

Captain Sargent recorded the following in his diary: We arrived about eight8 o'clock in the morning, thoroughly exhausted, yet our hearts beat high with exultation and triumph. I am certain that the part of the picket line of which I was in command was the first infantry in the city and the first troops of any kind, except a squad of the Fourth Massachusetts Cavalry, to whom the mayor and council surrendered about thirty minutes before.

General Weitzel and Captain Warren Kelley, commander of the picket line of the Second Brigade have both testified to the much disputed fact that the pickets of the Second Brigade were first in the city, leaving for the seven mile trip to Richmond shortly after 4:00 a.m. without halting until they reached Richmond.

However, there is one Union soldier who, against orders, may have arrived at Richmond before anyone else. His name is Corporal Newell Davidson.

Corporal Davidson left his picket post, stripped himself of all encumbrances from the waist up and ran all the way to Richmond. It is believed he was the first soldier to enter the city.

From Corp. Newell Davidson: I was the first live man, wearing the blue, to enter Richmond on the morning of its capture, and there are many who can testify to it. Then was the "Old Twelfth" represented there ahead of any other.

I ran all the way ahead of the rest, stripping myself but for shirt and pants. I went up Main street all alone, but citizens, black and white, were on the street, with now and then one in Rebel uniform, but unarmed. I began to wish that some of my comrades were with me, for I did not feel quite safe; but everyone seemed to be too busy caring for his own or plundering from some one else to take much notice of me. The city was on fire in several places, and from this cause, and the expectation that our army was coming, the whole population seemed wild with excitement. I got a little boy to show me Jeff Davis' house, and I think I was the first Union soldier to enter it. Jeff himself had skipped, but some of his servants remained. I then went to the State Capitol building. There were none of our colors flying there then, or anywhere else in Richmond yet.

There was a young girl at the state house square, standing guard over her uncle's goods that they were bringing from his house near the fire. She told me that she came from New York to visit her uncle, and the war breaking out, she could not get back home. She gave me presents for remaining with her, for she was much frightened at the scene around her. Among the things she gave me was a ring, a pack of cards, a box of fine combs, and a canteen full of "applejack." She told me not to take any whiskey from the Rebel residents as they might put poison in it. She said that most of the citizens were very bitter against the Northern soldiers, but there were some who in their hearts would welcome us into the city. She said that I was the first blue-clad soldier she had seen that morning. I left after some of her folks had joined her.

I was in Richmond a long time, as it seemed to me, before I saw a soldier wearing the same uniform as myself. Now I want to tell you what I know. That the pickets of our brigade, the Second, were the first to enter the Rebel capital after the Massachusetts cavalry squad, any claim or talk to the contrary notwithstanding, for I was there to see for myself and know whereof I affirm.

Corporal Davidson's testimony is given ironic credence in the *Final Roster Listing* of the 12th Regiment which states **"Escaped en route to Richmond."**

B. B. L. 6-0.
CORP. NEWELL DAVIDSON.

Newell Davidson had learned well the art of running and escaping. At Chancellorsville he ran ahead of the regiment right into the Rebel ranks from which he also ran and escaped into the woods. While sitting on a log to catch his breath, he was captured again by a Rebel guard whom he convinced that he'd been left behind by his first captors and was sitting there trying to plan a way to desert from the Union. "If ya' got no heart for the work, what did ya' come down here to fight us for?" inquired the Rebel guard. "Three hundred dollars and a cow," replied Davidson—at which the Rebels in the party laughed heartily, followed by a free interchange of queries and jokes in which the "Funny Yank" gained the good will of his captors. The captain of the provost guard that had captured him had a sister in New York to whom he was anxious to send word, and Newell promised to bring a letter and wishes in person to her on his "escape to Canada" if the guard would assist him. Before dawn, the officer sent Davidson in a small skiff across the Rappahannock, from which, with lighter feet, he found his way to General Hooker's headquarters and on to the camp of the 12th Regiment.

A Blazing Celebration

Regardless of who first entered the burning city, all agreed that pandemonium reigned.

As the city was being evacuated, the Rebel army set fire to the principal buildings and store houses, and the flames spread rapidly. The poor and lawless elements were fighting for bread at the store houses, or sacking the stores for plunder, while whisky, which ran in the gutters by order of the mayor, was being gathered up and drunk by those who craved it.

One of the Twelfth found his tent-mate, who had imbibed at the expense of his deportment and dignity, sitting on the steps of a store building and the following exchange took place:

"Why, Joe, what are you doing here?"

"Oh, Dan, is that you? I'm so glad (hic) to find you. I've been a-huntin' and 'untin' for the bo-bo-boys till I can't s-s-stand any longer."

"You are evidently in a bad condition, Joe."

"Yes, the condi-d-dition is (hic) very, very bad . . . but the s-s-sit-situation is glorious."

Pen cannot describe the scene in Richmond when our troops entered, yet letters and journal recordings written at that time have tried:

From Sergt. Clarke: [Penciled during a brief halt of the brigade on Tree Hill]: "This is the greatest day I have seen yet in this war. Thank God. Richmond is ours, and the stars and stripes are now floating over the doomed city. Some of the pickets have already entered the city, but the rest of our brigade has not yet entered. It lies before us all in flames, and there has been a continual roar of bursting shells and exploding magazines all the morning.

We are now on a hill just outside of the city, which is in full view; we passed through the outskirts of the city as we came up.

We started from camp at seven o'clock and got here at nine. We came straight up on the New Market road. I write this on a leaf of a company book of the 19th Georgia, Company B.

The boys have caught a peacock and cut his tail off, and are sending pieces of his feathers home in their letters that nearly all are engaged in writing while we are waiting.

The Rebels blew up three gun-boats on the James river just before we started, and there were two or three heavy explosions earlier in the morning, the first about 2 o'clock.

From Captain Bartlett: Richmond, the long sought and fought for, is at last within our grasp. The Sevastopol of the Confederacy has fallen, and but a single act remains to close the bloody drama of the great rebellion of 1861-5.

The war-weary veterans of the Twelfth, plainly seeing their country saved, rush into each other's arms with smiles and tears of gladness, grasp hands, then throw high in air their caps, and give three long and loud resounding cheers, to be taken up and echoed and re-echoed along the lines from one command to another until the whole heavens are filled with shouts and cheers of victory.

Till life's last day will this day last, vivid and distinct in our memories. It makes the boys think of the gladness that the glorious news will carry home; and so they write letters to those nearest and dearest to their hearts.

From Colonel Barker: I am so overjoyed with this day's success of our arms, that I can hardly keep still enough to write. Captain Sargent, as he was passing Jeff Davis' house, halted his command and ordered three groans for the arch traitor who left last night.

Before leaving, the Rebels set fire to some of the public buildings and storehouses and a great part of the city was destroyed before we could arrest the progress of the flames.

MUSTERED!

Shells and torpedoes have been exploding all day. Thousands of people are homeless.

The indignation of the citizens at the soldiers of their army for setting the city on fire is great. They seem ready to own that they were secessionists, but are now loud in denouncing their leaders and desire to return to their allegiance. I never expect to see but two bigger days than this—one, when peace is declared, and the other, best of all, when we return to our homes.

General Weitzel, who assumed command of the city as provost marshal, directed his attention to extinguishing the flames and in saving most of the city. It would seem that the city had suffered enough from its occupation for a year by the Confederate forces and the effect of the siege, and that the Confederate government would have desired to save the city, especially in view of the fact that its destruction could not aid what was already a lost cause. It may be that the fires were set by the lawless who remained in the city. Who the real authors were has not yet been established.

A Starving City

Richmond was a starving city, and some of the richest and proudest of the aristocracy were obliged to beg of those whom they most strongly despised and bitterly hated, despite their southern chivalry. Thus the first duties of the military authority after extinguishing the flames and restoring order was the feeding of the citizens, rich and poor, white and black.

"Of all the sights I ever saw," wrote Sergeant Clarke, "Richmond, on the 3^d of April, was the hardest. The people were literally starving. The market looked as if it had not had a pound of meat in it for years. The stores were all empty or burned, women and children were begging for something to eat."

To those so long residing securely within the seemingly impregnable fortifications of their capital city, it was a blow as severe and crushing as it was sudden.

Unwelcome Captors

The choice the aristocracy of Richmond was forced to make was humiliating. For women dressed in silks were obliged to welcome Union officers to their homes that they might procure meat and flour enough for the servants to cook and feed both themselves and their detested Yankee boarders.

Several officers of the 12th Regiment found board and lodging in just such families, but never dreamed of their destitution until made known to them by painful necessity. All the male members of such families able to carry a sword or a gun were in the Rebel army; thus, fear of being molested by our soldiers was always present in the women tolerating the polluting presence of our officers.

Yet these southern-bred ladies soon found that not all Yankees were thieves and villains, for they were not blind to the scene before them and the cause of it and were obliged to give the "Yankee devils" their due for saving their property and feeding their starving families.

The following relevant footnote to this topic is given by Captain Bartlett in the regiment's history:

> As one of our aides was riding through the streets engaged in gathering together the able-bodied men to assist in extinguishing the fire, he was hailed by a servant in front of a house towards which the fire seemed to be moving. The servant told him that his mistress wished to

speak with him. He dismounted and entered the house and was met by a lady who stated that her mother was an invalid, confined to her bed, and as the fire seemed to be approaching, she asked for assistance. Subsequent conversation developed the fact that the invalid was none other than the wife of General Robert E. Lee, and the lady who addressed the aide was the daughter, Miss Lee. An ambulance was furnished by Colonel E.H. Ripley, of the 9th Vermont, and a corporal and two men guarded them until all danger was over.

Welcome Heroes

However unwelcome the greeting of Union troops was from the residing elite, there was another class, degraded yet delighted, who "welcomed us with smiling faces and many a 'God bless you,' and mingled their cheers with ours as we marched through the streets of Richmond between crowded sidewalks of these dark-faced sons of unrequited toil," wrote Captain Bartlett, who recorded for posterity the voices of freed slaves, till then unheard:

It was from this patriotic race that exclamations of joy and praise – many queer and comical expressions and ejaculations – greeted our ears upon every side:

"*Who's boss, now?*" "*We's all black and blue, yer see, but isn't we uns been beaten.*" "*Yankee Doodle forebber!*" "*But one mo'e jump to Heben!*" "*I's a white woman now! Here, take dis chile!*"

An aged negro stood with a broad grin upon his ebony face, waving a big bandanna fastened to the end of his cane as the troops marched by. "'*Pears though de jubilee has come at last, and de Lord be praised!*" he shouted as we passed by, and Colonel Barker, Captain Bohonon, and I returned his greeting with our best, most dignified, salute.

No soldier in blue ever asked for food or shelter from them in vain, even though they did so at the risk of their own lives. In perfect trust and confidence the Union soldier had learned to seek aid or refuge within the hovel of the slave, for he knew he would neither be denied nor betrayed by them. Surrounded by traitors, they alone stood loyal, and as soon as permitted to do so, they fought brave and true for the stars and stripes. And it was upon this flag that they now looked through tears of joy in the bright sunlight of that April morn over the dome of what, but an hour before, was the capitol of the slaveholder's Confederacy.

Libby Prison

One of the chief objects of interest to the soldiers was Libby prison. Its doors were first opened by the 4th Massachusetts Cavalry, the first Federal troops to enter the city. From filth, starvation, torture and death, the captured stepped unexpectedly into the pure, free air of unrestricted freedom.

Quite an excavation was found under the building, which led some to believe that the report of its being mined and ready to blow up when the rescue of its inmates was strongly threatened by Sheridan's cavalry was probably true.

Though the doors of Libby prison swung quickly open to the Union captives, including some from the Twelfth, they closed quickly again upon some who had held them there.

Veterans of the Twelfth who were imprisoned there well remember the large bloodhound, "Nero," which had been kept at the prison, and who was too brave to imitate the example of many of the citizens and run away at the approach of the Yankees. [This dog is supposed to have been the same one that confronted Thompson and Bacheler on the night of their escape.] After the war he was taken north and exhibited in some of our large cities.

President Lincoln Arrives

At nine o'clock on April 4th, President Lincoln arrived at the landing called "the Rocketts" upon Admiral Porter's flagship, the *Malvern*.

Without ceremony, the President walked ashore and started off up town, looking about with an interested air and taking in everything. As soon as Admiral Porter was informed that the President was already ashore, a marine guard was ordered to follow as escort, but in the walk of about two miles prior to the marines' arrival, he was directed by negroes. For most of the march, he was accompanied by Admiral Porter and other naval officers.

It was one triumphal march from The Rocketts to General Weitzel's headquarters at the late residence of Jefferson Davis. Crowds surrounded the Davis house and sent up cheer after cheer.

After the officers were presented to him, the citizens were allowed to take his hand in theirs. He was dressed in a long, black overcoat, high silk hat, and black pants, giving to his form a very commanding appearance.

Thomas Thatcher Graves, General Weitzel's aide, accompanied the President into the house, and it is from his account that the following events became known.

At the Davis house President Lincoln was shown into the reception room, with the remark from the housekeeper that "this room is President Davis' office." As he seated himself he said: "And this must have been

President Davis' chair," and, crossing his long legs, he looked far off with a serious, dreamy expression. Upon learning that the housekeeper had left, he jumped up and said in a boyish manner, "Come, let us look at the house." He seemed interested in everything, but when General Weitzel came, in breathless haste, President Lincoln's face at once lost its boyish expression, and duty resumed.

Shortly afterwards Judge Campbell and General Anderson. both Confederates, called and asked for an interview with the President. It took place in the parlor behind closed doors.

Afterwards, President Lincoln and General Weitzel went to Libby prison and Castle Thunder. Here General Weitzel asked the President what he should do regarding the conquered people of Richmond. President Lincoln replied that he did not wish to give any orders on that subject, "but if I were in your place, I'd let 'em up easy, let 'em up easy."

Later the President with a cavalry escort of colored troops appeared on the square, drawn in a carriage and four, and was driven round the works. Everywhere the reception was the same—bands played and crowds besieged the grounds anxious for a closer inspection of the occupant of the carriage.

It was in Jefferson Davis' chair and upon his desk that President Lincoln later sat and wrote his famous order for the reassembling of the Virginia legislature which, though never carried out in the manner and spirit intended, nevertheless showed his statesmanlike wisdom and noble magnanimity which is only allied with human greatness.

As soon as the excitement and enthusiasm of taking the Rebel citadel had subsided, the soldiers became greatly interested in what Grant and his corps commanders were doing to cut off Lee's retreat. There were fears that the Rebel Army of Northern Virginia would elude the pursuit of our forces and escape into some mountain region of the south to prolong the war.

General Lee had succeeded in escaping from Richmond with his army and marching southwest till he reached Appomattox, but while on this march such was the hopelessness of his cause that his army had shrunk by desertions from fifty thousand to twenty-five thousand men.

General Lee Returns Home

Early one morning a few days after the capture of Richmond, General Lee arrived at his house in the city. General Weitzel, calling his aide, Thomas Thatcher Graves, into a private room, took out a large well-filled pocket-book, and said: "Go to General Lee's house, find Fitzhugh Lee and say to him that his old West Point chum Godfrey Weitzel wishes to know if he needs anything, and urges him to take what he may need from that pocket-book."

Upon reaching General Lee's house, Graves knocked, and General Fitzhugh Lee came to the door dressed in a Confederate uniform. He was so overcome by Weitzel's message that for a moment he was obliged to walk to the other end of the room. He excused himself and passed into an inner room where General Robert E. Lee was sitting with a tired, worn expression upon his face. Fitzhugh Lee knelt beside his General and placed a hand upon his knee. After a few moments he came back and assured Graves that he did not require any loan of money and that he sent his love to General Weitzel. He stated that General Robert E. wished only for a pass for some ladies of his household to return to the city. The ladies were back in the house by the next morning.

On the 9th of April at Appomattox, Lee surrendered to Grant the Army of Virginia. When on the evening of the 9th the news came to the troops in Richmond that Lee's whole army were prisoners of war, they knew that the end of the Rebellion was imminent and that they would soon be allowed to go home for their work was accomplished.

CHAPTER XVII

Manchester and Danville

April 1865. The 12th Regiment was not numbered among the troops that followed General Lee and his retreating army. It remained in Richmond doing provost duty. On the 14th, they crossed the river and entered Manchester, a smaller city on the southern side of the James.

That night as the men slept content in the peace and safety of the nation none dreamed of the tragedy being enacted in Washington. They awoke early in their new quarters to a rallying cry by Colonel Barker. By eight o'clock on the following morning, the news that President Lincoln had been shot at Ford's theatre was announced to the tearful troops.

Assassination of Lincoln

General Meade received the astounding news from General Grant, then in Washington, early on the morning of the 15th; but so fearful was its supposed effect upon the army that it was given out in piecemeal, and the whole truth was not known even to some staff officers until two or three days afterward.

Captain Prescott, then an aide-de-camp to General Weitzel, said: "If the army had been told the whole story at once, not a stone in all Virginia would have been left unturned. Yet it was humiliating to the soldiers to think that they had been deceived from fear of their commanders that they could not be trusted."

Another bit of news was also being withheld from the soldiers, particularly those in the Twelfth Regiment— That one of their own was the first man to reach the President after the fatal shot was fired and that a warrant for his arrest had been issued.

Captain Bedee, who had earned a reputation among the rank and file for being at the right place and time with the wrong consequence, was in Washington on special leave and was sitting in the second row on the left, back of the orchestra, where he had a full view of the President's box on that woeful night.

Hearing a pistol shot, his quick eye caught sight of Booth as he leaped from the box upon the stage. In an instant the terrible truth flashed through Captain Bedee's mind. He jumped from his chair over the row of seats in front of him and with a rush and bound was past the orchestra and over the footlights before the assassin had disappeared behind the scenes. Following him across the stage to the rear, he heard someone beyond cry out, "*They've got him!*" (which he later found was done by an actor accomplice to stop pursuit). He returned to the stage beneath the President's box. Mrs. Lincoln was screaming, "*My husband is shot!*" Bedee mounted the railing of the stage box and climbed into the President's box above. Close behind, a person claiming to be a physician was rushing up, and Captain Bedee lifted him into the box.

Others were trying to enter the President's box by the rear door through which Booth had entered, but it had been locked by Booth before he leaped upon the stage.

When Captain Bedee and the physician entered the box, the President was reclining in his chair with his head far back, much as if he were asleep. The doctor immediately began to search for the wound, stripping back the President's coat and unbuttoning his vest. Nothing could be seen of any blood or any place where the bullet had entered the head or body.

While the doctor was searching vainly for the wound, Captain Bedee, who was supporting the President's head, felt something warm trickling into his hand, and exclaimed, "Here is the wound, doctor," and at the same instant, he put one of his fingers into the hole in the back part of the head where the ball had entered and from which "the precious blood of the great martyr had just commenced to ooze out," in Captain Bedee's words.

In pulling back the President's coat to find where he was hit, some papers fell from one of the pockets onto the floor, and Mrs. Lincoln, who was remarkably calm and self-possessed, picked them up and handed them with others about to fall from the same pocket to Captain Bedee, saying to him as she did so, "You are an officer, and won't you take charge of these papers?" The captain took the papers as requested, putting them carefully into his own pocket.

He next assisted in removing the unconscious President from the theater and conveying him across the street into the house, where he died at 7:20 a.m. the next morning. Captain Bedee remained in the room with the dying President until nearly three o'clock in the morning while Vice-President Johnson, Secretaries Stanton and

Chase, Senator Sumner, and several others arrived. Then at the request of Stanton, he went to the War Department to carry a message for the Secretary and from there carried orders for preventing the assassin's escape to the officer in command at Chain Bridge.

Having executed his orders and reported back to Stanton, *to whom he had delivered the papers given him by Mrs. Lincoln,* he received praise and thanks from the Secretary for all he had done and was told that he could report to his place of duty.

Captain Bedee's Lament

The next evening Captain Bedee returned to Manchester and his comrades in the 12th Regiment. But hardly had he recovered from the tragic scene in which he had taken so prominent a part before the provost marshal received an order from Washington for his arrest.

When the arresting officer showed his order to Bedee, there was a forcible cry of innocence and indignation from the captain for the bungling attempt to connect him to the crime of murdering the President. On Captain Bedee's behalf, Colonel Barker telegraphed General Hardie who had sent the order and suggested that a blunder had been committed upon an innocent man.

In a short time came a telegram for Bedee's release. But this did not satisfy Captain Bedee who wanted an explanation and complete exoneration from all blame, for the order of arrest had cast suspicion upon him among his comrades and their trust was pre-eminent in his mind and heart.

The following correspondence from and to Captain Bedee tells the rest of the story:

MUSTERED!

HEAD QUARTERS 2D BRIG., 3 DIV., 24 A. C.
IN THE FIELD, VA., April 26, 1865.

SIR, — I have the honor to report that on the evening of the 18th an order from Washington was received by telegraph at Gen'l Ord's head quarters for the arrest of Capt. Bedee, 12th N. H., to the effect that Capt. Bedee had failed to deliver the President's papers, saying: "He will be arrested, the papers taken from him, sealed and forwarded to Washington."

By Order of
SECRETARY OF WAR,

(Signed) JAMES A. HARDIE,
    Bvt. Brig. General, etc.

In compliance with the above I was arrested and remained under arrest until the evening of the 20th.

When arrested and taken before Gen. Devens on the morning of the 19th, I stated to him that I delivered the papers of the late President to your Honor on the morning of the President's death, April 15th, at the house opposite Ford's Theatre, where the President was then lying, which you will probably remember as your Honor at the time of my delivering said papers noted my name, regiment, and corps upon the wrapper which you placed around said papers.

On the evening of the 20th the following telegram was received at General Patrick's head quarters:

U. S. MILITARY TELEGRAPH,
April 20th, 1865.

By telegraph from Washington to Gen. Patrick:

I have seen the Secretary who now says that Capt. Bedee did give him certain papers. Major Hay was not aware that the papers were so disposed of by Capt. Bedee.

Please release the Captain from arrest.

(Signed) JAMES A. HARDIE,
    Bvt. Brig. General, etc.

Doubting that your Honor approve, of the public disgrace of an officer who has endeavoured for the past three years to earn an honorable name in the defense of his country, I take the liberty of laying this case before you, hoping your Honor's sense of justice will induce you to set the matter right with the command with which I am connected. I am Sir,
Very Respectfully,
Your Obedient Servant,
E. E. BEDEE,
Capt. 12th N. H. V's and
A. D. C. 2d Brig., 3d Div., 24 A. C.

To The Hon. E. M. STANTON,
    Secretary of War, Washington, D. C.

WAR DEPARTMENT,
WASHINGTON CITY, May 5, 1865.

CAPTAIN,— On the 18th of April last, word came to me from Maj. John Hay, Assistant Private Secretary to the late President, that certain papers taken from the person of Mr. Lincoln on the night of his assassination, which had on that occasion come into your possession, had not been delivered by you as promised; and, further, that you could not be found in this city, and that upon inquiry it was learned that you had left town for the army. I then telegraphed, believing the matter required immediate action, to General Patrick, in the name of the

Secretary of War, an order for your arrest, and that the papers in question should be taken from you, sealed up, and forwarded to Washington. Upon this order you were arrested. Ascertaining subsequently that you had delivered the papers to the Secretary of War upon the same night on which you became possessed of them, I telegraphed an order for your release, and you were released.

In view of your entirely honorable conduct with regard to the papers in question, and of the mortifying position in which you were placed by the accusation and the arrest, I desire to express my serious regret at my action; and cheerfully make you the reparation of a full and free acknowledgement of my mistake, which is conceded in the light of my present knowledge of the circumstances of the case to have been an act of serious though unintentional injustice to yourself.

In conclusion I beg that you will please make such use of this letter as may in your opinion be necessary to repair as far as possible the evil occasioned by my action of the 18th of April. I remain, captain,

Very respectfully,
Your obedient servant,
JAS. A. HARDIE,
Bvt. Brig. Genl. and Inspector Genl., U. S. A.

WASHINGTON, D. C., May 5, 9.20 P. M.

CAPT. E. E. BEDEE, *12th N. H. Vols., 2d Brig., 3d Div., 24 Army Corps, Care of Maj. Gen. Devens:*

Your note of April 26 has just reached me, and I hasten to reply by telegraph. The order for your arrest issued by General Hardie was without my knowledge or authority, and was unjust to you. The papers found on the person of the late President were delivered by you to me on the morning of his death and immediately sealed up, your name and address endorsed thereon, and placed by my clerk in the safe of the War Department where they remained until delivered to Judge Davis and opened in his presence.

When informed by General Hardie that he had issued an order for your arrest, I immediately directed the order to be revoked, and an acknowledgement made of the injustice done you. Your conduct in the matter was in every respect becoming your rank and personal character, and I deeply regret that the hasty and unauthorized act of General Hardie should have subjected you to a moment's pain or reproach. If he had informed me before using my name, the error could not have happened. You are at liberty to use this explanation in any way you may deem useful to yourself.

General Hardie has been directed to make a proper acknowledgement to you, which he will no doubt take pleasure in doing, in order to relieve you as far as possible from the pain you have innocently suffered.

EDWIN M. STANTON,
Secretary of War.

Thus was Captain Bedee completely exonerated from all blame and suspicion.

MUSTERED!

On the 25th the regiment with its Division marched into Richmond to receive the First and Second Divisions of the Twenty-fourth Corps on their return from the extreme left where they had marched and fought night and day in helping to capture Lee's army.

Rations and water were plenty and with enough time to rest and care for themselves, the men regained their health quickly. But more than anything to help their healing was the thought that the war was over and that they would soon be going home.

April 29th Lieutenant Colonel Marsh came down from Washington where he had been on detached duty since receiving his wounds at Chancellorsville. He found the boys healthier and in much better spirits than when he last saw the battle-worn regiment on its return from the Gettysburg campign. And the men were feeling even better than they looked — for they had just been released from the Army of the Potomac.

May 6th the regiment again crossed the river into the capital city to receive the Second and Fifth Army Corps of the Army of the Potomac; and on the 11th the trip was repeated to exchange cheers and congratulations with the Fourteenth and Twentieth Corps of Sherman's army on their way to Washington.

For several days there was almost a constant tramp of different corps of both armies into and through Manchester and Richmond, all returning from fields of conquest and victory. Sherman's army had "beat the bush," while Grant's had "bagged the game."

The regiment continued police and provost duty in Manchester till May 19th when orders came from General Ord, then commanding the Department of Virginia, for the 12th Regiment to proceed by rail to Danville, Virginia, a distance of nearly one hundred fifty miles. The men remained in the train cars until the next morning when temporary quarters were found in an old tobacco building near the depot.

On that same day Colonel Barker issued the following orders:

GENERAL ORDER NO. 1.

In obedience to instructions from Headquarters, Department of Virginia, the undersigned hereby assumes command of Danville, Virginia and vicinity. It is expected that the inhabitants will render their willing and cheerful support to preserve order. Any act of violence . . . will be promptly punished. Officers and enlisted men of this command will be careful to avoid all unnecessary interference with the inhabitants. Private property will be protected; and it is hoped that the men who have exhibited so much bravery on the field will readily recognize the necessity of protecting the private rights of peaceful citizens.

Here Colonel Barker with his trusted few left in the 12th Regiment proved themselves worthy of confidence and showed that they could wisely rule as well as bravely fight.

Danville was at this time a city of between three and four thousand inhabitants and was before the war an important business center on the Richmond & Danville Railroad running through Petersburg, Danville, Weldon, and Goldsborough to Wilmington, North Carolina. It was situated on the Dan river near the head of navigation. It was here that Jefferson Davis and his cabinet made their first step to re-establish the headquarters of the Confederacy after being driven out of Richmond; and it was here that Davis issued his last proclamation.

MUSTERED!

On the 24th of May Colonel Barker received by telegraph an order from General Ord to assume command of not only Danville but also the counties of Pittsylvania, Henry, Fairfax and Patrick and to administer the oath of allegiance to citizens within those borders.

In compliance with this order, Captains Ricker, St. Clair, and Bohonon were sent with detachments to the county seats of Patrick, Pittsylvania, and Henry counties, while Lieutenant Bacheler was sent to Fairfax county. They established provost headquarters, and the greatest vigilance was exercised to maintain order and protect life and property. In effect, the Twelfth again constituted an independent command, relying upon nothing but themselves in wisdom to direct or power to execute and being responsible for everything within each jurisdiction.

This section of Virginia had been intensely disloyal, and there was an unsettled, chaotic condition of civil and social affairs. Everything had been taken from the people to feed their army, and thousands of families had not eaten for months. More than this, the white citizens, mostly old men, women and children, had for a long time been living in constant fear of an uprising among their slaves. Thus, they not only carefully avoided anything being disclosed to the slave population, but purposely misrepresented the facts and deceived them in the prospect of the Union's final success against their masters. Most slaves in these counties still did not know they were free or even the result of the conflict.

The men soon learned more of southern life in its every day forms and practices than ever before while in the army. And they learned by personal observation how true was the penned picture by Harriet Beecher Stowe in <u>Uncle Tom's Cabin</u> *which many of them had read. Yet it was only the brighter tints and the lighter shades that they saw, for between slave life in Virginia and slave life in the gulf states there existed a world of difference.*

"In the absence of legislation to the contrary," wrote Captain Bohonon, in charge of the district of Henry, "it is presumed that a very large proportion of this class [freed slaves] . . . will remain with their former masters, and will aid in farm labor for wages, for so strong is their attachment to the house and neighborhood in which they were born and raised that very few will voluntarily leave."

The duties of the officers and men were arduous and trying, not in fighting or making long marches as of yore, but in restoring and preserving order, settling differences among the people, administering the oath of allegiance and caring for the many cases of suffering and want among both whites and colored.

The unexpected fruit of their labors among the "enemy citizens" came in June from the citizens themselves:

TESTIMONIAL TO THE 12TH REGIMENT
NEW HAMPSHIRE VOLUNTEERS

To Lieutenant Colonel T. E. Barker, Commanding:

Sir, — It was suggested by citizens that there should be some expression of our appreciation of the proper and gentlemanly bearing of yourself, your officers, and your entire command while on duty here.

The unsettled state of feeling since the war has ended naturally hinders the free interchange of friendly tokens between those who so lately and so sternly met as enemies . . . and time has not yet blunted the keen sense of the failure of hopes we dearly cherished; but we are not willing you should pass away from among us without some testimonial that may serve to show you and your friends in the far North that Southern men can estimate and appreciate worth without heeding lines of separation, whether geographical or political.

It is proper that you, Colonel, and the officers and men serving with and under you, should know that you and they possess our respect as soldiers and our esteem as men for the manner in which you and your command have discharged duties which might have been, in another spirit, painful or annoying to our community; and we deeply regret your removal from this post while a military occupation is continued. We request you to make known to the men of your command our high appreciation of their uniform good conduct, their quiet and unassuming deportment, and their prompt and efficient service in the protection of private property.

In hope that when this reaches you, you and your regiment will be once more enjoying the comforts of home and the blessings of peace not soon again to be broken, and believing that we convey to you the common sentiment of this community, we have the honor to subscribe ourselves your friends and fellow citizens.

(Signed) J.W. Walker, Mayor

The testimonial was forwarded to Washington, the citizens thinking that the regiment was on its way home and would be forwarded to wherever the regiment might be. It was received by Colonel Barker while still in Virginia awaiting the completion of regimental returns preparatory to its final muster out.

CHAPTER XVIII

Concord—Home!

WAR DEPARTMENT,
WASHINGTON, D. C. May 29, 1865
To Maj. Genl. H.W. Halleck,
Commanding Military Division of the James

The Secretary of War directs that all volunteer organizations of white troops in your command whose term of service expires between this date and September 30 next, inclusive, be immediately mustered out of service.

THOMAS M. VINCENT, *A.A.G.*

June 1865. The first order issued from Washington on May 29, 1865 for the discharge of troops took a long and circuitous route before reaching Colonel Barker on June 2, 1865. It went from Major General Halleck in Washington, to Major General Ord, Commander of the Department of Virginia in Richmond, to General Gibbons, Commander of the 24th Army Corps, to General Devens, Commander of the Third Division, 24th Army Corps in Manchester, and finally to Colonel Barker and Captain Heath in Danville.

MUSTERED!

On the 4th of June Colonel Barker telegraphed General Gregg: "I have the honor to request that my command, which is now on duty at Danville and vicinity, may be relieved. Our term of service expires before the 30th of September 1865, consequently the company and regimental records should be made so complete that the muster out rolls can be made immediately."

The last marches that any of the Twelfth made were from their county detachments in Henry, Pittsylvania and Patrick counties to Danville. They started on the morning of the 11th of June, some marching thirty-one miles before midnight and the remaining twenty miles the next day. Never was a march so gladly tramped by the men, for they understood they were scuffing Virginia dust for the last time.

On the 13th of June the regiment left Danville by steamboat to Manchester. The next morning after arriving, they marched three miles to Ruffin's Farm, pitched tents, and went into camp for the last time upon Virginia's soil.

The Stars and Stripes now floated once more over the capital of every southern state, and a muster-out roll and homeward ride were impatiently awaited.

The first general order ever issued to the Twelfth had come at Concord on September 25, 1862 stating: **"You will proceed . . . to Washington, D.C. . . . at 7 o'clock a.m. and report there to the commanding general."** The last order ever issued to the Twelfth came on June 21, 1865 – Special Order No. 153: To leave Richmond, Virginia and return home to Concord again:"**The 12th Regt. N.H. Vols, will be mustered out of service . . . and will at once proceed to Concord, N.H. for final payment and discharge. By command of Maj. Gen. John Gibbon."**

"Will be mustered out of service" and "will at once proceed to Concord, New Hampshire." These were the words, wrote Colonel Barker in his last letter, "that were brightly promising to the eye, sweetly sounding to the ear, and filling the whole heart with a feeling of gladness. 'Concord' meant *Home!*"

On June 21, 1865, the 12th New Hampshire Regiment was mustered out of service. Howard Taylor, the Little Corporal, who had "faked" both his age and height during the mustering in ceremony, stood beside his trusted accomplice, Dr Fowler. He did not need to try nearly as hard this time, but the same excitement filled him, though he had grown from a "boy" into a "man" both personally and legally.

Tears of gladness and regret filled each heart, for they must leave behind them the silent dust of those once as fond and hopeful of Home as they, but who would never return.

So it was that of the 1,463 officers and enlisted men who had been mustered in at Concord on September 9, 1962, only 218 remained on June 21, 1865 to hear the poetic words penned by Captain Asa Bartlett and read by Colonel Barker:

> *Good-by, Sunny South, now clouded with gloom,*
> *We leave thee alone in sadness to rest;*
> *Thy streams have run red, each valley a tomb,*
> *But the viper is slain that nursed at thy breast.*
>
> *Good-by to thy cannon-ploughed fields, where the soil*
> *Is stained with the blood of the Blue and the Gray;*
> *We've watched in your trenches of danger and toil,*
> *Through the dark night of war to the bright peace of day.*
>
> *Good-by, sacred soil, aye, sacred indeed,*
> *Where mingles the dust of the brave and the true;*
> *Long, long shall the heart of the poor mother bleed*
> *For him who here sleeps 'neath the sod and the dew.*

MUSTERED!

Farewell, comrades dear, with a farewell tear
We leave you to rest till the bugle's last call
Shall bid them arise, without danger or fear,
Who fell that no star of our Union should fall.

Farewell, patriots dead, though your cause shall survive
The ruin and the wreck of war's desolation;
Till man 'gainst his brother no longer shall strive,
But peace and good-will make the whole world a nation.

For we go to our homes, once more there to live
By the bright crystal lakes 'mid mountains that stand
As watch-towers of freedom the warning to give,
If danger again shall e'er threaten our land.

The 22nd of June 1865 was a beautiful day. Early in the morning the Twelfth broke camp for the last time upon Virginia soil, and in company with the Tenth and Thirteenth New Hampshire formed a little home-bound brigade about half the size of a full regiment and marched to The Rocketts. At 8:00 a.m. they embarked onboard the steamer *State of Maine* bound for Home.

They cruised down the river past dismantled forts which but a short time before were crowded with Rebel batteries. Soon they rounded out upon the broader river below its confluence with the Appomattox at City Point. Down the river to Fortress Monroe they glided. Two days later at eight o'clock in the evening, they dropped anchor in New York harbor.

The next morning they departed for New England, arriving in Boston Harbor on the night of the 25th of June. By nine o'clock in the evening, the three small battalions were marching through the gas-lighted streets of the

"Hub" to Faneuil Hall within whose honored walls they found quarters for the night. It was a warm evening, much too warm for an in-door bivouac of old veterans from the tented field, and most of them chose to sleep upon the steps and entrance-walk in the open air. Passers-by thought those lying upon the cobblestone were drunk, but some citizens, learning the real cause, invited them to their homes, promising a nice soft bed. But the men, conditioned soldiers, now preferred the soft side of a stone to the softest feather bed.

At nine o'clock the following morning they left by rail for New Hampshire. After waiting impatiently in Nashua overnight, where the Tenth and Thirteenth New Hampshire had enlisted, they embarked for the city of Manchester. Here another enthusiastic reception awaited them and a sumptuous dinner was prepared for them beneath the shade trees on Merrimack Common, near where now stands the monument erected to commemorate their deeds. Thomas J. Whipple, who had once so ardently desired to command them, spoke. They marched back to the depot, and at three o'clock boarded the rail and started on their final journey to Concord.

Just before reaching Hooksett the train was thrown from the track. This accident delayed the train so that it did not arrive at Concord until nearly sunset. The delay had been telegraphed ahead, and anxiety filled the large number of relatives and friends who had gathered in Concord to greet them.

As the train pulled into the depot, cheers went up from the assembled thousands. It was only the second time they had heard cheers other than their own since leaving Concord on September 27, 1862. They marched amidst a continuing ovation from the depot to the State House yard following their tattered and bullet-rent battle flags. Two years and nine months before they had marched, led by glistening new colors, from the Concord Plains to the same depot on the morning they had left for the front—more than a thousand strong and stalwart men. The *Twelfth New Hampshire*—the same regiment in name, but, oh, what a change less than three years had wrought among its ranks.

They were escorted from the depot to the Capitol by the Veteran Reserve Corps, led by a band of music; and after listening to welcome speeches by Governor Smith and others, arms were stacked, equipments hung thereon, and the men, in lighter marching order of mind and body than ever before, marched to the Eagle and Phoenix hotels. Yet many encamped for the night in the State House yard.

The next forenoon, the regiment marched down to Camp Gilmore where headquarters were established for a few days until final discharge papers could be prepared and muster rolls completed.

Handing Over the Colors

On the afternoon of July 3d the boys of the 12th Regiment marched for the last time under the colors of their flag, led by Sergeant Joseph Stockbridge, selected by the men for his enviable record as a soldier to be the last color bearer of the Twelfth New Hampshire. The colors were delivered up to the Adjutant General of the State by Colonel Barker. But not before the Colonel gave a vivid summation of the colors in front of his tearful veterans:

> Sergeants Jon Tasker, William Howe, and Marquis McDuffee . . . carried the Stars and Stripes, regimental colors and State flag through the battle of Fredericksburg and into the battle of Chancellorsville where all were pierced with bullets. Sergeant Tasker, though wounded, still bore up his

country's flag by leaning against a tree for support; Corporal William Straw . . . picked up the regimental colors when Sergeant Howe fell in front of him and was found lying a few rods back from the battle-line with the flag-staff still firmly grasped, the blood flowing fast from the side of his head; Sergeant Asa Bartlett snatched the Stars and Stripes from his hands, the Rebels pouring out of the woods close behind him. Sergeant McDuffee, severely wounded but refusing to yield the colors, brought the State colors safely from the field by crawling on his back until he reached the river and found the remnant of our Regiment. . . . In this battle all the colors were many times perforated with bullet holes which still remain.

At the battle of Gettysburg, where all color bearers were shot down almost at the same instant, Corporal Samuel Brown took the colors from the bullet-riddled Luther Parker just as he himself fell dead. Even then, the Stars and Stripes hardly touched the ground, serving as a covering sheet of the brave guard who fell and lay beneath its folds until it was rescued from capture by Lieutenant Charles Emery. Corporal John Davis and Andrew Heath snatched the other two flags from the dead. Sergeant Howe made a death grasp for the flag, and so firmly were his fingers closed upon the fabric that in the Sergeant's death-clinched hands remained a remnant about one foot wide and fifteen inches long. Private Bacheler, carrying a wounded comrade, was the last to leave the battleground, and while doing so, he noticed the piece of flag in Sergeant Howe's fingers. Not willing that the fragment should fall into the enemy's hands, he stopped, under a destructive fire of bullets, to unclinch the dead sergeant's fingers, one by one, and thus saved the precious fragment.

In the Fall of '64, the national and state colors that had been through three great battles were sent home for preservation and we are now united with them once again. Sir, these standards that have been so gallantly borne and so bravely defended are worthy of as proud a position as is in your power to give it. Their tattered folds speak volumes to the heroic few who still remain to tell the sad story of those who have fallen in their defense.

Sergeant Charles Hoyt and Sergeant Sweatt took turns carrying the regimental banner through the battles of Wapping Heights, Swift Creek, Relay House, Drury's Bluff and Port Walthall and into Cold Harbor where Sergeant Hoyt was cut down in the fateful charge. Seeing his own death coming, he tossed the colors to Sergeant Sweatt, who clung to them by dodging from tree to tree until wounded nearly at the breastworks, where he surrendered them to Corporal William Wallace, who carried them off the field. He presented the flag, stained with the blood of Sergeants Hoyt and Sweatt, to me saying, "Here, Colonel, are our bloody old colors. Sergeants Hoyt and Sweatt send them to you with their compliments." The blood and bullets that mortally wounded Sergeants Hoyt and Sweatt are still on the flag staff. Corporal Wallace was made sergeant and entrusted with the colors he had helped save and carried them longer than any other color bearer. He carried them during the remainder of Cold Harbor, through the Siege of Petersburg, the battle of Cemetery Hill, at Bermuda Front, and, most proudly, into the City of Richmond on that glorious day of April 3rd. Just before the Regiment left for home, he was taken dangerously ill. His hope and privilege of carrying the colors home to the capital of his native State was reluctantly relinquished to the trust of Sergeant Joseph Stockbridge, the last color bearer of the Twelfth New Hampshire.

So it was that on the eve of Independence Day 1865, Sergeant Stockbridge, his eyes flashing with the memory of those past bearers, bore aloft and then relinquished the glorious war-torn banner, the sacred token of their patriotism and valor which they had vowed to uphold so long as a single thread remained.

Independence Day Farewell

On that most glorious of Independence Days, July 4th, 1865, the officers and men of the 12th Regiment were formed in dress parade line for the last time to listen to Colonel Barker's farewell address.

FAREWELL ADDRESS TO THE 12TH REGIMENT
THOMAS E. BARKER, COL. 12TH N.H. VOLS

SOLDIERS, The day to which we have all looked forward so long and anxiously has at last arrived. The great work in which we engaged almost three years ago is accomplished, and . . . we have been permitted to return to our dear native State.

YOU have served your country long and nobly. By your deeds you have won a name that shall live forever. From the bloody fields of Fredericksburg, Chancellorsville, Gettysburg, Front Royal, Swift Creek, Drury's Bluff, Port Walthall, Cold Harbor, Petersburg, Cemetery Hill, Bermuda Front, and your triumphant entry into Richmond, ages hence will view your deeds, and the generations of centuries to come will honor and bless you for the legacy gained by your valor and bequeathed to them.

FOR HONOR and bravery in battle you are second to no regiment that has ever been sent to the field, and there is no State that can boast of braver troops than our own rock-bound Granite State. For discipline and drill you have ever excited the admiration of military men . . . [and] have been particularly complimented in General Orders by President Lincoln. . . .

WE have delivered up to the State our old war-worn and blood-stained colors which have been made dear to us through toil, danger, and sacrifice. Nobler blood never coursed in the veins of man or was sacrificed on a country's altar than has been poured out on many a crimsoned field for them. God bless the noble dead, our comrades still, who have fallen in their defense!

YOU have been faithful and brave, valiant and true soldiers. . . . Our last duties have been performed. And I ask only that you will ever greet the bereaved friends and family of our comrades buried in a distant land or sent home to rest beneath their native sod with kind words and helping hands.

SOLDIERS, I am proud! And the highest honor that I ask is that when the History of the Rebellion is written my name may be recorded as the Commander of the Twelfth New Hampshire.

Farewell.

With moistened eyes and broken utterances, the men of the 12th New Hampshire Volunteers gave three final cheers for their beloved and trusted commander.

And then, with a loud resounding clap of hands, the Boys of the 12th New Hampshire threw their caps high in the air and broke ranks once more and forever.

THE END